ISRAELIS and JEWS

The Continuity of an Identity

BY THE SAME AUTHOR

The Reaction of Jews to Anti-Semitism
American Students in Israel

CONTEMPORARY JEWISH
CIVILIZATION SERIES

In cooperation with
Institute of Contemporary Jewry,
Hebrew University of Jerusalem

MOSHE DAVIS, *Editor*

ISRAELIS
and
JEWS

The Continuity of an Identity

by Simon N. Herman

THE JEWISH PUBLICATION SOCIETY
OF AMERICA
Philadelphia/5731-1971

1943

This volume is based on studies made possible by a research grant from the Israel Office of the American Jewish Committee to the Institute of Contemporary Jewry (Social Psychology Division) of the Hebrew University of Jerusalem.

*This edition published for members
of the Jewish Publication Society
by arrangement with Random House*

To Segula, Ephraim, Benzion and Avital

Acknowledgments

THIS volume is based on a series of studies on the social psychology of contemporary Jewish life undertaken by the Institute of Contemporary Jewry at the Hebrew University of Jerusalem in cooperation with the Department of Psychology. I owe much to the wise counsel and friendly encouragement extended at all stages of these studies by Professor Moshe Davis, head of the Institute of Contemporary Jewry.

In the conduct of the research I had the benefit of the able collaboration of Drs. John Hofman and Yochanan Peres, both of the Hebrew University. A team of graduate students gave loyal service to the project, and while it would be invidious to single out members of the team by name, mention needs to be made of the special responsibilities which devolved on the shoulders of Uri Farago, David Katz, and Yoel Yinnon.

Our work was greatly facilitated by the ready cooperation extended by Mr. Joseph Schochat, Deputy Director-General of the Israel Ministry of Education, who assisted us in our contacts with the schools.

A sabbatical year in the United States as Philip W. Lown Fellow in Education at the Graduate Center of Contemporary Jewish Studies, Brandeis University, allowed me the opportunity to continue my research on Jewish identity. I am grateful for the helpful cooperation extended by Professor Leon Jick, Director of the Center.

A number of colleagues readily gave of their advice during the course of these studies and my thanks are due in particular to Professors Ben Halpern and Marshall Sklare, both of Brandeis University, and to Drs. Shlomo Breznitz, Hayyim Cohen, Charles Greenbaum, and Ozer Schild, all of the Hebrew University.

The research was made possible by a generous grant from the Israel Office of the American Jewish Committee. I am grateful for the sustained interest in the research on the part of members of the Committee— in particular Dr. John Slawson, Dr. Simon Segal, Judge Theodore Tannenwald Jr., and Mr. Gerard Weinstock. On my visits to the American Jewish Committee offices in New York many friendly courtesies were extended by Mr. George Gruen and other members of the staff. In Israel Mr. Maximo Yagupsky, the first Director of the Israel Office of the AJC, was very helpful in facilitating the initiation of the project.

Research grants to several of our graduate students by the Blumenson Fund enabled them to contribute to the project by exploring special topics in the field of Jewish identity.

I appreciate the help given in the technical preparation of the manuscript by Mr. Morris Levy and by Mrs. Deborah Baker and Miss Adena Silver.

Simon N. Herman
Hebrew University
Jerusalem
June 15, 1970

Contents

PART III
Four Profiles

PART IV
The Future of Jewish Identity

Appendices

Tables

List of Tables

PART I

*The Study of an
Ethnic Identity*

CHAPTER 1

Jewish Identity in the Contemporary World

Although problems of identity have been the subject of considerable popular interest (as reflected in the frequent discussion of topics such as "alienation" and the "search for identity") and latterly have received increased scientific attention, there is a surprising dearth of social psychological studies dealing specifically with *ethnic* identity.[1] The very proper preoccupation with the easing of racial and other tensions has resulted in numerous studies of ethnic prejudice and of other facets of intergroup relations. A systematic social psychological analysis of the structure and dynamics of an ethnic identity has, however, still to be undertaken.[2]

The emergence of so many new national and regional units in recent years in Africa and Asia—in the wake of liberation from the constraints of colonial rule—may well bring about an enhanced interest in the understanding of ethnic identity.[3] Already it has become evident in these countries how tortuous can be the process of integrating segmental loyalties into more inclusive ones and how vital it may be to know how to do so without suppressing the segmental cultures. The Nigerian-

Biafran conflict was a tragic illustration of how there can be no effective political integration if ethnic diversities are not properly accommodated.

The Persistence of Ethnic Diversity

In other parts of the world, too, indications multiply that ethnic peculiarities cannot be disregarded. If it was believed that in an age of rapid intercommunication and growing interdependence between all peoples there would be a reduction in ethnic diversity, events have belied these expectations. A glance at the realm of language would show that while small nations may find it necessary to learn one of the major world languages, they remain as zealous as ever in the cultivation of their own national tongue.[4] Where two ethnic groups live side by side in the same country there may be alternating periods of harmony and of tension; the period of conflict will inevitably be accompanied by a sharpening of ethnic divergences, but even in the times of harmonious cooperation the groups will not readily forego their separate identities. The confrontations between Flemings and Walloons in Belgium and between French and English in Canada are just two of many instances of the persistence with which ethnic identities continue to assert themselves throughout the years.

In exploring the varied role of ethnicity in the life of New York City, two American sociologists (Glazer and Moynihan) have documented their point that "the melting pot did not happen." They show how the principal ethnic groups maintain "a distinct identity, albeit a changing one, from one generation to the next."[5] Their analysis leads them to the conclusion that "religion and race seem to define the major groups into which American society is evolving as the specifically national aspect of ethnicity declines." They see as the four major groups: Catholics, Jews, white Protestants, and Negroes.[6]

If the ethnic divisions were clearly visible in 1963 when Glazer and Moynihan made their observations, they have become even more sharply drawn in the few years that have followed. One of the most remarkable developments in the field of ethnic relations has been the dramatic *volte face* in the policy of substantial sectors of the Negro community. After initially seeking integration as individuals in American society, many Negroes have turned round in their tracks and are now stressing that which sets them apart from others. The epithet "Black" has been invested with a new pride, and scorn is heaped upon the Negro accommodating himself to the norms of White society. Serious criticism has been leveled against some of the more militant assertions of Black identity, but there is little doubt that a deep need exists for Blacks to hammer out an identity which can serve as a source of the self-esteem they so sorely lack. It remains to be seen whether the attainment of a more complete Black identity will or will not be accompanied by a constructive integration into a common American framework. But in any event the change in Black strategy is already having an impact on the thinking of other ethnic groups in the United States, who have been emboldened in the expression of their own identities.[7] The foundations of American pluralism are undergoing reexamination, and it is likely that as a result the ethnic subcultures will find fuller expression and be subordinated in lesser degree than before to the majority culture.

The Peculiarities of Jewish Identity

In spite of centuries of dispersion, the Jewish people has preserved its identity with peculiar tenacity. The

Jewish communities, located in so many diverse environments, and yet everywhere maintaining, despite the diversity, a kernel of sameness which can be termed "Jewish,"
constitute a subject of special interest to the social scientist engaged in the study of ethnic identity. The study of
the similarities and differences between these communities has gained enhanced interest since the establishment of the State of Israel. The Jewish community of
Israel has acquired a status radically different from that
of the others, all of whom are in the position of minorities.

The problems which beset efforts to maintain a Jewish
identity have become increasingly complex in recent
decades. The cultures of the Western world, in which
the greater part of the Jewish people now lives, exercise
a powerful attraction, and Jews in many countries are
either searching for ways to preserve a distinct Jewish
identity in these cultures, or, where it is preserved, to
give it meaningful content.

Let us glance—even if cursorily—at what has become
the largest of the Jewish communities, that of the United
States. In a pluralistic society of the kind America has
hitherto been, Jews have the opportunity to develop
their own subculture, but the pervasive non-Jewish majority culture inexorably exerts its influence.[8] There is no
crystallized ideology of assimilation among American
Jews—such as existed in European Jewry—but it is difficult for them to resist the forces making for uniformity.
Evidence does exist to support the multidimensional
model of the assimilatory process suggested by social sci-
entists, i.e., there may be a complete acceptance of majority norms in certain areas of behavior and at the same
time an identification with the Jewish group in others.[9]
But there is a closer interrelation between the various
facets of assimilation than is sometimes presumed, and
the general trend is in the direction of a loss of Jewish
distinctiveness.

There has been speculation as to whether the trend persists in the third generation.[10] While the second generation of American Jews may have been tormented by the conflict between the world of their immigrant parents and the new world into which they were born, this conflict apparently subsides in the third generation. There are indications, however, that while the third generation may quite readily accept the fact of their Jewish affiliation, the content of this Jewishness has been considerably diluted for many of them. They look upon themselves as Jews, they are looked upon by others as such, their social contacts generally are mainly with Jews. But "each new generation is in part the product of its inheritance,"[11] and the homes of their second-generation parents already had less Jewish content than those of their immigrant grandparents. The problem of many members of this third generation is thus not one of identification with the Jewish group; it is rather one of giving distinctiveness to their identity as Jews.

There are indeed members of this generation who have benefited from improvements in Jewish education—Jewish day-schools, the more Jewishly-oriented summer camps, departments of Jewish studies at some universities —but the great number have little in their lives to which they can point as being significantly Jewish. The percentage of Jews who attend institutions of higher learning is very considerable and the college subculture whose norms they accept has in many cases further weakened the specific Jewish content in their lives.[12] The decline in religious observance has left them without the moorings supplied by an ancestral faith which gave substance and direction to a Jewish identity. There are obviously gradations in the Jewish identity of members of so heterogeneous a community as that of the United States but it would seem that there are appreciable numbers of Jews who have no clear view of what "being Jewish" means—

no satisfying answer to a question which the march of
events in a world in turmoil makes it increasingly difficult
to avoid.

Two great upheavals in contemporary Jewish life have
made it necessary for Jews in the United States—as for
Jews everywhere—to reexamine and redefine their Jewish
identity in the light of the changed conditions these events
have produced. First came the destruction of six million
Jews in Europe. The implications of this vast tragedy re-
verberate unto this day throughout all sections of the
Jewish people, profoundly influencing all their conceptions of Jewish collective existence and of relations between Jews and the Gentile world. In the wake of the
tragedy came the emergence of the State of Israel, pro-
claimed and regarded as a "Jewish State." No Jew can
escape the necessity of defining his Jewish identity in
relationship to Israel, particularly so after the Six Day
War when Israel as a geo-political entity achieved increased prominence in the affairs of nations and in the
minds of men the world over. There is evidence that the
compelling impact of these events has brought about a
renewal of identification with the Jewish group on the
part of many marginal Jews who had been on their way
outward.

If we turn our gaze from the Jewish community of the
United States to the second largest in the Diaspora—the
two-and-a-half million Jews in the Soviet Union—we
become aware of how fateful for an individual can be
his designation as a Jew. In the USSR the campaign
against religion and the subsequent erosion of religious
practices, the prohibition of the teaching of Hebrew, the
curbs on contact with Israel and with Jews outside of
Russia, all these have left many Russian Jews with a Jewish identity devoid of positive content. In the consciousness of some of them it means little more than the mere
word "Jew" stamped on their identity cards. But the implications of such identity, even when devoid of its proper

substance, have been far-reaching.[13] Bearers of this identity are debarred from certain offices, they are among the first suspects if there is any expression of non-conformity with the totalitarian regime, they are singled out for ominous warning if there is any likelihood of sympathy with Israel, they are ever potential victims of one of the recurring tides of anti-Semitism. On the part of some of the youth who can know so little about their Jewishness there have been poignant expressions of their Jewish identification, as on Simchat Torah (the festival of the "Rejoicing of the Law") when young men and women congregate singing and dancing around the synagogue. Pleas to be allowed to immigrate to Israel have become more insistent in recent years. If the time comes when the Jewish identity which develops in an anti-religious totalitarian society can be systematically studied, it is likely to provide significant points of contrast and yet also of similarity with the Jewish identity in the Western democracies.

The Jews of the United States and of Soviet Russia are just two of the Jewish communities living under conditions which differ so radically. In each of the others there are local variations of one kind or another to the problems they face as Jews but there is everywhere a quintessential sameness to the mark their Jewish identity leaves on them.

In Israel, Jews have been free to shape their identity in whatever way they will. What form the Israeli-Jewish identity is taking is of concern not only to Israel but to Jewish communities throughout the world, who see in Israel the center of contemporary Jewish life. One of the motivations of Jews in establishing a Jewish state was their conviction that they as individuals could not be the equals of their non-Jewish neighbors as long as the Jewish group was unequal among peoples. They feel Israel has given them new dignity and self-respect. Already the many thousands who come to Israel each year for a longer or shorter sojourn find that it lends an added dimension to their identity as Jews.[14] But the emerging Israeli-Jewish identity has an interest which transcends Jewish circles. It is a dramatic illustration of how from diverse strands drawn from all corners of the earth a people can be reshaped under the impact of common historic memories and common constructive purposes.

While the present study will concern itself with the Israeli-Jewish identity only, it was quite clear that the peculiar nature of this identity could be properly understood only if viewed against the broader background of Jewish life the world over.[15] Indeed, apart from the interest in the Israeli-Jewish identity *per se,* the study was conceived to serve also as a springboard for a worldwide comparative study of Jewish identity. With this orientation in mind we shall point up likely contrasts and similarities between the Israeli-Jewish identity, which is the immediate subject of our investigation, and the Jewish identity of the Diaspora communities. This leads us into an even wider domain—the points of difference between majority and minority identities. While the conceptual framework we shall try to develop in this study is designed for the purpose of an investigation of a Jewish identity, it may have applications to the study of other ethnic identities as well.

There has as yet been no comprehensive social psychological study of Jewish identity. The nearest approaches to such a study have been limited investigations of, primarily, Jewish *identification,* i.e., of the extent to which Jews in a particular community are prepared to stand up and be counted as such. What has been of interest in these investigations to the social scientist as well as to the Jewish practitioner has been the degree to which Jews—when exposed to the influences of the majority culture, either to its allurements or to the forces of rejection—accept their membership in their minority group or prefer affiliation with the majority, and, furthermore, whether their attitudes and behavior are determined by the Jewish group or whether they turn to the majority as a source of reference. Only few studies go beyond this to analyze what being Jewish means, what kind of Jew and what kind of Jewishness develop in the non-Jewish majority culture.[16] In Israel, where Jews constitute the majority society and their Jewish identification is taken for granted, interest naturally shifts from the study of identification to the problems of the emerging Israeli-Jewish *identity*.

CHAPTER 2

Conceptual Contours for the Study of Jewish Identity

While the study of ethnic identity can obviously not be divorced from that of identity in general, we shall skirt the broader field and limit ourselves to the specific ethnic aspects. With the Jewish identity as the focus of our attention we shall seek to erect a series of guide-posts which will be followed in the subsequent empirical exploration.

Although there is this limitation to the study, it would seem to us that the manifestations of ethnic identity have a more tangible and less elusive quality than the expressions of some of the other facets of identity. If—as we believe—the study of ethnic identity will receive increasing attention in the future, such investigations may constitute useful vantage points from which to make contributions to the understanding of identity in general.

The Definition of Ethnic Identity

The ethnic identity (or more precisely, subidentity) of an individual is, of course, just one of the subidentities which constitute the total identity and which develop around its core. A person who speaks of himself as a Jew, a teacher, a father, is describing only three of the sub-identities which go into the making of the kind of person he is. The core, as Miller has defined it, is "the organizing part of the identity in that its traits interact with all the other traits outside the core."[1]

Emphasizing that a person's conception of his self develops in the course of social interaction, Miller distinguishes between objective public identity (a person's pattern of traits as they appear to others), subjective public identity (his perception of his appearance to others), and self-identity (the person's private version of his pattern of traits). Self-identity is, of course, influenced by subjective public identity. Miller prefers "self-identity" to the more common term "self-concept" which, as he points out, sometimes lacks the connotation that the self is a social object.[2]

In her review (in 1961) of studies of the self-concept, Wylie pointed out that the theories on the subject "are in many ways ambiguous, incomplete, and overlapping and no one theory has received a large amount of systematic empirical exploration."[3] In a more recent 1965 paper, French and Sherwood have suggested that a major explanation of the limited research output may have been the lack of systematic theory to provide the basis for systematic research.[4]

Behind the diversity of theories is a wide array of definitions. We shall derive our definition of ethnic identity by basing ourselves on definitions of identity provided both by Miller and Erikson. Miller refers to identity as "the pattern of observable or inferable attributes 'identifying' a person to himself and others."[5] Erikson (who despite his insightful studies of identity admits to the difficulty of definition) states in *Childhood and Society* that "the ego identity develops out of a gradual integration of all identifications."[6] Discussing elsewhere Freud's formulation of his own "inner identity" with Judaism, Erikson speaks of the reflection in the individual of "an essential aspect of a group's inner coherence."[7]

Depending upon the particular context we shall use the term ethnic identity, and, more specifically, Jewish identity to mean either (1) the pattern of attributes of the ethnic group as seen by its members, i.e., what "being Jewish" is seen by them to mean, or (2) the reflection in the individual of these attributes, i.e., how the individual sees himself by virtue of his membership of the ethnic group.

While it is useful to bear in mind the distinction between "identification" and "identity," the two terms will frequently intertwine in the analysis which follows.

Marking-off and Alignment

Identity implies both sameness and uniqueness. A person who has a certain ethnic identity is aligned with members of a particular group and at the same time is marked off from members of other groups.

In a study of a Jewish community in the Diaspora special attention would have to be given to the marking-off implications of an identity. Members of a minority— much more so than members of a majority—are conscious of being marked off from certain others. One of the most significant divisions of their world for members of a Jewish community is that between themselves and the non-Jews around them. Indeed the negative ascriptive category "non-Jews" comes tripping off their tongues more readily than would categories such as "non-Christians" or "non-Americans" from the tongues of the respective majorities. In their introduction to a recent study by Stember, *Jews in the Mind of America,* Sklare and Solotaroff observe that ". . . while the image of the Jew may no longer be expected to possess much significance in the mind of the secularized American Gentile, the image of the Gentile will remain central in the mind of the Jew, however acculturated and secularized his own life may become. For to be a Jew in any meaningful sense of the term means that one must establish and respect a certain boundary between Jews and Gentiles, an act of self-definition that is hardly as necessary for a Christian in America."[8]

Where the marking-off group is negatively evaluated, the evaluation of the Jewish group is likely to gain by comparison and distinctive Jewish characteristics may be highlighted to prevent any mistake in identity. Where the marking-off group is positively evaluated, distinctive Jewish characteristics which run counter to its standards may be looked on askance or may deliberately be slurred over. Evaluation by Jews of their non-Jewish neighbors differs from country to country and has differed throughout history. The Jews herded together and humiliated in the ghettos of medieval Europe nonetheless felt their own culture to be superior to that of their detractors.[9] The Jews living in freedom in the advanced technological societies of the West generally view the majority culture with considerable deference. Of special interest is the position of Jews where they are wedged in between two distinct subgroups of the non-Jewish population and where they accordingly need to make what may be for them an invidious choice of a source of reference.

The individual members of a Jewish minority will differ in their relation to the non-Jewish majority according to their position in their Jewish group. Those who readily accept their Jewish affiliation are more aware of their distinctiveness, of what sets them apart, while those on the periphery who wish to leave the group are more anxious to stress what they have in common with the majority. The former will tend to be conscious of intergroup dissimilarities, of the differences between the Jewish and Gentile groups, while the latter will underline intragroup dissimilarities, that not all Jews are alike and should not be branded as the bearers of identical "undesirable" characteristics. Jews on the periphery would indeed have wished the lines of demarcation to have been drawn differently so that they could be aligned with those from whom they are now marked off.

Unlike Jewish minorities, the Jews living in their own majority society in Israel are not in daily juxtaposition with an omnipresent non-Jewish group. In every meeting with a stranger a Jew in the Diaspora automatically asks himself the question: "Is this person a Jew or a non-Jew?" And if he concludes the other is a non-Jew the first question is followed by further queries addressed silently to himself: "Is he cognizant of my Jewishness?" "Does it affect his relationship to me?" The Jew in Israel takes the Jewishness of others for granted (unless there are clear indications to the contrary) and he knows that this does not serve as a differentiating factor between him and those he meets in daily intercourse. Although non-Jews undoubtedly come to mind from time to time, they are not likely to feature as prominently in the consciousness of the Jewish majority as in that of a Jewish minority; they do not serve in the same way as a constant reminder to Jews in Israel that they are marked off as different.

The Basis of Alignment

While we shall examine how and by whom Israeli Jews see themselves marked off, what would seem to be more important in a study of the Jewish majority society in Israel is the basis of the alignment between its members inside Israel and between them and Jews elsewhere.

In his incisive pioneering studies of group life, Kurt Lewin has stressed the fact that group belongingness is based on the dynamics of interdependence rather than on similarity. At the same time he has indicated how much misconception exists on the subject both in scientific and popular thinking. "Stressing similarity or dissimilarity, rather than interdependence, is typical of the descriptive 'classificatory' epoch, which can be observed in a relatively early stage of development in practically every science. It governs also, to a large degree, the everyday thinking concerning groups. The discrepancy between what people should do if they would be guided by their real interest, and what they actually do is frequently caused by the fact that a person feels himself belonging to those to whom he is similar or to whom he wishes to be similar. On the other hand, his 'real interest' would demand that he should feel belonging to those upon whom his dependence is greatest."[10]

Wide divergences of opinion may exist among Jews as to how the Jewish group should be defined and as to whether they are similar to other Jews or not. On the other hand, the facts of Jewish existence are such that a feeling of a common destiny or fate can be more easily invoked. If interdependence is recognized as the basis of belongingness, even some of the Jews who see themselves as dissimilar from other Jews may regard themselves as belonging to a Jewish group.

Our study will need to examine the part played respectively by the feeling of similarity and by the feeling of interdependence in determining alignment. As between Israelis and Jews elsewhere, our hypothesis is that it is the feeling of interdependence that binds together. Israelis are likely to be aware of the dissimilarities between themselves and Jews socialized in other environments, but are likely to accept their common Jewishness in situations where interdependence comes to the fore. Within the majority itself, i.e., among Israelis, the feeling of similarity may have more of a part to play, but even in this case it is likely that the alignment is based primarily on interdependence.

We are using interdependence in the sense of a change

in the state of any part of the whole affecting the state of
all the other parts. In the context of Jewish life this will
be taken to mean that whatever happens to Jews *qua*
Jews anywhere has implications for Jews everywhere.
Related to the feeling of interdependence is likely to be a
sense of mutual responsibility, and the question will arise
in this study to what extent Israelis recognize the existence of such mutual responsibility between Israel and the
communities of the Diaspora. Similarly, there can be no
proper study of the Jewish identity of a Diaspora community without consideration of what obligations it sees
as arising from its relationship to Israel.

There are, of course, kinds of interdependence as well
as degrees of interdependence. Thus, there is the interdependence which results from promotive cooperation
in the pursuit of a common goal, as well as the interdependence in the face of an external threat.[11] Sensitivity
to insult of Jews is a reflection of the latter kind of interdependence. There is likely to be a high degree of such
sensitivity among members of a minority who may feel
personally insulted wherever there is even the slightest
hint of an insult directed against their group. We shall
examine how far Israelis still experience this sensitivity
when Jews elsewhere are insulted.

When we turn from insult to praise, our hypothesis will
be that praise of Jews will not be as readily perceived as
pertaining to all members of the group. It may be that
sensitivity to praise exists to the extent that there is a
feeling of similarity between members of a group.

A comprehensive investigation of Jewish identity will
need to go beyond the examination of the perceived basis
of alignment and explore additional facets of the belongingness to the Jewish collectivity. The question that immediately arises is how is the Jewish group defined by its
members—as a religious entity, as a national entity, or
as both? The Jewish people is a unique blend of religious
and national elements; both Jews and non-Jews often fail

to grasp this complexity and consequently draw fallacious parallels with other groups. Does a particular individual regard himself included within the terms of the definition he gives of the group, and how does he see his position vis-a-vis other members?

The Source of Self-esteem

What is there about the Jewish group which attracts and what is there which repels members? Some — but not necessarily all — attributes of the Jewish identity may be so evaluated by members of the group as to serve as a source of self-esteem.[12] Again, among these attributes some may contribute more than others to self-esteem. Under what circumstances then does "being Jewish" foster self-esteem, and when — and for what type of members — are feelings of inferiority associated with it? How do tendencies to leave the group develop, and when, on the other hand, do members tend to draw closer to it? In what ways do individuals who are on the periphery differ from those at the center of the group? What are the relationships of the occupants of the respective positions to out-groups?

Members of a minority are indeed often ambivalent about their group. They may disparage the group in its entirety or specific segments of it. There may also conceivably be a liking of the collectivity and a dislike of the members. The study of these variegated facets of ethnic belongingness are of particular interest in the case of so widely dispersed and diversified people as the Jews. Some Jews think in terms of "one Jewish people," while there are others whose relationship is primarily with their local community and who have little concern for Jews elsewhere. There are differences of opinion, and at times animosities, between religious and non-religious Jews, between European and Oriental Jews — as once there were, for example, between German and East

European Jews. And so the analysis of group belongingness leads to questions about the extent to which there
is a differentiation into subgroups and how these subgroups are evaluated. In this study we shall give particular
attention to the way in which the Israelis view Jews from
different countries of the Diaspora.

To what extent does the Jewish group serve not only as
a membership group but as a source of reference, and, if
so, on what issues? Many of the psychological problems
of the Diaspora Jew arise from the fact that he often tends
to accept as a source of reference the norms of the non-
Jewish majority culture which may run counter to those
of his Jewish membership group. One of the merits of
Israel as a majority Jewish society lies in the fact that it
may avoid this conflict.

The Content of "Being Jewish"

In discussing the group as a source of reference we need
to examine the content of "being Jewish" and the attributes of "a good Jew" as seen by members of the group.
The emphasis in Jewish life has been on observance
rather than on belief, and this brings us to an examination
of the behavioral expressions of "being Jewish." There
are wide differences in this respect among Jews in the
Diaspora—from the Orthodox Jew observing the many
mitzvot (religious commandments) to the marginal Jew
whose limited Jewishness may find expression merely in
some measure of association socially with other Jews.[13]
Since the Jewishness of the Israeli is taken for granted
unless there are indications to the contrary, he does not
need to demonstrate his Jewish identification in order to
be seen as a Jew. In regard to association preferences,
his social environment is such that these associations are
in any case with other Jews. In what ways then does the
Israeli specifically express his Jewishness? In the case of

the Orthodox Israeli, distinctively Jewish practices are a regular part of his daily life. But how does being Jewish express itself in the lives of Israelis who are not religious? To what extent, for example, is participation in certain ceremonies and festival celebrations seen by them as an expression of Jewishness? Thus, the *bar mitzvah* is widely celebrated even in non-religious circles, but there are variations in the "Jewish" significance attached to the celebration.

One of the behavioral facets of being Jewish is the readiness or otherwise of members of the Jewish group to appear in the eyes of others as Jews. Marginal Jews meeting non-Jews will tend to avoid presenting themselves as Jews even in situations where such presentation is necessary. Jews at the center of their group may sometimes present themselves as Jews in situations not requiring such presentation. In presenting a "visiting-card" as an Israeli to non-Jews, the Israeli proceeding abroad is in fact presenting himself and is being seen as someone who is also a Jew. But even in cases where he simply states "I am an Israeli" and implicitly presents himself as a Jew, he may— by nuances in tone (emphasis on the word "Israeli") and otherwise—indicate whether as an Israeli he is "a Jew like these local Jews" or "a Jew who is different from these local Jews."

A study inspired by the desire to aid in the preservation of a particular identity (and this is indeed the bias of the present study) will pay special attention to the forces which strengthen or weaken that identity. Thus, we would explore what factors heighten the sense of interdependence and under what circumstances it is accompanied by a recognition of mutual responsibility. How do the home, the school, the peer groups contribute to identity development? Under what circumstances does a background factor such as the memory of the Holocaust (the destruction of European Jewry) add to the intensity of a Jewish identity?

Time Perspective and Identity

The alignment with an ethnic group implies a relationship to the group beyond a given moment in time—to the past and future of that group as well as to its present. An ethnic identity points, indeed, to an individual's link with "the unique values, fostered by a unique history, of his people."[14] In a study of alignment with so ancient a people as the Jews the interrelationship of past, present, and future merits special attention.

There have been several studies of the role of what may be termed "developmental time perspective," i.e., time perspective in the life cycle of the individual— studies of the young child who lives essentially in the present, of the adolescent standing on the brink of crucial decisions as the scope of his time perspective widens rapidly, the octogenarian with a shrinking future turning to the memories of the past.[15] But systematic exploration of the relationship between what we may term "historical time perspective" and *ethnic* identity has still to be undertaken. It would seem to us that this exploration would be facilitated by an analysis of time perspective into its various dimensions. We would suggest that the relevant dimensions in a discussion of the relationship between historical time perspective and ethnic identity are those which relate to past, present, and future orientation, to scope, to structurization, to selectivity, to continuity, and to probability of locomotion.

Let us first examine what is implied by the *past, present, and future orientation*. This dimension is concerned with whether the orientation of the members of the group is primarily to the past, to the present, or to the future, or whether there is a more balanced view embracing the three time sequences.

A people may tend to dwell on the glories of its past, and disconsolately see no relation between the past, a bleak present, and an unpromising future. On the other hand, it may find in the past a source of inspiration for the planning of a brighter future, the hope of which in turn makes tolerable the hardships of the present. In recent Jewish history an example of the latter orientation is provided by the Zionist movement. Acting on their analysis of the Jewish problem of their time, the Zionists harnessed the forces arising out of a distressful present situation to an age-old yearning and canalized them into a constructive program for the building of a Jewish state.[16] How crucial a role an historical time perspective could continue to play was dramatically illustrated in the early stages of the movement. At the beginning of the present century, Russian Zionists refused—despite the dire need of a haven of refuge after the Kishinev pogrom—to accept a British offer of territory in Uganda lest it deflect them from Zion. And, indeed, it would seem that the settlement of no other territory would have released such reservoirs of energy and dedication as did the restoration of an ancestral homeland.

There will obviously be significant differences in orientation to the future between some of the small Jewish communities in Europe, pathetic remnants of the Holocaust, striving, with little prospect of success, to maintain some semblance of Jewish corporate existence, and the larger, vigorous communities, such as that in the United States, seeking to extend further the foundations of their Jewish life through improved educational and other facilities.

Scope refers to the range, or span, of the time perspective. It may be narrowly limited to events which occurred only a short while ago or which are immediately impending, or it may be broad, i.e., stretching extensively into a more distant past or future.

The Israeli Jew is in an unusual position on this dimension. His past time perspective as an Israeli is of relatively short scope; as a Jew he may look backward to a past spanning thousands of years.

There may be instances in which members of a group

find solace in hopes which may be realized only in an indeterminate future[17]—as do some deeply religious Jews waiting patiently for the coming of the Messiah—but generally morale is low where there are no clear boundaries to the scope of the future time perspective. This brings us to a consideration of two further dimensions which are concerned with the structure and with the clarity of the boundaries in the time sequences.

Structurization refers to the organization of the time perspective. A time perspective is said to be structured when there is an understanding of how the past has led into the present, or, in regard to the future, when there is some vision of the paths that lead to the hoped-for goals, of how and when the aspirations can be realized. There is likely to be a positive relationship between morale and the structuredness of the future time perspective.[18]

Differentiation relates to the division of the past or the future into a series of distinguishable segments. The number of such segments determines what is known as the *density* of the time perspective.[19] There will obviously be a relation between familiarity with the history of a particular period and the degree of its differentiation.

Selectivity is concerned with the differential attitudes which may exist toward these segments of the past. Are some referred to with pride, others with shame? Is there a tendency to concentrate on some epochs and to obscure others? In order to bolster self-esteem ethnic groups tend to seek out events in their history which shed luster on their past, and at times may go further and interpret these events in a way which fits the temper of the present.

As the situation of Israelis is so radically different from that of Jews in the Diaspora, they are likely—in referring to various periods of Jewish history in the Diaspora—to show considerable selectivity, and in this study we shall explore the direction in which the selectivity goes. If this were also a study of a Diaspora community, say of American Jewry, we would encounter a time perspective which is likely to be less selective than that of the Israelis in regard to the centuries of Diaspora life. But a certain selectivity—related to current ideologies in American Jewish life—will nevertheless be found. Thus, the existence in the past of centers of Jewish cultural creativity outside of Eretz Israel (Land of Israel) is often stressed. In regard to the future, as the tragic experience of so many other Diaspora communities contradicts their hopes for a bright Jewish future in the United States, they are likely to indicate why "America is different."

The Israeli and the American Jew will each tend to interpret the Jewish historic past from the vantage point of his own present.

Continuity concerns the interrelatedness of past, present, and future. Is a particular event (such as the destruction of European Jewry) relegated to the limbo of the historic past, or is it seen as exercising a continuing influence through the present into the future? A key question in the present study will be whether Israelis see the Israel of today and tomorrow as the projection into the present and future of the past of the Jewish people and whether they regard themselves as the bearers of the Jewish historic tradition.

A past cannot be "adopted." It is only when it consists of memories which still live on in the lives of men and impinge on the present life-space that it plays its proper part in the development of an ethnic identity. (Black identity, understandably in search of its past, will need to reactivate memories of this kind.)

Probability of locomotion pertains to the anticipated attainability of the goals of the group within a reasonable time in the future. One of the contributions of the Zionist movement was its transformation of a centuries-old yearning into a series of concrete goals seen as achievable through defined forms of action.

The Confluence of Two Subidentities

The study of ethnic identity gains in both complexity and interest when there is need to examine two subidentities (in our case, the Jewish and the Israeli) coexisting side by side and interacting with one another. The proper comprehension of any one subidentity requires that it be seen in the context of its association with the other. A Jewish identity anywhere in the Diaspora bears the impact of the other ethnic identity with which it is associated. (Pertinent to this subject, as to others, is the thesis propounded by Lipset "that the comparative study of the Jew must be linked inseparably with the comparative study of the Gentile.")[20]

It would seem to us that the relationship of two such subidentities can best be analyzed by regarding the person (the Israeli Jew) as being in overlapping situations, i.e., as subject simultaneously to influences from two (or more) psychological situations.[21] Adopting, with some modifications, the analysis by Barker[22] of the properties of overlapping situations, we shall explore the extent of overlap between the two subidentities, the degree of consonance between them, the extent of their centrality, their salience in differing situations, their valence and relative potency.

Of particular importance in our study is the extent of the *overlap* between the subidentities, i.e., their pertinence to identical regions of the person's life-space.[23] The larger the overlap, the greater, obviously, will be the measure of reciprocal influence. Of significance too will be the clarity or otherwise of the boundaries between the subidentities and the permeability of these boundaries.

Our hypothesis is that there is likely to be a larger measure of perceived overlap between Jewishness and Israeliness than there is between Jewishness and Americanism, or between Jewishness and any other ethnic sub-identity with which it may be associated. It is conceivable, furthermore, that crucial differences exist between Israelis who perceive such overlap and those who regard their Jewishness and Israeliness as things apart.

Consonance refers to the extent to which two situations are seen as giving rise to psychological forces moving in the same direction. Barker has pointed out that types of overlapping situations vary along a continuum at the one extreme of which are situations leading to consonant behavior and at the other extreme situations requiring completely antagonistic behavior. At points between these extremes are situations determining behaviors of varying degrees of compatibility or of interference with one another.[24]

In addition to the interconnectedness between Israeli-ness and Jewishness we may anticipate a high degree of consonance between them. The Israeli is accordingly less likely to experience the dualism which enters into the life of a Diaspora Jewish community where the Jewish subculture exists as something different from the majority culture.

The central regions in the life-space have been de-scribed as "the more intimate, personal regions" in which the individual is more sensitive than in the peripheral.[25] The centrality of a region is related to the proximity of that region to other regions within a whole. The more central a region, the more readily does it influence other regions and the more readily is it influenced by them.[26] Centrality may thus be said to correspond to breadth or extensity of influence.

Membership of an underprivileged minority has reper-cussions in many spheres. There can be no doubt about the centrality of "being Black" or "being a Jew" in the life of a person, quite irrespective of whether or not he rec-onciles himself to the fact of his minority membership.

Salience refers to prominence in the perceptual field,

the "figure" against the ground, the extent to which an object or activity catches the person's attention at a given moment.[27] Several experimental studies have been conducted on the salience of group memberships.[28] After heightening the subjects' awareness of their membership in a specific group by vivid reminders, the researchers investigated the effect of the increased salience of the group's norms in the given situation in producing change or resistance to change.

Certain "behavior settings,"[29] such as the synagogue, will bring to the fore, i.e., enhance the salience of, the Jewish identity of a person in Israel or the Diaspora. Again, the Jew in the Diaspora may be reminded of his Jewishness in a particular situation by an anti-Semitic remark or some form of discrimination. The frequency of these reminders over a wide variety of situations contributes to the centrality of the Jewish identity. There is indeed a relationship between salience and centrality although at the same time the distinction between the two should be observed. "Salience is a short-term phenomenon, i.e., a function of the immediate situation; centrality refers to a much more durable interest on the part of the individual in certain kinds of objects, with these objects remaining important for him through many differing specific situations,"[30]

Valence denotes the attractiveness (positive valence) or repulsiveness (negative valence) of a goal-object or activity.[31] The valence of his Jewishness for an individual is likely to be related to the degree of his proximity to the center of the Jewish group. Salience, on the other hand, will frequently be related to proximity to the non-Jewish group, i. e., location near the border between the two groups. The marginal Jew often looks around anxiously to determine whether the non-Jews he meets classify him as Jewish or whether the behavior of other Jews casts an opprobrium also on him. The negative valence of his Jewishness accompanied by high salience produces severe tension in these situations. For the Jew at the center of his group, i. e., for whom his Jewish subidentity has high positive valence, the salience of his Jewishness may also be high (for reasons other than proximity to the non-Jewish majority) but is likely to be less anxiety-provoking.

Although members of a Jewish community in the Diaspora may see their Jewishness as relevant only in specific, limited regions of the life-space, non-Jews may at times discriminate against them as Jews in regions in which Jewishness should ordinarily be irrelevant, e. g., application for a job or admission into a social club. This leads to an ambiguity and consequent tension in Jew-Gentile relationships.

Potency is defined as the weight, or influence, of a situation relative to all simultaneously acting situations.[32] While centrality referred to the breadth of influence, potency relates to the intensity, or strength, of influence.

Barker has suggested that "potency" and "valence" together determine behavior in overlapping situations.[33] We shall regard the potency of a situation as corresponding to the *effect* that situation has on behavior, and we shall then treat valence as *one of the determinants* of potency. We would submit that the other determinant is salience.[34] Thus, in one of the experiments on the salience of group memberships, the reminder to the students gathered in a room when a questionnaire was administered that they were Catholics resulted in more answers conforming to the Catholic norms than were given by students in another room who received no such reminder. It could be assumed that the valence of their Catholicism was equal for the students in the two rooms, but the heightened salience of their membership in the first case contributed to the higher relative potency of the Catholic group in determining the responses.

It may be that when valence differentials are extremely high, differentials in salience will be relatively unim-

portant (and possibly also vice versa, i.e., with high
salience differential, differentials in valence may be
relatively unimportant).[35] Usually, however, both factors
will be in operation and each will make a contribution to
potency.

An Application of the Conceptual Framework

Following the conceptual contours which we have out-
lined we shall seek to analyze the Israeli-Jewish identity
in the light of data obtained from high school students
and their parents. After introducing in the next chapter
the issues which are the main concern of this enquiry, we
shall proceed to examine the relationship between the two
subidentities—we begin with the presentation of this
part of the material, since the failure to grasp the peculiar
interrelatedness between the two subidentities often leads
to basic misconceptions about the Jewishness of the
Israeli. We shall then explore the marking-off and
alignment implications of the Israeli-Jewish identity, the
historical time perspective of Israeli Jews, their definition
of their Jewish group and of its attributes, their view of
the Gentile world and of anti-Semitism.

There is a need to go beyond the welter of what are
often contradictory impressions and to assemble systematic data on the attitudes of a representative sample of
Israel's Jewish population. No such study has been
previously undertaken and sweeping generalizations have
been made on the basis of what little has been known
about the attitudes of individuals or groups who were not
necessarily representative of the population at large.
It is conceivable that significant differences exist in the
strength of Jewish identity between generations, between
religious and non-religious Jews, between members of the
Ashkenazic and Oriental communities, between veteran

settlers and new immigrants. Statements about the identity of the Israeli which do not take proper account of these differences are likely to represent partial and misleading views.

The present study seeks to fill a void in the knowledge about this crucial area in the life of the Israeli community. While it too suffers from a limitation, in that it does not encompass the whole of Israel's Jewish population, it is based on a representative country-wide sample of defined sectors of that population. The composition of the selected sectors is such that it reflects the generational, religious, communal, and other variables necessary for an understanding of the Israeli-Jewish identity.

The study focuses on Israeli school-going youth born in the year the State of Israel was established. It is based on the data obtained from a representative sample of all the eleventh graders—the sixteen- to seventeen-year-old group—in schools within the framework of the Israel Ministry of Education in the 1964–65 school year. The sample comprised 3679 students in 117 schools.[36]

Questionnaires were administered to classes in schools sampled on a stratified basis according to four criteria: (a) type of school (academic, vocational, etc.); (b) religious status (secular or religious); (c) recency of immigration (children of veteran settlers, new immigrants); and (d) communal origin (Ashkenazic, Oriental). Interviews were conducted with a number of the students so as to enable them to explain and amplify responses on the questionnaire.

In order to view the attitudes of the students in a comparative generational setting, it was decided to study their parents as well. A questionnaire containing the key questions given to the students was administered to the parents of a subsample of the students. The parents, who were located in all parts of the country, were visited personally by members of the interviewing team; completed questionnaires were obtained from 443 of the 539 parents, i. e., 82 percent.

In addition to the major study carried out in 1965, two supplementary small-scale studies were conducted in 1968. One study had as its subject 255 eleventh graders in seven schools in Jerusalem and Haifa; the other study was of undergraduates at the Hebrew University.

The importance of the religious variable in determining identity became evident from the outset, and the principal comparison made throughout is between subjects (among the parents as well as the students) who indicated in the questionnaire that they were *dati'im* (religious), *m'sorati'im* (traditionalist), and *lo dati'im* (non-religious) respectively. In referring to these categories we shall use the literal translation of the three terms. It should, however, be noted that in the Israel context the terms relate to degrees of religious *observance*. *Dati* implies a strict observance of religious obligations; *m'sorati* indicates a positive orientation to Jewish tradition accompanied by varying degrees of laxity and selectivity in regard to observance; *lo dati* means non-observant (although here too some customs may be honored).

We have not dealt in the study in any systematic way with the dynamics of the factors which go into the shaping of an ethnic identity, such as the process of socialization in the home, the influence of the school, of peer groups, of the wider social milieu. We shall, however, present a series of profiles of religious, traditionalist, and non-religious students in which an attempt will be made to reflect the operation of these factors. These profiles are based on detailed case studies of students and their parents. We shall, furthermore, compare the attitudes of the students with those of their teachers.

CHAPTER 3

An Old-New People in an Old-New Land

When the State of Israel was established just over two decades ago, Jews—for the first time after the long centuries of Dispersion—constituted a majority society. The first generation of children to be born "Israelis" have completed their schooling and fought in the Six Day War. What form is their Israeli-Jewish identity taking, and how does it differ from that of their parents, most of whom were born in the Diaspora? What is the relation between the Israeli and the Jewish components of this identity? Do the Israelis see themselves as part of the continuity of Jewish history? How strong are the bonds between them and Jews of the Diaspora?

Continuity or Discontinuity

It would seem strange that questions of this kind should arise at all in relation to a people which has been characterized throughout the vicissitudes of time and place by a unique sense of unity and continuity. Many Jews—even if they have never seen Jerusalem—could with sin-

cerity state about their own lives what the Israeli writer,
S. Y. Agnon, said so succinctly in his speech at Stock-
holm, accepting the Nobel Prize for Literature. "As a
result of the historic catastrophe in which Titus of Rome
destroyed Jerusalem and banished Israel from its land,
I was born in one of the cities of the Exile. But always
I regarded myself as having been born in Jerusalem."[1]
And just as Jews longed for Jerusalem, so one of the primary purposes of the State of Israel has been the "in-
gathering of the Exiles," and on its statute book is the
Law of Return which accords to every Jew the privilege
of entry into Israel and automatic extension of Israeli
citizenship.

But while this "in-gathering" is the raison d'être of the
State of Israel, there has been considerable unclarity
about the attitudes of the new generation of Israelis to
Jews who remain abroad, and indeed to the Jewish past
in the Diaspora. In the Diaspora a people yearned through
the centuries for its distant homeland; the young generation of Israelis who have grown up in that homeland
are now being required to define their relationship to a
people in the far-flung lands of the Diaspora.[2]

An eminent French sociologist, Georges Friedmann,
a marginal Jew whose own sense of Jewish identity was
deeply stirred by his visit to Israel, concludes in his book
The End of the Jewish People? that "a new people is
being created every day in Israel; a young people that
is neither an appendage nor the center of the now-legen-
dary 'Jewish people.'"[3] Can this be said to be a correct
appraisal?

Writing of the children of the one kibbutz he studied
in the Valley of Jezreel, an American anthropologist,
Melford Spiro, states in *Children of the Kibbutz:* "In
effect, the sabras feel no tie—other than a negative one—
with much of Jewish tradition or with peculiarly Jewish
values; they want little to do with the last 2000 years of
the Jewish past; and they wish to dissociate themselves
from those Jews, who, actually or symbolically, represent

those values and that past."⁴ To the extent that such sharp negation of the past exists, is it peculiar to the "sabras" of this particular type of kibbutz, affiliated with a specific ideological movement, or does it prevail in wider circles as well?

These are the impressions of observers from the outside who may be said to lack an intimate acquaintanceship with Israeli youth. But inside Israel, too, growing concern has been expressed across the years about the Jewish component in the identity of the youth of the country. While the emergence of a distinct Israeli nationality brought the question of the relationship between Israel and the Diaspora more strongly to the fore, the alarm had been sounded before the establishment of the State. "Is there in the soul of the youth of Eretz Israel the capacity, and the need, to share the feeling of a common Jewish destiny, to experience a kinship with the Jewish people . . . ?" anxiously asks a revered leader of the Jewish community of those days, Berl Kaznelson, in an address delivered in 1944.⁵

How widely felt was the anxiety about Israeli youth's possible estrangement from their Jewish heritage was evidenced in the debate in the Knesset in 1959 on a proposal by the Ministry of Education about the inculcation of "Jewish consciousness." Even the majority of the non-religious members of the Knesset were of the opinion that schoolchildren should become acquainted with Jewish religious beliefs and practices—without the requirement (in the secular schools) that they personally adopt these beliefs and practices.⁶

But the acceptance of the program (the effects of which were never assessed) did not completely allay anxiety. Indeed the questions which had been asked through the years assumed more than their usual pertinence a few years later when Eichmann was kidnapped in the Argentine by Israeli agents and brought to stand trial in Jerusalem.

The Eichmann Trial

In the Eichmann trial a chapter of history was pro-
jected with peculiar intensity from the past into the present as the story of the Holocaust of European Jewry was
retold—and, in a sense, relived—by its survivors. The
presence of the accused, a chief agent in the destruction,
sitting in the glass cage in the courtroom facing his judges,
contributed to this impression of the past being lifted
into the present. The confrontation of Eichmann with
his accusers was more than the retelling of a tragic tale;
it was as if battle had been joined again between Eichmann, the Nazi system and ideology he represented, and
the representatives of the people who were among the
main victims of that system and ideology. It may be that,
at any rate for those who were not in Europe at the time,
the impact of the Holocaust, seen in the perspective of
the trial, was stronger than that of the stories which fil-
tered through piecemeal soon after the actual events.

In bringing Eichmann to stand trial in Jerusalem, Israel
again gave dramatic expression to its peculiar link with
Jews the world over—not only with the living but also
with the dead, "the six million accusers" in whose name
the prosecutor in the trial spoke.[7]

The trial, which across a number of months became
an overwhelmingly salient fact in the lives of the Jews
of Israel, old and young, evoked no small measure of
heart-searching among them. It uncovered some of the
deeper recesses of the attitudes of Israelis to Jews the
world over and afforded additional glimpses into the
tortured inner dilemma of sections of Israeli youth about
their relationship to their people's immediate past. There
were expressions of perplexity on the part of some young
Israelis that the Jews in Europe should have gone meekly
to their doom "like sheep to the slaughter"—for so it
seemed to these Israelis viewing the past from their par-

ticular vantage point. What did they have in common, they asked themselves, with Jews of that kind?

In the years following the trial increasing emphasis has been placed by educators and others on the Warsaw Ghetto revolt and other instances of resistance. Such acts of resistance Israeli youth readily admire. But questions still remain. What of their relationship to Jews who showed only passive resistance or who did not—often could not—resist at all? To what extent do they identify with them for what they were and as they were? And a further crucial question in any enquiry about the sense of continuity—do Israeli youth see themselves as if they are survivors of the Holocaust, a surviving remnant of a Jewish people charged with a special responsibility for ensuring its future?

A Majority with a Minority Past

Israeli youth is indeed in an unusual psychological position. They have grown up in independence as members of a majority in their own sovereign state, but their Jewish past is to a considerable extent the annals of a dependent Jewish minority in the Diaspora. They have no difficulty in relating themselves to the warriors led by Bar Cochba at the fortress of Masada or even much further back to the Jews of the earliest Biblical days. But there is an understandable problem in identifying with the long period of Jewish minority existence so different to the conditions of their own life. Do they find it possible to view the past as a continuous chain including the years of Dispersion or is there a mental leap from ancient statehood directly to the modern Israel?

The absence of systematic information on these questions has resulted in exaggerated attention to any and every report of the views of young Israelis, however unrepresentative they might be. Thus, disturbing newspaper

accounts of interviews with Israeli students led, as recently as January 1967, to questions from members of
both the Coalition and the Opposition in the Knesset and
to the referral of the subject for further exploration by
the Knesset's Committee on Education and Culture.

Only a few months later the behavior of Israeli youth
during the stirring events of the Six Day War seemed to
disprove the more extremely critical appraisals of Israeli-
Jewish identity. Not only were there indications that in
those days they were deeply conscious of the bonds that
linked them with other Jews, but there were also manifestations of a sense of historic mission on behalf of a
Jewish people.

Writing in 1964, Georges Friedmann commented: "In
spite of their willingness to come to an understanding
with the Arabs, the sabras are prepared to fight to re-
establish the integrity of Palestine under the Star of David
and to recover the ancient city of Jerusalem. But if there
is a holy place to which they are indifferent, it is the Wail-
ing Wall, the symbol of a past all trace of which, in their
view, should be obliterated."[8] Yet in 1967 hardened paratroopers wept when they reached the Wall—it was beyond
doubt the most emotion-laden event of the War.

What then is the real nature of the emerging Israeli-
Jewish identity? What are merely expressions of an
ephemeral enthusiasm, what indications of a deeper,
more lasting sense of Jewish identity?

These questions will be the burden of much of the
enquiry which follows.

Forces Shaping the Israeli-Jewish Identity

In seeking an answer to these questions the study will
concern itself with the attitudes, the subjective reports,
of the young Israelis and their parents. But although the
comparison between the parents and their sons and
daughters does introduce a developmental dimension,

the picture which is unfolded still has the limitations of
a cross-sectional view obtained at a given moment in
time. The historical background to this picture has been
elaborated in a number of studies,[9] and while we now
focus on the contemporary expressions of the Israeli
identity it should be borne in mind throughout that
the distinctive characteristics of this identity have been
shaped by forces which long antedate the establishment of the State of Israel. So, for example, some of
the tensions in the Israeli identity are latterday expressions of crosscurrents which have coursed through the
Zionist movement from its earliest years—emphasis on
the religious leitmotif by some and a revolt against religion by others; by some a negation of the *Galuth* as
degrading and corrupting coupled at times with a condemnation of the Jews who remained there under such
conditions, by others a conception of Israel as a cultural-
spiritual center providing dignity and uplift to the Jews
who are seen as continuing to live in large numbers in the
Diaspora; on the part of some an embittered withdrawal
from the Gentile world, but on the part of others a decision to renew contact with it on a basis of equality.
Again, while Israel is an amalgam of Jews who have come
from all parts of the world bringing with them the ways
of thought and behavior of the countries of their origin,
there are obviously strands in the population which are
more dominant than others. Thus, in many spheres the
tone was set by the pioneers of the second *aliyah* (immigration wave) who came from Eastern Europe at the turn
of the century.[10] In consequence of the leadership role
of these and other settlers from Eastern Europe, the
Israeli identity has stamped on it the imprint of the Jewish
life which prevailed in those countries as well as of the
ideologies that the immigrants brought with them. At
the same time the orientation of present-day Israel is
increasingly to the modes of thought and to the systems
of the Western democracies. The early settlers extolled
the virtues of a "return to the soil" but in an increasingly

industrialized society new emphases have become necessary. The image of the pioneer has been extended to include spheres other than agricultural settlement—it can
apply to a scientist in the laboratory, an officer in the
army, and an industrialist in his factory.[11]

The tensions which run through the Jewish identity
of the Oriental sector, who were far removed from some
of the ideological debates of the Zionist movement, have
peculiarities which require additional attention. In adopting the values of Israeli society they do indeed find a distinct Jewish kernel with which they can be familiar, but
they are strangers to the East European molds into which
many of its practices have been cast, the Western outlook
of this society, and its conceptions of technological progress. The parents may still find security in the maintenance of the accustomed traditional patterns of their
life; the sons and daughters, at times without such anchor-
age, are required to adjust to a social milieu sharply different to that of the homes of their parents from Yemen
or the Atlas mountains.

And finally, a seeming contradiction in the character
of all Israelis—a nation which has prided itself through
the centuries on being the "People of the Book," eschew-
ing all vestiges of militarism, has been compelled to develop the skills of war. The history of modern Jewish
settlement from its beginnings is also the story of Jewish
self-defense—from the rudimentary Hashomer organization, through *Haganah* and the Jewish Brigades in the two
world wars to the Israel Defense Forces (Z'va Haganah
Le'Israel) which came into being with the establishment
of the State. If, despite the pride in the victories and in
the acknowledged prowess of its army, Israel remains
essentially non-militaristic and seeks peace with its neighbors (though not a peace without security), we may see
in it the supremacy of certain more enduring values which
the exigencies of a particular period do not easily erase.

PART II

The Empirical Study

CHAPTER 4

The Interweaving
of Jewishness and Israeliness

Nowhere in the world does a Jewish subidentity exist
in isolation as an individual's exclusive ethnic identity.
It is everywhere linked with another ethnic subidentity
with which it interacts and by which it is influenced. And
so the Jewishness of the Israeli can be adequately com-
prehended only if seen in the context of its association
with his Israeliness—just as the Jewishness of an American Jew needs to be examined in the context of his
Americanism.

Jewishness and Israeliness
as Overlapping and Consonant

The great majority of our subjects regard their Jewishness and their Israeliness as interrelated.[1] Less than a
third of the students—and a much smaller minority of
parents—fail to observe any overlap and declare there
is no connection between feeling Israeli and feeling Jewish (see tables 1 and 2).

Table 1 Overlap and Consonance
When I feel more Jewish:

	All Respondents		Religious		Traditionalist		Non-Religious	
	Parents	Students	Parents	Students	Parents	Students	Parents	Students
1. I also feel more Israeli	83	70	81	83	88	76	76	62
2. There is no relationship between my feeling Jewish and my feeling Israeli	17	27	19	15	12	22	24	36
3. I feel less Israeli	-	3	-	2	-	2	-	2
Total %	100	100	100	100	100	100	100	100
N	434	2980	147	680	165	942	122	1358

Table 2 Overlap and Consonance
When I feel more Israeli:

	All Respondents		Religious		Traditionalist		Non-Religious	
	Parents	Students	Parents	Students	Parents	Students	Parents	Students
1. I also feel more Jewish	84	67	84	87	85	72	79	54
2. There is no relationship between my feeling Israeli and my feeling Jewish	15	29	16	10	13	24	18	41
3. I feel less Jewish	1	4	-	3	2	4	3	5
Total %	100	100	100	100	100	100	100	100
N	434	2980	147	680	165	942	122	1358

The perception of overlap is widely shared by all categories of parents—whether religious, traditionalist, or non-religious. While the perception of the religious students closely resembles that of the parents, a gap begins to appear between traditionalist students and traditionalist parents (the latter of whom are particularly high in the perception of overlap). The difference between parents and students widens still further when we examine the responses of the non-religious students, as many as 41 percent of whom declare there is no connection.

There is thus a not inconsiderable minority of students who view their being Israeli and being Jewish as separate compartments in their life-space. This points to a basic difference between the structure of their ethnic identity and that of the other students, in particular the religious students, with whom the Jewish and Israeli identities are closely interwoven. We shall later examine the implication of this difference.

Not only do the majority perceive an overlap between the Israeli and Jewish subidentities. If we take a further look at the responses in Tables 1 and 2, we note the large degree of perceived consonance or compatibility. "Feeling more Israeli" is seen as implying "feeling more Jewish," and vice versa. Here again the parents (84 percent) recognize more than do the students (67 percent) the consonance between the subidentities; similarly, the religious students (87 percent) do so more than the traditionalists (72 percent), and the traditionalists much more than the non-religious (54 percent) (see table 2). In the interviews the religious students are the most frequent proponents of the view that their Israeli subidentity is a reinforcement of the Jewish subidentity and that the Israeli Jew is the more complete type of Jew. What is most striking, however, is the almost total absence on the part of all students, non-religious as well as religious, of any experience of dissonance between the two elements. For only few of them (no more than 4 percent) does feeling more Israeli mean feeling less Jewish, or feeling more Jewish imply feeling less Israeli.

Typical remarks in the interviews:

"As a religious person, I see Jew and Israeli as one and the same thing. Therefore the more Jewish the more Israeli and vice versa. It is easier to be a good Jew in Israel and there is a connection."

"As a Jew I was taught to love Israel. 'Israeliness' is one of the duties imposed on a Jew."

Not only are Israeliness and Jewishness seen as entering into identical regions but there is no clear demarcation between them. Insofar as lines of demarcation can be observed they are clearer to overseas-born parents and to the religious students. In the case of the parents (unlike their children who were Israelis from birth) the Israeli subidentity was superimposed at a later stage of their lives on the preexisting Jewish subidentity. In the case of the religious students, clearly defined regions of religious observance are seen as pertaining primarily to the Jewish subidentity. At the same time these students see their Israeliness as an extension of their Jewishness and the line between the two is blurred. In the non-religious sector those students who feel that their Jewishness and Is-raeliness overlap have difficulty in defining in what ways their "being Jewish" specifically expresses itself.

It would seem that nowhere else is the Jewish subiden-tity interwoven so closely with another subidentity as it is with the Israeli subidentity. The Jewishness of a Jew in the Diaspora is generally limited to specific spheres of his life and there are relatively clear boundaries be-tween his Jewishness and his other ethnic subidentity.

When questions parallel to those asked of the Israeli students were addressed to a group of American Jewish students spending a year in Israel[2] more than 60 percent of the group maintained there was no connection between their feeling Jewish and feeling American (see tables 3A and 4A).* A group of visiting students is, of course, not representative—neither of American Jewry nor necessarily even of American Jewish students. But other studies[3] too suggest that American Jews, located within a prestigious majority culture dominating many areas of their lives, regard their Jewishness as pertinent only in certain settings and on particular occasions, and it would seem a reasonable hypothesis that an American Jew would find less of a connection between his Americanism and his Jewishness than would an Israeli between his Israeli and Jewish subidentities. As an American psychologist (Isidor Chein) has observed: ". . . A competitive situation thus develops and one can do (or think, or feel) something Jewish only by giving up or withdrawing from something in the stream of general activities."[4]

The lack of specificity about the Jewishness of the Israelis does not necessarily mean that it plays a less important role in their lives. Indeed, while the Jewishness of the Jew in the Diaspora relates only to specific, delimited regions, the Jewishness of many Israelis is more pervasive, i.e., it enters—along with their Israeliness— into a large number of regions.

Centrality: The Importance of Being Jewish or Israeli

From an exploration of the perceived interrelatedness of the two subidentities we now proceed to examine their centrality (which we shall in this context equate with "importance"). To what extent is being Jewish and being Israeli important in the lives of the students and their parents?

As was to be expected, the parents are much more emphatic (62 percent "very important" and another 29

*Tables which appear in the Appendix of Tables A but not in the body of the text have an "A" suffixed to the number.

percent "important") than are their sons and daughters (23 percent "very important" and 45 percent "important") about the part being Jewish plays in their lives (see table 5). Not only have the parents experienced the deprivations to which members of a Jewish minority have been subject in the Diaspora, but it is precisely because of the fact of their Jewishness that they either chose, or were obliged, to transplant their lives to Israel.

When the students amplify their responses their comments are often typical of the feeling of members of a majority in their own land whose day-to-day life is not characterized by a special awareness of problems of ethnic identity. This is so as long as their thoughts focus on their position inside Israel, but when they look beyond their own country a different note is sometimes sounded.

"I am like everybody else over here. Perhaps if I am outside the country, it will be different."

"As long as I am in the country it doesn't matter much. But the moment I leave (and I know because I once was overseas) it will matter a good deal."

The afterthoughts some of them express indicate that they indeed share the historical time perspective of a people which for centuries has been (and a large part of which still is) in a minority situation.

"In Israel, no, because the majority are Jews. Outside of Israel possibly yes, because there may be some prejudice against me. Here all are like me and there the majority are different."

"I think yes. Because overseas if there was anti-Semitism I would be amongst those suffering from it."

The religious students attribute much greater importance to being Jewish in their lives than do the traditionalists or non-religious; considerable areas of their daily conduct are governed by Jewish codes of observance and they see their Jewishness as an all–encompassing way of life.

Table 5 Centrality of Jewishness
"Does the fact that you are Jewish play an important part in your life?"

	All Respondents		Religious		Traditionalist		Non-Religious	
	Parents	Students	Parents	Students	Parents	Students	Parents	Students
1. It plays a very important part	62	23	79	62	58	18	52	7
2. It plays an important part	29	45	15	36	33	60	33	39
3. It is of little importance	8	25	6	1	9	18	9	44
4. It plays no part	1	7	-	1	-	4	6	10
Total %	100	100	100	100	100	100	100	100
N	434	2980	147	680	165	942	122	1358

"My whole way of life is determined by Judaism."

"I am all the time a Jew and cannot conceive of myself thinking otherwise."

"It expresses itself in every detail of my life . . . to what school I go, what sort of education I receive . . . whom I visit, who are my friends, everything!"

For the traditionalists it means less than this. While they are on the whole positively oriented towards Jewish tradition, they do not see their daily practice as guided by a comprehensive religious code. Such religious proclivities as they possess find expression mainly at the time of the festivals and other ceremonial occasions.

The non-religious students differ sharply from the religious students on the question of the part played by being Jewish. They also differ sharply from their non-religious parents. As many as 44 percent feel that being Jewish "is of little importance" in their lives and another 10 percent say "no part at all" (see table 5). For some of them, indeed, "being Jewish"—in the context of this ques-

tion—carries a strong, though not an exclusively, religious connotation.

"I am non-religious and Judaism appears to me to be mainly
a religion. Therefore the fact that I am Israeli matters more
to me [than the fact of being Jewish]."

The parallel question on the importance of "being
Israeli" elicits a far higher endorsement by traditionalist
and non-religious students than does the question about
being Jewish. While the religious students are more emphatic about the role of their Jewishness than about that
of their Israeliness, they at the same time do not fall below
the other categories of students in the importance they
attach to the part played in their lives by "being Israeli."
(see table 6).

Differing views about the relative importance of "being
Jewish" and "being Israeli" are reflected in the following
remarks by students in the interviews:

"I always have to think about the fact that I am a Jew and
as such have to carry out *mitzvot* [religious obligations]. I don't
have to think so much about being an Israeli."

"Being Israeli obliges me to be loyal to the State. Being Jewish obligates me to much more."

"Both are important. They are linked together. As Jews we
have been yearning two thousand years for our country."

"I attribute more importance to being Israeli, more love for
the country. I live in a country surrounded by enemies and do
not intend to leave. By contrast, a Jew can live in any country."

Noteworthy is the high percentage of parents (70 percent) who see being Israeli as playing "a very important"
part in their lives—considerably higher than the corresponding percentage of students (see table 6). The
parents who have come to Israel from the Diaspora have
had to acquire the Israeli identity which the students obtained by birth. It would seem that the importance of

Table 6 Centrality of Israeliness
"Does the fact that you are Israeli play an important part in your life?"

	All Respondents		Religious		Traditionalist		Non-Religious	
	Parents	Students	Parents	Students	Parents	Students	Parents	Students
1. It plays a very important part	70	43	73	44	73	43	64	42
2. It plays an important part	22	47	15	48	23	49	30	48
3. It is of little importance	6	7	9	5	2	5	6	8
4. It plays no part	2	3	3	3	2	3	-	2
Total %	100	100	100	100	100	100	100	100
N	434	2980	147	680	165	942	122	1358

being Israeli is highlighted for them as a result of the comparison they make with the period of their lives in which they were not Israelis.

Valence: The Attractiveness of Being Jewish or Israeli

A renunciation of identity is regarded by Israeli students as an act of cowardice—irrespective of whether such identity is attractive to them or not. In order to obtain some measure of the valence, or attractiveness, of their Jewishness for the students we accordingly placed them in a hypothetical situation in which they were called upon to choose their ethnic identity anew. The question was worded as follows: "If you were to be born all over again, would you wish to be born a Jew?" This was followed by the further question: "If you were to live abroad, would you wish to be born a Jew?"

Seventy percent of the students would wish to be born again as Jews; for 28 percent it is a matter of indifference (see table 7). When it becomes a question of living outside of Israel, only 54 percent would wish to be born again as Jews, for 25 percent it is a matter of indifference, and 21 percent answer "no" (see table 8).

A breakdown on the basis of the religious factor shows significant differences between the three categories of students. The religious students are staunch in their desire

Table 7 Valence of Jewishness
"If you were to be born all over again, would you wish to be born a Jew?"

	All Respondents		Religious		Traditionalist		Non-Religious	
	Parents	Students	Parents	Students	Parents	Students	Parents	Students
1. Yes	80	70	97	94	82	76	61	54
2. It makes no difference to me	16	28	-	6	18	23	27	43
3. No	4	2	3	-	-	1	12	3
Total %	100	100	100	100	100	100	100	100
N	434	2980	147	680	165	942	122	1358

Table 8 Valence of Jewishness In Life Abroad
"If you were to live abroad, would you wish to be born a Jew?"

	All Respondents		Religious		Traditionalist		Non-Religious	
	Parents	Students	Parents	Students	Parents	Students	Parents	Students
1. Yes	73	54	86	84	71	57	58	37
2. It makes no difference to me	9	25	4	8	12	23	12	34
3. No	18	21	10	8	17	20	30	29
Total %	100	100	100	100	100	100	100	100
N	434	2980	147	680	165	942	122	1358

to be born Jews—whether they would be living in Israel (94 percent) or outside of it (84 percent). The great majority of traditionalist students (76 percent) would wish to be born Jews, but only 57 percent give a positive answer when it means life outside of Israel. Among the non-religious students a slight majority (54 percent) would wish to be born as Jews. When it comes to life outside of Israel, however, only a minority (37 percent) of the non-religious students give an affirmative response while the others either declare it would not matter to them (34 percent) or would prefer not to be born Jews (29 percent).

It would seem that the responses to this question—whether they would wish to be born Jewish if they had to live abroad—provide an index to fundamental differences among students in feelings about Jewishness. There are those for whom the attractiveness of their Jewishness is sufficiently high for them to wish to be Jewish wherever they reside, even if being Jewish in another setting may subject them to discrimination or other disadvantage. By contrast with these students, the attachment of a considerable minority to their Jewishness is predicated on their living in Israel; their Jewishness loses its attraction for them when removed from the context of life in Israel.

Students in this latter category give a variety of explanations for not wishing to be born Jews in the Diaspora. Thus, some recoil at the thought of living as members of a minority:

"In Israel I prefer to be a Jew but in the Diaspora I would prefer to be a non-Jew so as not to be a member of a minority."

Others feel that the expression of Jewishness in the Diaspora is mainly religious and as such has no meaning for them if they themselves are non-religious.

"Jewish religion has no meaning for me. In Israel where all are Jews I don't mind also being a Jew. But outside of Israel—why be a Jew?"

A few others in the interviews express distaste or shame
at the picture of the Jew of the Diaspora as it is conjured
up in their minds:

> "The image of the Jew in the Diaspora arouses negative feel-
> ings in me. In Israel the Hebrew is proud and prepared to fight
> for the State." (Note how the student differentiates in this con-
> text between "Jew" and "Hebrew.")

The parents show a greater readiness to be born Jews
than do the students. While the parents—like the students
—are less ready to be born Jews abroad than in Israel,
the percentage (73 percent) who prefer to be Jews even
in such circumstances remains high. The attitudes of
religious parents and students are close to one another
in their highly positive response to both questions. In the
question on life outside of Israel the gap widens between
traditionalist parents (71 percent) and students (57 percent) and even more sharply between non-religious parents (58 percent) and students (37 percent).

A third question was added in order to ascertain the
attractiveness of the Israeli subidentity. Would they wish
to be born again as Israelis?

Table 9 Valence of Israeliness
"If you were to be born again, would you wish to be born an Israeli?"

	All Respondents		Religious		Traditionalist		Non-Religious	
	Parents	Students	Parents	Students	Parents	Students	Parents	Students
1. Yes	89	81	86	79	93	78	82	83
2. It makes no difference to me	10	17	10	17	7	18	18	17
3. No	1	2	4	4	-	4	-	-
Total %	100	100	100	100	100	100	100	100
N	434	2980	147	680	165	942	122	1358

The great majority of both parents (89 percent) and students (81 percent) express a desire to be born Israelis (see table 9). This is somewhat higher than the percentages (80 percent of parents and 70 percent of students) desiring to be born Jewish. While the percentage of religious students wishing to be born Jews (94 percent) is higher than the percentage expressing a desire to be born Israelis (79 percent) and while the percentage of traditionalist students is approximately equal for the two questions (76 and 78 percent respectively), there is a marked difference in the position of the non-religious students. Eighty-three percent would wish to be born Israelis as against the 54 percent who would wish to be born Jews.

Relative Salience: Which Subidentity is in the Forefront of Consciousness?

In order to ascertain which of the two subidentities will actually determine behavior or attitudes in a given situation, it does not suffice to know their relative valence. There are situations which will bring the one rather than the other subidentity to the fore of consciousness, i.e., heighten its salience. Thus, the students in the interviews indicate that they are particularly conscious of being Israeli on Yom Ha'atzmaut (Independence Day), or when border incidents are reported, or when they are thinking about their enlistment in the Israel Defense Forces after matriculation. The salience of their Jewishness rises on the Jewish festivals, or when they study the Bible or Jewish history, or when they hear about the Holocaust, or when they read about attacks on Jews in any part of the world. (There are students for whom the attacks on Jews also heighten the salience of their Israeliness. As one of them remarked: "I then realize how good it is to be an Israeli.")

Relative Potency: Which Subidentity Determines Attitudes and Behavior?

We proceeded to juxtapose the two component elements in the ethnic identity of the Israeli in order to determine their relative potency or strength. Strictly speaking, relative potency is a function of the relative valence of the two elements and of their relative salience in a particular situation. But, straining the use of the term somewhat, we sought to obtain a rough general measure —over and above situations—of relative potency by asking the students to locate their position on a seven-point Israeli–Jewish rating scale. The instructions read as follows:

"Below is a rating scale, at one end of which appears the word 'Jewish' and at the other end the word 'Israeli.' Indicate your position on this scale by placing a checkmark X within the appropriate compartment on this scale. To the extent that the mark is nearer to 'Israeli' it means that you feel yourself so much more Israeli than Jewish. To the extent that the mark X is nearer to 'Jewish' it means that you feel yourself so much more Jewish. Please note that the mark X should be placed inside the space between the points on the scale.

Israeli   :___:___:___:___:___:___:___: Jewish
          1   2   3   4   5   6   7

Table 10 indicates the distribution of responses. When forced into a choice a third of the students and 40 percent of the parents locate themselves at the midpoint 4. The rest choose the one or the other side of the scale.

A glance at a table of the mean scores (see table 11) facilitates a comparison between the various categories of students and parents. The mean position (3.5) of the entire sample of students is to the Israeli side of the scale, but not extremely so. The religious students are on the Jewish side (mean 5.1), the traditionalist students slightly to the Israeli side (mean 3.6), and the non-religious stu-

dents more pronouncedly to the Israeli side (mean 2.6).
The parents are near the center, inclining slightly to the
Jewish side (mean 4.2). Religious parents and students
and traditionalist parents and students are close to one
another; the gap is wider between non-religious parents
and students.

Table 10 The Israeli—Jewish Continuum

	All Respondents		Religious		Traditionalist		Non-Religious	
	Parents	Students	Parents	Students	Parents	Students	Parents	Students
Israeli (1–3)	32	44	3	7	38	40	45	69
Midpoint (4)	40	32	42	33	42	38	39	27
Jewish (5–7)	28	24	55	60	20	22	16	4
Total %	100	100	100	100	100	100	100	100
N	434	2980	147	680	165	942	122	1358

Table 11 The Israeli—Jewish Continuum (mean scores)

	All Respondents	Religious	Traditionalist	Non-Religious
Parents	4.2	5.5	3.4	3.3
Students	3.5	5.1	3.6	2.6

The scale was then broken up into two separate scales
and the respondent was asked to rate himself according
to the extent he felt Jewish or just "a private individual"
and similarly to locate himself on an Israeli-"private
individual" continuum. The parents reveal both the
stronger Jewish and the stronger Israeli orientation as
opposed to a "private individual" orientation. The religious students, as would be expected, have a stronger
Jewish orientation than the other students; at the same

time, their Israeli orientation is not weaker than that of
the others—indeed it is slightly stronger than that of the
non-religious students (see tables 12 and 13).

When No Connection is Seen
Between Being Jewish and Being Israeli:
A Comparison Between Two Subcategories

It will have been noted that as many as 41 percent of
the non-religious students saw no connection between
their feeling Israeli and feeling Jewish (see table 2, sup.).
A majority of the students asserted, on the one hand,
that the two elements in their identity were compatible
and mutually reinforcing; on the other hand, a substantial
minority separated them into distinct compartments.
This seemed to betoken a crucial difference in the structure of the identity of the two categories of students. We
accordingly proceeded to compare those students who
maintained that they feel more Jewish when they feel
more Israeli (we shall term them the "compatibles") with
those who saw no connection between feeling Israeli
and feeling Jewish (we term them the "separatists"). The
main focus of our comparison was on the non-religious
students in the two categories but we shall also make reference to the traditionalist and religious students (of
whom only a small number fell into the separatist category). We compared them in regard to their position on
the Israeli-Jewish continuum, the centrality, and the
valence of their Jewishness.

In regard to the Israeli-Jewish continuum, it could be
expected (i) that the compatibles would show a preference
for the midpoint of the scale and that a much greater
percentage would choose that point than would be the
case with the separatists, and (ii), conversely, that the
separatists would be found nearer to the edges of the
scale, i.e., the non-religious separatists would choose

Table 12 The Jewish—"Private Individual" Continuum

	All Respondents		Religious		Traditionalist		Non-Religious	
	Parents	Students	Parents	Students	Parents	Students	Parents	Students
Jewish (1–3)	73	45	81	75	69	47	67	29
Midpoint (4)	10	18	12	16	18	20	15	20
Individual (5–7)	17	37	7	9	13	33	18	51
Total %	100	100	100	100	100	100	100	100
N	434	2980	147	680	165	942	122	1358

Table 13 The Israeli—"Private Individual" Continuum

	All Respondents		Religious		Traditionalist		Non-Religious	
	Parents	Students	Parents	Students	Parents	Students	Parents	Students
Israeli (1–3)	79	57	82	65	82	61	76	54
Midpoint (4)	14	24	4	16	12	21	15	27
Individual (5–7)	7	19	14	19	6	18	9	19
Total %	100	100	100	100	100	100	100	100
N	434	2980	147	680	165	942	122	1358

the Israeli edge of the scale more frequently than the non-religious compatibles, while the religious separatists would choose the Jewish edge more frequently than the religious compatibles. The traditionalist students could be expected to reflect the same trend as the non-religious students but less sharply so. The responses of the students bore out these expectations (see table 14A).

The most frequently chosen point by the compatibles (38 percent) is indeed the midpoint 4, whereas it is the position most infrequently chosen by separatists (19 percent). There is an appreciable veering away by separatists either to the Israeli edge (traditionalists and, more particularly, non-religious students) or to the Jewish edge (religious students).

Our next comparison was in regard to the centrality of their Jewishness. As could be anticipated, there was a sharp difference between the non-religious compatibles and separatists. While 62 percent of the compatibles regard their Jewishness as playing either "a very important" or "an important part" in their lives, only 27 percent of the separatists express such views. The same trend is discernible among the traditionalist students (see table 15A).

Turning now to the question on valence, the disinclination of non-religious students to be born Jews if they have to live outside of Israel is clearly more marked among separatists than among compatibles. Only 25 percent of the non-religious separatists would positively wish to be born Jews under such circumstances as against 49 percent among non-religious compatibles (see table 16A).

The differences we have elaborated between compatibles and separatists show how the tendency among non-religious (and traditionalist) students to separate or compartmentalize the two subidentities is associated with a weakening of the Jewish subidentity. The converse of this is that the tendency to see the two subidentities as overlapping and consonant is associated with a stronger Jewish identity. Looking now at the measures of association between the responses on the questions testing consonance and the other variables we find that there are indeed positive relations between consonance, on the one hand, and centrality of Jewishness (.54), valence of Jewishness (.38), a Jewish orientation on the Jewish–"private individual" scale (.39), and a sense of interdependence between Jews (.33).

The compatibles are those who assert that when they feel more Jewish they also feel more Israeli (see table 1, sup.). Is this feeling, which implies that the stronger Jewish identity is associated with a stronger Israeli identity, borne out by other data? The measures of association between responses on parallel questions testing Jewishness and Israeliness bear out the hypothesis that the students who are more "Jewish" are likely also to be more "Israeli." Thus, there is a positive relation between centrality of Jewishness and centrality of Israeliness (.46), between position on the Jewish–"private individual" scale and position on the Israeli–"private individual" scale (.51), between valence of Jewishness and valence of Israeliness (.21), between the feeling of interdependence with the Jewish people and the feeling of interdependence with Israel (.47).

The Israeli–Jewish Identity: A "Wholeness" or Two Mutually Exclusive "Totalities"?

In his discussion of identity Erikson distinguishes between "wholeness" and "totality." "As a gestalt . . . wholeness emphasizes a sound, organic mutuality between diversified functions and parts within an entity, the boundaries of which are open and fluid. Totality, on the contrary, evokes a gestalt in which an absolute boundary is emphasized; given a certain arbitrary delineation, nothing that belongs inside must be left outside, nothing that must be outside can be tolerated inside."[5]

When the Jewish and Israeli subidentities are perceived as overlapping and consonant, as a "wholeness" in Erikson's terms, the Jewish subidentity is strong—and so also is the Israeli subidentity. Where there is this overlap, the Jewishness is suffused with Israeliness, and the Israeliness suffused with Jewishness. The one gathers strength from the other, and together they enter into a large number of regions of the life-space. Where, however, they

are separated and compartmentalized, a weakening of
the Jewishness becomes evident. It tends then to be seen
as pertinent to limited regions only.

The direction the emerging Israeli–Jewish identity
will take is fraught with far-reaching consequences. In
the case of the majority of students, our analysis reveals
an Israeli–Jewish identity which is a "wholeness" with
permeable boundaries between the parts. In the case of
the minority, the two subidentities are developing into
two mutually exclusive totalities coexisting side by side.

Taken to its extreme the sundering of Jewishness and
Israeliness leads into the paths pursued by two small
fringe groups—at opposite poles from one another—in
the life of Israel. The one group are the so-called "Canaanites" who would wish to see an Israeliness completely divorced from the Jewish people and from the
Jewish past in the Diaspora. The other group are the
Netorei Karta ("Guardians of the Walls") who see themselves only as Jews and not as Israelis and who do not
"recognize" the existence of the "profane" State of Israel.

CHAPTER 5

Marking-off and Alignment

An ethnic identity aligns with some and marks off from others. From whom do the Israeli Jews see themselves marked off as Israelis and as Jews? To what extent, and on what basis, do they regard themselves aligned with other Jews?

A minority tends to be very conscious of the majority from which it is marked off. The constant juxtaposition of Jewish minorities in the Diaspora with an omnipresent non–Jewish majority heightens their awareness (i.e., increases the salience) of the fact that they are Jews in contradistinction to their Gentile neighbors. Since in Israel Jews constitute the majority, the group from which they are marked off obtrudes less in their consciousness than it does in that of Jewish communities elsewhere. The statement "I am an Israeli" will for many be tantamount to saying "I am an Israeli Jew." It will be more natural for a member of the minority to qualify his description of himself by saying "I am an Israeli Arab" (Arabs in Israel are in fact so designated when the intention is to differentiate between them and Israelis who are

Jews, on the one hand, and between them and Arabs in the neighboring countries, on the other hand).

The Marking-off Group

When Israelis do think of themselves as marked off as Jews it is not so much in relation to any minority in Israel but as part of a Jewish people in the Gentile world; they place themselves in a global context. The "marked-off from" group is the general category of Gentiles, at times the Gentiles of whom they learn in Jewish history, at times the Gentiles in countries from which reports currently come of anti-Jewish discrimination. But these are Gentiles who are at a distance and of whose existence they do not have a constant reminder.

The Arab minority and other non-Jews living in Israel serve only a limited marking-off function. The Arabs serve this function more in relation to the Oriental Jews than in relation to the Ashkenazic Jews; the Oriental Jews have lived in the Arab countries, in many cases the Arabs are the only non-Jews they have personally encountered, and, moreover, in Israel they are anxious to be seen as different from Arabs. At the same time they too—like the Ashkenazic Jews—are conscious of the wider Gentile world from which they are marked off as Jews. When the students (in a substudy) were presented with the following statement: "We are Jews but they are . . ." and were asked to supply the missing word, the most frequent response—on the part of both Ashkenazic and Oriental students—was "goyim" (Gentiles), with smaller numbers inserting terms such as "non-Jews" and "Christians." A minority of subjects inserted "Arabs"; within this minority the proportion of Oriental students loomed large (see table 17A). This substudy was carried out after the Six Day War and we were in a position to compare the findings for the Ashkenazic subjects with an earlier study in which the same questions had been put to largely similar groups of Ashkenazic high school students. In the earlier study only a minute fraction (3 percent) of the students had inserted "Arabs."

When the students were presented with the statement: "We are Israelis but they are . . ." there was less agreement as to the marking-off group than when they were asked to mark themselves off as Jews (see table 18A). Broad negative ascriptive categories, such as "non-Israelis" and "other nations," appear among the responses. The Arabs (supplementary interviews show these to be the Arabs outside of Israel) serve as one of the marking-off groups—more so after the Six Day War and more so for students from the Oriental than the Ashkenazic communities. Gentiles again feature as one of the marking-off groups. A few of the non-religious students inserted "Jews."

The Bases of Alignment: Similarity or Interdependence

When we now turn to the alignment implications of the Israeli-Jewish identity we need to determine whether such bonds as are seen to exist between Israelis, and more particularly between them and Jews in other parts of the world, are based on a perception of similarity or of interdependence, or of both.

The question assumes special importance in the light of the obvious increase of dissimilarities between Israel and other Jewish communities. Thus, only a few decades ago, there was much that was similar between the Jews of what is now Israel and the largest of the Diaspora communities—American Jewry. To a considerable extent they were immigrants from Europe (principally Eastern Europe) who had taken different routes. In the years that have followed, new generations have grown up undergoing a process of socialization in two different environments. In addition, a considerable proportion of the Jewish population of the Israel of today have come from the countries of the Orient and not from Europe. Dissimilarities have developed even in the field of religious practice where the closest bonds would be expected to exist.

In a series of questions the students were asked whether they thought Jews similar in regard to (a) customs and culture, (b) characteristics and behavior, and (c) appearance. Identical questions were asked about similarity (1) between Israelis, and (2) between Israelis and Jews abroad.

The students perceive similarity more readily—as could be expected—between Israelis. This is so in regard to customs and culture and also characteristics and behavior, but little similarity is seen in appearance. They find less similarity between Jews than they do between Israelis. When Israelis and Jews abroad are juxtaposed as two groups, the dissimilarities rather than the similarities become salient in the minds of the students (see table 19).

Table 19 Perception of Similarity (N = 1430)

	Customs and culture			Characteristics and behavior			Appearance		
	Very similar or similar	Slightly similar or not at all similar	Total %	Very similar or similar	Slightly similar or not at all similar	Total %	Very similar or similar	Slightly similar or not at all similar	Total %
Israelis	70	30	100	63	37	100	28	72	100
Jews	52	48	100	45	55	100	27	73	100
Israelis & Jews outside of Israel	22	78	100	19	81	100	15	85	100

To the extent that they do see similarity between Jews, what do they regard as its source? They perceive similarity more in customs and culture than in the two other facets, and when supplementing their responses in the interviews, both religious and non-religious students (the former with greater emphasis) specify as the main source of this similarity the religion Jews share in common. But while there is some perception of similarity, it does not constitute a sufficiently wide base for alignment between Israelis and other Jews. Just as the Israelis are conscious of the considerable measure of dissimilarity, so too (in the parallel study we conducted) were American Jewish students taken aback by the differences they found when they met the Israelis during a study sojourn in Israel.[1]

When we now examine the feeling of interdependence we find this to be strongly present. To the question whether they feel their fate is bound up with the fate of the Jewish people, 82 percent of the students answer either "yes definitely" or "to a large extent" (see table 20).

Table 20 Common Fate of Jewish People
"Do you feel your fate is bound up with the fate of the Jewish people?"

	All Respondents	Religious	Traditionalist	Non-Religious
1. Yes definitely	39	58	41	50
2. To a large extent	43	35	47	22
3. To some extent	14	7	10	21
4. No	4	-	2	7
Total %	100	100	100	100
N	776	166	242	368

Related to the feeling of interdependence is the high sensitivity to the insult of the Jewish group or its members. It is particularly high when the collectivity to which they see themselves as belonging—the Jewish people—is insulted. In response to the question: "When an important overseas journal insults the Jewish people, do you feel as if it was insulting you?" 87 percent of the students reply either "always" or "often" (see table 21A). When the insult is directed against "Jews abroad" the sensitivity is somewhat lower but still quite high (see table 22A).

The sensitivity of the religious students is more pronounced than that of their non-religious peers. On both questions the parents show even higher sensitivity than the students; this is particularly so in regard to the insult directed against "Jews abroad"—many of the parents were themselves at one time in this position.

There is also a strong feeling of being personally praised when there is "praise of the Jewish people," although identification on this score is not as frequent as when there is an insult (see table 23A). Compared with their sensitivity to the insult of "Jews abroad" a sharp falling-off is noticeable in the number of students who accept praise of "Jews abroad" as praise for themselves (see table 24A). They explain in the interviews that an insult directed against any group of Jews always has a sting in it for Jews everywhere while there are more likely to be occasions where praise is limited to the individual Jews on whom it is bestowed. Although the parents too differentiate in this way between insult and praise, the discrepancy in the reactions to the two is far less pronounced among them.

An insult directed against Israel is "always" resented by the great majority of students—by an even greater number than react in such manner to an insult of the Jewish people (see table 25A). The religious students, however, more frequently react to the insult of the Jewish people than to the insult of Israel.

The students distinguish between an insult of their country, Israel, and an insult of their fellow Israeli Jews, in which latter case a considerable number prefer to endorse "often" instead of "always" (see table 26A). On the part of the parents, however, there is a heavy endorsement of "always" in relation to an insult of Israeli Jews as well as of Israel.

The frequencies among students for resentment of an insult to Israeli Jews are somewhat less than for an insult of the Jewish people and approximately the same as for

Jews abroad. There is appreciably less identification when the insult is directed against Israeli non-Jews (see table 27A).

Interdependence Between Israel and Jewish Communities Abroad

The interdependence is seen by students to exist between Jewish communities as well as between individual Jews. American Jewry and Israel are regarded as interdependent, but while 80 percent feel that a deterioration in the prestige of American Jewry would "almost always" or "often" have detrimental effects on Israel, only 54 percent feel this way about the effects of a lowering of Israel's prestige on American Jewry (see table 28A).

This divergence does not appear in regard to the reciprocal influences of Israel and World Jewry. The latter is seen as more affected by a lowering of Israel's prestige (78 percent say "almost always" or "often") than is what the students consider to be the less dependent American Jewish community (see table 29A).

As against 78 percent who feel that World Jewry will be affected "almost always" or "often" by a deterioration in the prestige of Israel, only 42 percent feel that it will be similarly affected by a lowering of the prestige of American Jewry (see table 30A).

The students look upon Israel as the center and the Jewish communities of the world are seen as radii around it. The links are seen to exist between Israel and each of the communities of the Diaspora rather than directly between Diaspora communities. But Israel is seen as being more likely to be affected by changes in the prestigious American Jewish community than in any of the others.

A decline in the prestige of Jews is regarded as having a more widespread effect than a rise in prestige (see table 31A).

The students view these questions against a background situation in which a critical, and at times hostile, world is seen as ready to exploit any Jewish failing to the detriment of all Jews. The following are typical remarks:

"A lowering of Jewish standing has adverse consequences because according to history when there were anti-Jewish outbreaks in one place it resulted in an increase of anti-Semitism in others as well."

"A lowering of Jewish prestige is always bad because there exists a certain opinion about Jews and whenever there is a 'puncture' (things go wrong) it affects other Jews, including Israel."

Related to the feeling of interdependence is the view of the students about the mutual obligations of support between Israel and Jews abroad (see tables 32 and 33). That there is such mutual responsibility is widely accepted

Table 32 Mutual Responsibility: Israel's obligation to Jews abroad
"Do you think it is the duty of the State of Israel to help the Jews abroad?"

	All Respondents		Religious		Traditionalist		Non-Religious	
	Parents	Students	Parents	Students	Parents	Students	Parents	Students
1. Yes, definitely	48	44	59	49	43	44	45	42
2. Yes, but only if the help does not result in a serious detriment to Israel	32	38	32	39	27	38	39	37
3. Yes, but only if the help does not result in any detriment at all to Israel	19	15	9	11	28	17	16	17
4. No	1	3	-	1	2	1	-	4
Total %	100	100	100	100	100	100	100	100
N	127	761	34	169	60	242	33	350

Table 33 Mutual Responsibility: Obligation of Jews abroad to Israel
"Do you think it is the duty of the Jews abroad to help Israel?"

	All Respondents		Religious		Traditionalist		Non-Religious	
	Parents	Students	Parents	Students	Parents	Students	Parents	Students
1. Yes, definitely	66	56	67	53	67	57	64	56
2. Yes, but only if the help does not result in a serious detriment to them	25	36	30	39	22	36	27	34
3. Yes, but only if the help does not result in any detriment at all to them	8	6	3	7	10	6	9	6
4. No	1	2	-	1	1	1	-	4
Total %	100	100	100	100	100	100	100	100
N	127	761	34	169	60	242	33	350

and is denied by very few (only 3 percent). On this issue there are no significant differences between religious, traditionalist, and non-religious students. The difference between students and parents is also less than it is on most Jewish issues. The responsibility of Jews abroad to help Israel is emphasized by a greater number of both students and parents than is the duty of Israel to the Jews abroad.

In the interviews, the students express the view that Israel is still sorely in need of help to consolidate economically and politically, that the consolidation of Israel is in the interests of Jews everywhere and that it is the obligation of the affluent Jewish communities to extend the necessary aid. These communities in their turn are exposed to the dangers of anti-Semitism and the inroads of assimilation, and it is the obligation of Israel as the center to give them spiritual and cultural sustenance and also to facilitate their *aliyah*.

The following are typical of remarks by those students stressing the obligation of Israel:

> "This is a Jewish state established in order to help Jews all over the world."

> "The question is what sort of help is more important— economic or spiritual. I think the Jews abroad are more in need of help."

Students emphasizing the duty of Jews abroad add remarks such as the following:

> "Jews of the Golah should be interested in helping because thereby they help themselves—those Jews who do not want to assimilate are interested in the preservation of Israel."

> "Israel helps them by its very existence."

> "A Jew should live in Israel and, if not, at least support it."

While all the students recognize the mutual responsibility that exists between Israel and the Diaspora, the religious students tend more than the others to place the emphasis on the spiritual and cultural aspects of the help that Israel should extend.

The sense of interdependence, of a common destiny or fate, seems to provide the widest basis for the alignment of the students with Jews in all parts of the world. In regard to the Jews inside Israel, this sense of a common fate is further reinforced by the constant threat posed by belligerent Arab states with whom three wars have been fought in the short space of twenty years.

Even though Israelis are seen as more similar to one another than are Jews in general, there are yet great diversities among them. There has been an "in-gathering" from almost all countries of the world, from the most advanced technological societies and from primitive peasant communities. These diversities continue to give rise to difficulties, but it would seem that the overriding sense of interdependence has hastened the *mizug hagalu-yoth,* the relatively harmonious integration of Jews from East and West into one people.

CHAPTER 6

Time Perspective:
Alignment Across Time

Do Israelis see themselves and the State of Israel as representing the continuation of a Jewish historic tradition, or are they—as some observers have asserted—a "new people" with little or no relationship to the Jewish past and to the Jews in the Diaspora?

The question of continuity does not arise in regard to the distant past within the Land of Israel. The enthusiasm which every archaeological finding arouses, the excursions by youngsters and adults alike to historical sites with Bible in hand, the intense popular interest in the conferences on Biblical themes and in the Bible study groups (one was initiated in the home of the then Prime Minister of Israel, David Ben Gurion, and another takes place in the residence of Israel's President Shazar) are just a few indications of the widespread concern with the remote past when, as now, Jews dwelt in their own land. Where the problem does arise is, as previously indicated, in relation to the Jewish past in the Diaspora and to the Jewish communities who live there.

When asked the question directly in a substudy, a majority of students (72 percent) view Israelis as representing a continuity of the Jewish people, and only a minority regard them as a new people (see table 1B).* There is a strong positive association (.60) between this sense of continuity and the feeling that Israeliness and Jewishness overlap. When the question turns on whether the State of Israel embodies in itself the continuity of the Jewish history of all periods including the Dispersion, or only of those periods in which Jews lived in the Land of Israel, the greater number endorse continuity *across all periods,* but here the majority declines from 72 to 54 percent (see table 2B). From the way they amplify their replies it is clear that, while most of the students recognize their relationship to the Jewish people, some among them feel that the new forms created in Israel have little or no connection with Jewish life as it is in the Diaspora and link up instead with the early history of Jews in their own land. The religious students recognize the existence of continuity on both questions more than do the non-religious.

A Selective Approach to the Past

A series of questions sought to gauge the attitude of the students to different periods of time in Jewish history, ranging from the period of the Second Temple to the Holocaust in Europe and to the establishment of the State of Israel (see table 34).

The resettlement of the country and the establishment of the State of Israel is a period of unalloyed pride for all. The feeling about two periods in the distant past—the period of the Second Temple and the "Golden Age" in Spain—is devoid of an element of shame (see tables 35A and 36A). But when it comes to other periods in Jewish history, the responses of some of the students mirror their

*Tables marked B appear in the Appendix of Tables B and relate to the substudy.

Table 34 Attitudes towards various periods in Jewish history (N = 775)

	Pride	Neither Pride nor Shame	Shame	Lack of Knowledge	Total percen
Second Temple	47	48	2	3	100
The "Golden Age" in Spain	65	30	2	3	100
The Jewish *shtetl* in Eastern Europe	27	46	18	9	100
The *Melah* (North African "Ghetto")	16	41	19	24	100
The entry of Jews into the social and cultural life of Western Europe	63	25	10	2	100
The behavior of Jews during the Holocaust	73	5	21	1	100
The resettlement of *Eretz Israel* and the establishment of the State	100	-	-	-	100

deprecation of the periods which relate to life in the Diaspora. The way they feel about the different periods is generally determined by two criteria which reflect the tenor of their own lives: first, the extent to which the period is one of Jewish activism and not of passivity; secondly, the extent to which it is characterized by efforts at the preservation of identity and opposition to its surrender.

The students select out as a source of pride the periods, or episodes within the periods, in which Jews are seen as hewing out their own destiny or as actively defending themselves, their land, or heritage. They find it difficult to identify with the picture of a Jew meekly accepting the blows of fate or allowing his destiny to be shaped by others. At the same time, they also show a derision for any surrender of identity. Whatever their views may be about the nature or the attractiveness of their Jewishness, the denial of self is seen as an act of cowardice—by religious and non-religious students alike (even though the measure of positive value they attach to the maintenance of the Jewish identity differs).

Thus, the entry of Jews into the life of Europe is, on the one hand, a subject of pride because of the Jewish contribution to the general cultural advancement, and at the same time there are some expressions of reservation— mainly by religious students—about the surrender of identity on the part of Jews in this period. The period of the *shtetl,* or Jewish village, in Eastern Europe conjures up for a number of students the picture of the weak, passive Jew. Those who react positively to this period— again, more particularly the religious students—do so because the Jews of the period are seen as faithfully maintaining a Jewish identity. There is likewise ambivalence about the *melah,* the Jewish ghetto of North Africa (about which a number of students profess ignorance) (see tables 37A-39A).

Feelings of ambivalence occur strongly when the students discuss the behavior of Jews during the period of the Holocaust. Twenty-one percent of the students stated that they look upon the behavior of the Jews with shame (see table 40A).

When students were asked in a substudy what the negative aspects in the behavior of the Jews in the Holocaust were, 55 percent of the replies referred to their "passivity," to the fact that they went "like sheep to the slaughter" (see table 3B). The instances of active resistance, such as that in the Warsaw Ghetto revolt, were singled out by a majority of students as examples of positive behavior. But while religious students, like the others, stress active resistance, they are much more prone to also refer admiringly to forms of passive resistance. Thus, they speak more frequently than the others of *Kiddush Ha-Shem,* (the "Sanctification of the Name"), of facing death with fortitude, of maintaining a belief in God, of observing the *mitzvot,* and maintaining a Jewish identity under inhuman conditions (see table 4B).

Since families of students from the Oriental communities did not suffer directly in the Holocaust—as did the families of many members of the Ashkenazic communi-

ties—the question arises how they differ in regard to
their feeling about the behavior of Jews during this period.
While there is an appreciable measure of pride on the
part of students from the Oriental communities in the
behavior of Jews in the Holocaust, it is less than is expressed by the Ashkenazic students (see table 41A). The
difference is particularly pronounced among the religious
students of the two communities (86 percent of the religious Ashkenazic students express pride as against 64
percent of the Oriental students). Again, there is more
of a tendency among Oriental students to express shame
than there is among their Ashkenazic peers.

Pride in the behavior of Jews during the Holocaust is
associated with a stronger, and shame with a weaker,
Jewish identity. Thus, 58 percent of those who express
pride would wish to be born Jews while only 38 percent
expressing shame would wish to be born Jews (see table
42A).

The Memory of the Holocaust

The Holocaust represents the most traumatic Jewish
experience in the Diaspora in modern times. "The memory of the Holocaust stirs to the depths the heart of every
Jew," observed the judges in the Jerusalem District Court
in the Eichmann trial.[1] We sought to explore whether
this is still the case with the generation born after the
catastrophe or whether the memory of that devastating
event has been dimmed.

The interviews with the students showed that the memory of the Holocaust simmered even in the minds of this
generation. The memory did not have the keen edge it
possessed for their parents, nor could the students be
expected to grasp fully how the destruction of the great
Jewish community in Europe had sapped the vitality of
Jewish life everywhere. But the memory was nonetheless

deeply embedded as a potent background factor in their Jewish consciousness. A number of them were sons and daughters of families of survivors, and the families of many others had lost relatives. But even students whose families were not among the six million murdered had a sense of involvement in the Holocaust. They were all aware of the Eichmann trial and some of them indicated with what intense interest they followed the course of that trial—they were then in their early teens.

The students indicate a high measure of identification with the suffering of Jews in the Holocaust, and this holds for the Oriental as well as for the Ashkenazic sector, albeit not quite to the same degree (see table 5B). The measure of identification with Jews who suffered from attacks in Islamic countries is considerable, although not as high as for sufferers in the Holocaust. The Oriental students here register—expectedly—a higher degree of identification than do the Ashkenazic students (see table 6B).

A majority believe that a repetition of the Holocaust is a possibility, at least in some countries. In a substudy 17 percent stated they believed it is possible in all countries, 11 percent in most countries, 56 percent in a few countries only, and 16 percent do not believe it to be a possibility (see table 7B). The countries in which the possibility is seen to exist are firstly the Arab countries, secondly, Soviet Russia and Poland, thirdly, Germany, and fourthly, the Latin American countries. Countries in which it is seen as unlikely are the United States, England, and the Scandinavian countries.

The students were asked what lesson they derived from the Holocaust. Most frequent were responses which stress the dangers inherent in the position of a Jewish minority subject to the caprices of a non-Jewish majority, the need for an "in-gathering" of Jews from all parts of the world in a homeland of their own, and the importance of consolidating that homeland. But what seemed particularly crucial to examine was the presence or absence of a feel-

ing on the part of this generation of young Israelis—
when they recall the extermination of one third of the
Jewish people—that they are in a sense in the position
of survivors charged with the responsibility of ensuring
the Jewish future.

A majority of students (59 percent) in a substudy gave
unqualified endorsement to the statement that every
Jew should see himself as if he were a survivor of the
Holocaust (see table 8B). The feeling of responsibility
for the future of the Jewish people runs strongly through
the interviews, and the views of many others are echoed
in the following remark by a student:

> "I think it is no exaggeration to say that everyone, or almost
> everyone, feels that the Holocaust imposed a duty which is
> perhaps the justification for our existence—to save whatever
> has remained and to prevent a repetition of what happened."

The memory of the Holocaust—probably more than anything else—sharpens the sense of a common fate among
Jews. The consciousness of being in the position of survivors is the strongest expression of the sense of interdependence, and it is associated with an intensity of Jewish identity.[2]

Justification for Israel's Existence

"The suffering of the Jews in the Diaspora as a people
without a homeland" is the most frequent choice of the
students when asked to choose from a list of reasons
justifying the existence of the State of Israel (see table
43). Next comes "the resettlement of the country in recent
times and the War of Liberation." Lowest on the list is
"the recognition by the nations of the world of the idea
of a Jewish state."

If we distinguish between the responses of categories

Table 43 Reasons Justifying the Existence of the State of Israel
esented in order chosen by all respondents. Students were asked to indicate
o reasons.)

	All Respondents	Religious	Traditionalist	Non-Religious
The suffering of the Jews in the Diaspora as a people without a homeland	55	52 (2)	54 (1)	57 (1)
The resettlement of the country in recent times and the War of Liberation	46	26 (4)	45 (2)	57 (1)
The aspirations of the Jews through the centuries to return to their homeland	37	44 (3)	38 (3)	33 (3)
The settlement of the Jewish people in the land of Israel in ancient times	35	56 (1)	34 (4)	27 (4)
The recognition by the nations of the world of the idea of a Jewish State	27	22 (5)	29 (5)	26 (5)
Total %	100×2	100×2	100×2	100×2
N	765	165	247	353

of students, we observe that the religious students most
frequently choose "the settlement of the Jewish people
in the Land of Israel in ancient times" (with a further
reason, "the suffering of the Jews," following closely).
A choice of low frequency on their part is "the resettlement of the country in recent times and the War of Liberation." The non-religious students, on the other hand,
place "the resettlement of the country in recent times
and the War of Liberation" high (alongside "the suffering
of the Jews"), while the "settlement of the Jewish people
in the Land of Israel in ancient times" comes low down.
In this, as in other contexts, we find an indication of differences in the time perspective of religious and non-
religious students. The former more than the latter look
backward over what is seen by them as an unbroken

stretch of Jewish history threaded together by a series
of unifying concepts. They see the right of the Jewish
people to Israel as primarily based in the distant past,
while the non-religious, though not oblivious of the past,
place greater emphasis on the events of recent years.

Attitude Toward Yiddish

As one of the indices of the relationship to the past,
we chose the attitude toward Yiddish. This language was
at one time a hallmark of the distinctive Jewish identity
of Ashkenazic Jewry.[3] It also became the expressive
medium of a rich literature.

In the United States and in other parts of the Diaspora
the number of Jews speaking or reading Yiddish has declined sharply from one generation to the next. Although
the number of Jews in the Diaspora who speak Hebrew is
still small, the study of Hebrew is part of many Jewish
educational programs, whereas Yiddish is studied much
less widely. As the language both of the Jewish liturgy
and of the Jewish renaissance in Israel, Hebrew is increasingly becoming the cultural emblem par excellence of
Jewish identity in the Diaspora.

While Yiddish is still spoken in the homes of many
Israeli families who come from Eastern Europe, the dominant language in Israel is Hebrew which has served as a
force unifying Jews from diverse cultural backgrounds.
Yiddish is no longer seen as a language competing for the
dominant position in Jewish life. Instead, there is a concern in some circles, who cherish highly the language,
its literature, and the associations they carry, at the possible disappearance of Yiddish from the contemporary
Jewish scene. At the same time there are others who
still look askance at Yiddish as one of the symbols of life
in the Diaspora, of a "Galuth existence," although the

erstwhile derision of the language seems to have lost its sharpness. A study carried out among university students reflected this ambivalence in the attitude toward Yiddish which was ranked eighth in order of prestige among fourteen languages in frequent use in Israel.[4]

In seeking to gauge the attitude of our students to Yiddish, we examined attitudes in the Ashkenazic and Oriental sectors. The majority of Ashkenazic students —many of whose parents doubtlessly know Yiddish— revealed an attitude of indifference to the language. A greater number of religious students (56 percent) than non-religious students (24 percent) maintain a positive attitude, and the traditionalists stand in between (40 percent) (see table 44A). A statistically significant relation was found to exist between a positive attitude toward Yiddish and the feeling that Israelis represent a continuity of the Jewish people (.32).

The students from the Oriental communities are overwhelmingly indifferent, while 23 percent go further and express a negative attitude (see table 45A). Yiddish is a language they do not understand; they see it as the peculiar possession of the Ashkenazic community which they do not share—as an Ashkenazic and not as a Jewish language. The negative attitude of the 23 percent may reflect the grievances of some of the students who feel themselves in the position of an underprivileged minority and regard Yiddish as symbolizing the specific culture of the privileged majority.

Neither Ladino nor any of the other languages of Jews in the Arab-speaking countries held such widespread sway among the Oriental communities as Yiddish once commanded among the Ashkenazic communities. The attitude of the Ashkenazic students to the languages of the Oriental communities has been found to be largely one of indifference, and this holds also for the students from the Oriental sector itself.[5]

Future Perspectives

The view that the students have of the future of Jewish communities in other parts of the world is determined to a considerable extent by what they have been told of the Jewish experience in the Diaspora, and the Diaspora of which they know most is that from which their parents came. It is—for the great majority—either Eastern or Central Europe, where Jewish life ended in destruction, or the countries of the Middle East and North Africa from which Jewish communities had to be evacuated. They tend to judge contemporary Jewish life by what they know of a Diaspora which in large part no longer exists. They have little comprehension of the life of the Jewish communities of America and other countries in the Western world in which the bulk of Jewry resides today.

Their outlook about the dangers of anti-Semitism tends to be pessimistic. Thirteen percent of the students are "certain," and another 52 percent incline to the belief that anti-Semitism is likely to endanger the existence of Jewish communities in the foreseeable future. The view of the parents who have lived part of their lives in the Diaspora is more emphatically pessimistic—32 percent are sure and another 46 percent incline to that belief (see table 46A).

In amplifying their responses the students differentiate between countries. The danger of anti-Semitism is seen as serious in Soviet Russia and countries in the Soviet bloc, in the Arab countries, in Germany and the Latin American countries. The danger is seen as much less in the United States, in the Scandinavian countries and in Britain.

When it comes to the retention by the Jewish communities of their Jewish character, the parents are more optimistic than the students. Twenty-six percent of the parents are certain that this will be so, another 38 percent

"think" so. The corresponding figures for the students
are 4 and 50 percent (see table 47A). In their amplifications to the question in the interviews the students (including the non-religious) see the weakening of religious ties
as the primary reason for the likely loss of Jewish character by communities in the Diaspora.

The approach of students throughout to questions
relating to the future of the Jewish communities in the
Diaspora is tinged with pessimism. They see these communities as threatened externally by anti-Semitism—in
some cases, to the extent of being exposed to the danger
of destruction—or as doomed to internal dissolution
through assimilation. The only solution they envisage is
Israel-centered—the in-gathering of Jews in Israel through
immigration. Such *aliyah* is seen by them as serving the
needs of Israel and also as a source of salvation to the Jews
of the Diaspora.

In contrast to the pessimism about the Jewish future
in the Diaspora, optimism is expressed about the continued Jewish character of the State of Israel. The parents
are much more emphatic in their optimism. Fifty-five
percent are certain, and another 36 percent think so; the
corresponding figures for the students are 28 and 53 percent (see table 48A). A typical explanation by a student:

"Israel is the ideal place for the maintenance of our Jewish
character since the majority here are Jews."

While they see Jews in the Diaspora as constantly subject to the influences of the majority culture, they feel
that in Israel they are shaping their own cultural future
which the majority believe represents a continuation of a
Jewish tradition (although some prefer to leap over the
centuries of the Jewish past which relate to life in the
Diaspora).

The students are future-oriented Israelis whose preoccupation is with the tasks that lie ahead. They are con-

fident about the prospects of Israel maintaining its independence (see table 49A).

When questioned in a substudy about their view of
Zionism, the students rarely referred to the philosophy
of Zionism as a movement concerned with the fate and
future of the Jewish people. Zionism was defined by them
as conterminous with *aliyah*, "upbuilding of Israel," "devotion to Israel." A majority stated that in the terms of
their definition they saw themselves as Zionists (see tables
9B and 10B). Some indicated that since they lived in Israel
there was no need for them to be Zionists. While in interviews before the Six Day War a few referred contemptuously to Zionists as persons prone to the utterance of
ideological platitudes which they do not always imple-
ment, this derisive note was absent in the more recent
interviews; it would seem that a more positive conception
of Zionism is developing.

Preserving Jewish Identity

The students desire Jewish identity in the Diaspora
to be preserved even though they are pessimistic about
the capacity of the Jewish communities to maintain their
identity. They do not hold the view that the alternative
to *aliyah* to Israel should be assimilation. When asked
what a youth abroad who is not prepared to immigrate
to Israel should do—maintain his Jewishness or assimilate—not only the religious students (99 percent) but also
the great majority (82 percent) of the non-religious students state that he should maintain his Jewishness abroad.
A minority of non-religious students (18 percent), however, favor assimilation (see table 50A).

"Assimilation" was a much-derided word among the
students and they spoke with contempt of "assimilation-
ist" Jews. But assimilation has many guises and it was
clear that the students had not given more than super-

ficial thought to this problem area. Our questions related
to two of the more obvious forms of assimilation—out-
marriages and conversion.

The growing rate of out-marriages in countries of the
Diaspora has been viewed with apprehension by the leadership of these communities as constituting a serious
threat to Jewish survival.[6] This apprehension is not
strongly reflected in the views of the students. The majority do indeed oppose out-marriages and only a mere
handful express a view favoring it, but at the same time
over half of the non-religious students (and about a third
of the traditionalists) refrain from any expression of opposition and regard this as the private affair of the persons
involved. Parents are, on the whole, more opposed than
students, but the non-religious parents are close to the
attitudes of the non-religious students. The question
asked for an opinion about "a Jew who marries a non-
Jew." The responses might have been different if they
had been asked specifically about the desirability of out-
marriages from the point of view of the future of the
Jewish community (see tables 51A and 52A).

When asked whether they would be prepared to marry
a non-Jew, fifty percent of the non-religious students,
differing sharply from the religious and traditionalist
students, express such readiness without requiring that
he/she convert to Judaism (see table 53A). Since the
majority of non-religious students, like their religious
and traditionalist peers, favor the preservation of the
Jewish identity, it appears that out-marriages are not
viewed by them—from their vantage point in their own
majority society—as an act of desertion or denial of identity, or as affecting the future of the Jewish group.

The conversion by a Jew to another religion meets with
opposition although a considerable minority of non-
religious students (41 percent) and also a number of traditionalist students (26 percent) regard this as "a private
affair" of the persons concerned. The opposition of stu-

dents is greater in the case of a Jew in Israel who converts than in the case of a Jew abroad who does so (see
tables 54A and 55A).

As members of an "incomplete" group the students see
the emigration of Jews from Israel (*yerida*—literally, "a
going down" as opposed to *aliyah*, "an ascent") as weakening the group and as an act tantamount in the minds of
some to undermining the Jewish future. There is accordingly considerable opposition to an Israeli who emigrates,
and on this issue there are no significant differences between the three categories of students. It is of relevance
that this condemnation is of *Jews* who leave Israel; Arabs
and others are not looked upon askance as *yordim*. The
number of non-religious students who are opposed to *yerida* is greater than those of this category who were
opposed to out-marriages or conversion and they are
also less inclined to regard it as a private affair. More
parents than students express opposition (see table 56A).

When the question is phrased personally "Would you
be prepared to emigrate from Israel?" the more emphatic
opposition of the parents is again manifested. A minority
of students—distributed equally between the three categories—indicate that they might be prepared to consider
the possibility of emigration (see table 57A).

CHAPTER 7

Defining the Jewish Group
and Its Attributes

In a Jewish identity the religious and national elements are inextricably interwoven. The students do not seek to separate out the inseparable; for the great majority of them the term "Jewish" has both a religious and a national connotation. At the same time, in certain situations the element of "religion" is salient and in others that of "people."

The religious aspect is salient when, for example, "Israeli" and "Jewish" are counterposed, as on the Israeli-Jewish scale in the questionnaire. In such cases the non-religious students see themselves as less Jewish—but not as un-Jewish, and certainly not as non-Jewish. Again, when the non-religious students see Jewishness and Israeliness as overlapping they would designate that part of Jewishness not included in the overlap as primarily religious.On the other hand, when a question relates to the Jewish people or to Jews, without reference, explicit or implicit, to their beliefs and practices, the peoplehood component is salient and their own Jewish attachment is more clearly seen.

With the religious students the two elements are more

fully integrated into a unified concept, but with them, too, a particular situation may heighten the relative salience of one or other of the elements.

Who Is a Jew?

While Israel is not a theocratic but a secular state, it has placed matters of personal status, such as marriage and divorce, within the domain of religious law subject to the jurisdiction of the rabbinic courts. (The Moslems and other religious minorities likewise have their special courts parallel to the rabbinic courts.) According to religious law (the *halacha*) a person is a Jew if he has been born to a Jewish mother or has undergone conversion to Judaism in accordance with the prescribed procedures. A mere declaration of faith or of a feeling of belongingness does not make a person a Jew. Nor does a person cease to be a Jew because of either lack of faith or of a sense of belonging.

A person may thus be Jewish either by heredity or by conversion. The conception of Jewish religious law is not racial: while it does not proceed with "missionary zeal" to seek converts, Judaism is prepared to accept anyone who wishes to enter the congregation and extends to the proselyte all the privileges of the Jew by birth. But it does not regard a declaration of faith by itself as sufficient— it insists upon established procedures of conversion.

Any decision taken in Israel about the question of "who is a Jew" is seen as bound to have implications for Jewish life elsewhere and particular care has accordingly been taken by responsible Israeli leadership to avoid definitions that may be divisive.

In 1958 the then Prime Minister of Israel, David Ben Gurion, addressed a letter to Jewish scholars—significantly to those in the Diaspora as well as in Israel—asking for their opinion on a matter relating to the registration of children of mixed marriages.[1] (The immediate occasion of the problem at the time was the arrival of immigrants from Poland with non-Jewish wives. The parents wished to register their children as Jews without their having to undergo the conversion procedures.) The question referred to the scholars was whether a child could be registered as a Jew on the basis of the expression of the desire of the parents and their declaration in good faith that the child did not belong to another religion, or whether any further ceremony was required.

The majority of the scholars objected to any departure from the *halachic* rules and a number of them pointed to the dangerous schism which might result between Israel and the Diaspora from the adoption of different norms in designating a person as "Jewish."[2]

Outside the domain of religious law the question "who is a Jew" has been the subject of countless discussions. It received incisive treatment in 1963 in a judgment of the Israel Supreme Court in the case of *Oswald Rufeisen v. The Minister of the Interior.*[3] The petitioner, Oswald Rufeisen, known since his conversion as Brother Daniel, was the son of Jewish parents in Poland and was educated as a Jew. During the Nazi occupation he, on a number of occasions, at great personal risk, rescued Jews from death at Nazi hands. Pursued by the Nazis he found refuge in a convent and during this time converted to Christianity. Despite his conversion he continued to regard himself as belonging to the Jewish people, and eventually came to Israel as a member of the monastic order which he had entered at the end of the War. The question before the Court was whether he could be considered a Jew in terms of the Law of Return.

According to Jewish religious law the fact of his conversion did not obliterate his Jewishness,[4] but the judgment pointed out that in the Law of Return the term

"Jew" had a secular meaning, that is, "as it is usually understood by the man in the street . . . by the ordinary plain and simple Jew."[5] The answer given by the Court was "that a Jew who has become a Christian is *not* called a Jew."[6] By the act of joining an antithetical group he had severed his connection with the Jewish group. "The meaning of this Law cannot be severed from the sources of the past from which its content is derived and in these sources nationalism and religion are inseparably interwoven. A Jew who, by changing his religion, severs himself from the national past of his people ceases therefore to be a Jew in the national sense to which the Law of Return was meant to give expression . . . He has denied his national past, and can no longer be fully integrated into the organized body of the Jewish community as such. By changing his religion he has erected a barrier between himself and his brother Jews. . . ."[7]

In the case of Brother Daniel two criteria were present, namely, descent from Jewish parents and a feeling of belongingness to the Jewish people, but a third criterion was not met, i.e., that of Jewish religion, by this being meant either conversion to Judaism of a person born of non-Jewish parents or non-conversion to another religion of a person born of Jewish parents.

The students in our study, to whose opinions we now turn, were given a series of cases built around these three criteria. In three of the cases one of these criteria is present while the two others are absent; in three other cases two criteria are present while one is absent.

The students do not regard Jews as an exclusive, racial group. The criterion of descent indeed has little weight if the two other criteria are both either present or absent. Thus, only 14 percent of the students regard as a Jew a person born of Jewish parents but who has converted to another religion and does not feel himself belonging to the Jewish people. On the other hand, 91 percent define as Jewish a person not born of Jewish parents but who has converted to the Jewish religion and feels himself belonging to the Jewish people (see table 58).

Table 58 Who is a Jew? Criteria applied by students (N = 775)

	% defining the person as a Jew	Religion	Feeling	Descent
Religion alone He converted to the Jewish religion; his parents are not Jewish, he does not feel himself belonging to the Jewish people	28	+	−	−
Feeling alone His parents are not Jewish, he has not converted to the Jewish religion but feels belongingness to the Jewish people	27	−	+	−
Descent alone His parents are Jewish, he converted to another religion and does not feel himself belonging to the Jewish people	14	−	−	+
Descent plus feeling. But conversion to another religion His parents are Jewish, he converted to another religion but feels belongingness to the Jewish people	54	−	+	+
Descent plus religion. Without feeling His parents are Jewish, he has not converted to another religion, but does not feel himself belonging to the Jewish people	66	+	−	+
Religion plus feeling. But not descent His parents are not Jewish, he converted to the Jewish religion and feels himself belonging to the Jewish people	91	+	+	−

Where in addition to descent another requisite is present a majority of students are prepared to regard the person as a Jew. Thus, Brother Daniel would have been regarded a Jew by 54 percent of the students. At the same time a considerable minority would have seen his conversion to another religion as a severance of his ties with the Jewish group—as did the Supreme Court. In a case where, in addition to descent, the religious component is present (without the feeling of belongingness) 66 percent regard the person a Jew.

If we now look at the definitions most acceptable to religious and non-religious students respectively, we observe the emphasis placed by the religious students on the religious criterion while the non-religious students attach most importance to the feeling of belongingness (see table 59).

Table 59 Who is a Jew? Percentage of students in each of the three categories regarding a criterion as sufficient (N = 775)

	Religious	Traditionalist	Non-Religious
1. Religion alone	41	23	25
2. Feeling alone	11	27	34
3. Descent alone	27	13	9
4. Descent plus feeling. But conversion to another religion	44	52	61
5. Descent plus religion. Without feeling	82	68	57
6. Religion plus feeling. But not descent	88	90	93

Where the person professes another religion and the parents are not Jewish, only 11 percent of the religious students are prepared to regard him as a Jew on the basis of his feeling of belongingness only. In the interviews the religious students stress the criterion of birth to Jewish parents (some specifically mention the mother) or conversion to Judaism. The feeling of belongingness is, however, seen as an important auxiliary criterion where one of the other two criteria—particularly the religious criterion— exists. Indeed if the religious criterion is met, the feeling of belongingness is regarded as a more important auxiliary than the factor of descent by the religious as well as by the other students (with whom it counts very heavily).

The Shalit Case

The differences that exist around the definition of "who is a Jew" were sharply reflected in a recent ruling of Israel's Supreme Court as well as in the controversy which followed the Court's decision and which culminated in Knesset legislation on the subject. In the case of *Benjamin Shalit v. the Minister of the Interior,* the petitioner, a Jew, asked that his children born to his non-Jewish wife (who had not converted) be registered as Jews in the Population Register under the item *"le'om"* (literally "nationality," here equivalent to ethnic affiliation or peoplehood). The Court, sitting as a full bench of nine judges, divided five to four on the issue, the majority holding that the children should be registered as Jews.

The decision gave rise to heated public debate, and a bill was submitted to the Israel Knesset in February 1970 and passed by a substantial majority to define as a Jew for the purposes of the Population Registry Law and the Law of Return "a person born to a Jewish mother, or who has converted, and who is not a member of another religion." At the same time, in order to facilitate immigration of families of mixed marriages, the benefits accorded by the Law of Return are extended to the members of the family of a Jew—to his spouse and children and even grandchildren.

It is noteworthy that in the discussion around the Shalit case the proponents of the differing views found it necessary to stress that their particular proposal was best calculated to avoid a rift between Israel and Diaspora Jewry. But wide divergences of view existed about the form "the act of identification" with the Jewish group should take—from opinions that a mere declaration of belongingness

should suffice to an insistence (with all manner of gradations in between) on the strict *halachic* requirement of
conversion according to prescribed requirements. Reflected in some of the definitions proposed in the debate
is an ahistorical view of the Jewish group as if it were a
sociological phenomenon of contemporary origin; against
this are the definitions which look at the group within
the framework of an historical time perspective. Basic
differences of conception appear about the structure of
Jewish ethnic identity; some participants in the debate
sought to separate out the "religious" and the "national"
components while others maintained that they could not
be disentangled. While it was widely agreed that there
needed to be—in the case of so dispersed a people as the
Jews—a commonly accepted criterion (applicable alike in
Israel and in the Diaspora) as to "who is a Jew," questions
arose about the extent to which it was feasible to speak
of "a Jewish *identity*" existing everywhere as a uniform
entity; it was argued by some that the variations which
had developed around the quintessential common core
were such as to make it more appropriate to think in
terms of a pluralistic Jewish society allowing for a diversity of "Jewish *identities.*"

The Knesset resolution requires an act of conversion
from a person not born to a Jewish mother who wishes to
be registered as a Jew. But it does not specifically state
that the conversion should be according to the strict
halachic procedures required by the Orthodox Rabbinate.
Soon after the passage of the resolution the controversy
took a further turn when the Orthodox Rabbinate and the
religious parties queried the validity of a conversion
performed by a Reform Rabbi in Israel.

The debate around "who is a Jew" has by no means
been terminated by the Knesset resolution. Indeed in
some quarters regret has been expressed that it had been
found necessary at this stage to undertake an act of formal
definition instead of allowing the process of historic
evolution to produce its own definitions.

The Attributes of "a Good Jew"

The students were given a list of activities and were asked to indicate to what extent they regarded them as important in order to be a good Jew (a) in Israel, (b) in the Diaspora.[8] A student could check one of the following four response categories: 1) Essential in order to be a good Jew; 2) Very desirable in order to be a good Jew; 3) Desirable in order to be a good Jew; 4) Irrelevant in regard to being a good Jew (see table 60).

As the students see it, the most important requirement to be a good Jew in Israel is to work for the in-gathering of Jews from the Diaspora (*kibbutz galuyoth*). Next in importance is "an ethical life." As the attributes of the "good Jew" in the Diaspora "an interest in the affairs of the local Jewish community" and "support of Israel" rank highest; then follows *aliyah* ("to settle in Israel or encourage his children to settle").

The students make more stringent demands on the Jew outside of Israel. The one exception is "to be a loyal citizen of the country in which he lives." In keeping with their perception of a special relationship between Israel and the Jewish people the students see a closer connection between being a loyal citizen of Israel and being a good Jew. In regard to each of the other activities, participation in it is regarded as more important for the Jew outside of Israel in order to qualify to be a good Jew. The view of the students as expressed in the interviews is that it is more difficult for a Jew to remain a Jew outside of Israel and accordingly deliberate activity is required of him to maintain his identity.

"Outside of Israel a Jew has to be careful not to assimilate. The gap between Jew and non-Jew narrows and in order to be a Jew there is need for really intensive efforts."

"In order to be a good Jew outside of Israel it is not enough to have the proper feeling. There is need for the expression of

Table 60 Requirements to be "a good Jew" in Israel and Abroad (N = 781)

(mean scores)

The Activity	All Respondents		Religious		Traditionalist		Non-Religious	
(ranked in order given for "good Jew" in Israel)	Israel	Abroad	Israel	Abroad	Israel	Abroad	Israel	Abroad
1. To work for the in-gathering of Jews from the Diaspora	2.26	-	1.91	-	2.17	-	2.47	-
2. To live an ethical life	2.36	2.27	1.73	1.83	2.32	2.30	2.67	2.45
3. A loyal citizen of Israel/of the country in which he lives	2.56	2.96	2.13	2.85	2.60	2.92	2.71	3.05
4. To take an interest in the fate of the Jews	2.64	2.36	2.25	2.20	2.51	2.38	2.90	2.47
5. To celebrate Bar-Mitzvah	2.66	2.21	2.12	1.97	2.45	2.06	3.05	2.43
6. To attend synagogue services	2.90	2.23	1.97	1.80	2.79	2.21	3.40	2.44
7. To take an interest in the fate of persecuted peoples	3.14	2.82	2.94	2.62	3.20	2.90	3.19	2.87
8. To take an interest in the affairs of the local Jewish community	-	2.04	-	1.77	-	2.07		2.15
9. To settle in Israel or encourage his children to settle	-	2.13	-	2.05	-	2.17		2.15
10. To support Israel	-	2.04	-	1.77	-	2.07		2.40

1 = essential—2 = very desirable—3 = desirable—4 = irrelevant.

that feeling. In Israel it is not difficult to be a Jew but outside of Israel you have to act as such—otherwise they will not even know that he is a Jew."

The difference between the requirements in the two environments is greatest for attendance at synagogue services, and a particularly sharp difference is discernible

in the approach of the non-religious students. Where the
Jew in Israel is concerned, attendance at synagogue services is regarded by them as almost irrelevant (mean 3.40),
but in regard to the Jew in the Diaspora it becomes desirable (mean 2.44)—in that context it is viewed by them as
an expression of identification.

The religious students are more demanding in their
requirements for a good Jew, both in Israel and outside
of it. All the activities—the general items as well as the
specific religious activities—are stressed more strongly
by them as desirable for the good Jew. What may appear
to some as a general item, such as immigration to Israel,
is seen by a number of religious students within the context of their religious conception of Jewish life. In the
interviews there is frequent reference to settlement in
Israel as the fulfillment of a religious commandment, and
one of them voices a widely-held view when he adds:

"A good Jew is a better Jew if he resides in Israel."

The rank order of requirements for the good Jew in Israel
and for the Jew in the Diaspora is highly correlated in the
case of religious students.

Evaluation of Jewish Communities

We have seen how high the students rate readiness
to immigrate (or to encourage his children to immigrate)
as an attribute of the good Jew in the Diaspora, and how
highly rated also is readiness to help in the in-gathering
of the immigrants as an attribute of the good Jew in Israel.
They feel close to Jews who are willing to immigrate to
Israel; on the other hand, they express a sense of distance
from those who are unwilling to come (see table 11B).

Using the terminology developed by the sociologist
R. K. Merton,[9] Israel may be likened to an open and

incomplete group. It is "open" in the sense that it wel-
comes the entrance into it of Jews from abroad whom it
regards as potential members; it is "incomplete" in the
sense that there are potential members who are still outside (i.e., are still non-members). The degree of incompleteness is the ratio of those already inside to all those
eligible for membership. Since Israelis tend to see all Jews
as potential members and there are many more Jews outside than inside, the degree of incompleteness is considerable.

The attitude of an incomplete group—particularly if
it feels itself beleaguered—is sharply critical of members
who leave it; they are at times seen as deserters. There
is a strong disapproval of *yerida* (emigration from Israel)
on the part of the great majority in all three categories
of students (see tables 56 and 57 sup.). (Despite the social
climate of disapproval, a small minority is nonetheless
prepared to consider *yerida*).

The readiness to enter, i.e., to immigrate to Israel, is
accordingly one of the main criteria determining the
attitude of Israeli youth to Jews abroad. Thus, since
American Jews are regarded, on the one hand, as eligible
and desirable members, but there are doubts, on the other
hand, whether any appreciable number will immigrate,
the attitudes toward them are ambivalent.

When the students were questioned about the esteem in
which they held six Jewish communities located in various
parts of the world, they ranked the Jewry of Soviet Russia
highest of all (see table 61A). The interviews reveal that
several factors account for the high rating. There is, first
of all, compassion for a persecuted Jewry and admiration
for their fortitude in adversity:

"I feel a sense of pity for Russian Jewry. When the Holydays
approach and I see what they have to endure and how they
stand up to it, my regard for them grows."

"I have a high regard for Russian Jewry. They are subjected
to tremendous pressure directed against Judaism, against Israel,

and yet there are people who go to synagogue, eat matzot on Pesach and also want to come to settle in Israel."

But in addition the view is held that Russian Jews would be more likely than American Jews to immigrate to Israel if given the opportunity to do so. While the reluctance of American Jews to immigrate results in a lowering of the esteem in which they are held, the question of *aliyah* does not confound the favorable attitude toward Russian Jewry. The following is a typical remark:

"I do not know what Russian Jews will do if given the choice. But I believe that a number of them wish to immigrate and would come to settle if they could. As against this American Jews can, but don't want to come."

Some students, themselves sons and daughters of East European Jews, recall the part played by Russian Jewry in the early days of the Zionist movement and in the settlement of the country. Furthermore, the image of the East European Jew as being closer to his Jewish heritage than the Jew of Western Europe or of America seems to linger on in the minds of the students.

"In Eastern Europe they have a more positive attitude to their Jewishness. In Western countries they are more like the others."

This image has been reinforced by the reports about the expression of fervent Jewish feeling by Russian Jews congregating in the synagogue and the streets around it on the New Year and Simchat Torah. Occasionally, however, doubts are expressed, albeit not in a critical vein, about the Jewish attachment of Russian Jewry.

"They are assimilating as time goes on; they don't know much about Judaism but this possibly is not their fault."

Second on the list of Jewish communities is American Jewry. The attitude to American Jewry is one of positive esteem.

"They are generous, they help Jews throughout the world."

"They support Israel."

"They are on a high cultural level."

"It is a flourishing Jewish community preserving Jewish values."

Some students, however, focus their attention on the inroads of assimilation in American Jewry. At a number of points ambivalences in the attitudes of the students are discernible—particularly in expressions of the feeling that American Jews are not prepared to settle and that their financial contribution, albeit considerable, cannot be a satisfactory substitute for their *aliyah*.

The evaluation of the remaining Jewish communities on the list—England, Iraq, Argentina and Germany—is still on the positive side, except for the community in Germany. The remarks of students are sharply critical of Jews who have remained in, or have returned to, Germany.

"I find it difficult to understand Jews who today can dwell in Germany."

"I am ashamed of every Jew who remained there."

"A Jew who returned to the country which murdered his brethren is no longer a Jew."

There were no significant differences between religious and non-religious students in the evaluation of the communities.

Do students whose families are from the West and those whose families are from the Orient evaluate the overseas communities differently? The communities are evaluated in the same order although there is a tendency for the students from the Oriental communities to give a slightly more favorable evaluation. An exception is the case of Russian Jewry where the evaluation given by the Ashkenazic students is higher, although not significantly so. A significant difference does exist in regard to the Jewish community in Germany. It is given the lowest place by both sectors but the evaluation of the students from the Oriental communities is not as sharply negative (see table 62A).

Closeness to Different Groups of Jews

A series of questions probed the feeling of closeness to different groups of Jews in Israel and abroad.

There is a very sharp difference in the feeling of closeness of the students towards Jews abroad who support Israel as opposed to those who do not (see table 63A).

In regard to a feeling of closeness to religious and non-religious Jews in Israel, the relative positions of the religious and non-religious students are as would be expected (see table 64). The traditionalist students express greater closeness to non-religious (46 percent feel "very close") than to religious Jews (only 27 percent feel "very close").

In regard to Jews abroad, the position of the traditionalist students is reversed. They feel greater closeness to the religious (35 percent "very close") than to the non-religious Jews (only 15 percent "very close") (see table 65).

Both non-religious and traditionalist students feel somewhat closer to religious Jews abroad than to religious Jews in Israel. From the interviews it appears that the relationship to Jews inside and outside of Israel is determined by different criteria. In regard to religious and non-religious groups of Jews in Israel, the students adopt the criterion of similarity. "They are like me," "I am one of them" were frequent remarks. In this context religious observance (or the lack of it) is salient as the source of the similarity or dissimilarity. When the question is one of closeness to Jews outside of Israel, the frame of reference becomes the relationship of the particular group to the

Jewish people and to Israel, and a number of the students
adopt another criterion, that of interdependence. They do
not feel themselves close to assimilating Jews. Religious
Jews are seen by these students as less likely to assimilate
than non-religious Jews and as likely to have a greater
attachment to the Jewish people and to Israel. Furthermore the conflict which exacerbates relations between the
religious and non-religious camps in Israel weighs less
heavily when the relationship to Jews abroad is considered. So a traditionalist student remarks:

"I feel a closeness to religious Jews in the Diaspora because
this (their religious observance) keeps them in the Jewish fold."

And a non-religious student observes:

"In regard to Jews in the Diaspora I feel a greater closeness
to religious Jews because they have a greater attachment to
Israel."

The broader criterion of relationship to the Jewish
people causes a number of students to indicate an equal
degree of closeness to the religious and non-religious
groups.

"We all belong to one people."

"What I regard as important is that they are Jews, irrespective of whether they are religious or not."

With religious students two considerations weigh:
firstly, religious observance, and secondly, residence in
Israel, which is seen as the fulfillment of a *mitzvah*. Non-
religious Jews abroad lack both desiderata while non-
religious residents in Israel possess at least one of them.
The order of closeness as experienced by religious students is, then, as follows: 1) religious Jews in Israel; 2)
religious Jews abroad; 3) non-religious Jews in Israel; 4)
non-religious Jews abroad.

The order of closeness as experienced by traditionalist students is as follows: 1) non-religious Jews in Israel; 2) religious Jews abroad; 3) religious Jews in Israel; 4) non-religious Jews abroad.

The order of closeness as experienced by non-religious students is as follows: 1) non-religious Jews in Israel; 2) non-religious Jews abroad; 3) religious Jews abroad; 4) religious Jews in Israel.

The religious students are more conscious than others of an overriding bond which unites all Jews. They feel less of a distance from non-religious Jews, both in Israel and abroad, than non-religious students feel from religious Jews. The following remarks by religious students are typical:

"Although I feel apart from them because of their views I also feel a sense of kinship because of the fact that they are Jews."

"The very fact that they are Jews brings us together. Even the non-religious have a feeling for Israel."

Thus, while 33 percent of the non-religious students indicated that they were "very close" or "close" to religious Jews in Israel, 78 percent of the religious students indicated these degrees of closeness to non-religious Jews in Israel (see table 64). Again, although non-religious Jews abroad fulfill neither the criterion of religious observance nor that of residence in Israel, the number of religious students (69 percent) who expressed degrees of closeness to them is about the same as—indeed, slightly more than—the number of non-religious students (64 percent) (see table 65).

A similar pattern is observable in questions relating to the feeling of closeness to Jews in Israel of the same, and of a different, communal origin. The religious students feel closer to Jews of the same communal origin and also to those of a different communal origin than do

Table 64 Feeling of closeness to (1) religious and (2) non-religious Jews in Israel

	All Respondents		Religious		Traditionalist		Non-Religious	
	Religious in Israel	Non-Religious in Israel	Religious in Israel	Non-Religious in Israel	Religious in Israel	Non-Religious in Israel	Religious in Israel	Non-Religious in Israel
Very close	30	55	90	30	27	46	6	72
Close	30	34	9	48	45	41	27	24
Not so Close	40	11	1	22	28	13	67	4
Total %	100	100	100	100	100	100	100	100
N	777	777	166	166	243	243	368	368

Table 65 Feeling of Closeness to (1) religious and (2) non-religious Jews abroad

	All Respondents		Religious		Traditionalist		Non-Religious	
	Religious abroad	Non-religious abroad	Religious abroad	Non-religious abroad	Religious abroad	Non-religious abroad	Religious abroad	Non-religious abroad
Very close	33	18	85	22	35	15	9	19
Close	30	48	13	47	42	52	29	45
Not so close	37	34	2	31	23	33	62	36
Total %	100	100	100	100	100	100	100	100
N	777	777	166	166	243	243	368	368

the non-religious students. Traditionalist students stand in between. At the same time, the students in all three categories feel closer to Jews of the same communal origin than to Jews of a different communal origin (see table 66A).

On this issue we divided the students into those from the Ashkenazic and Oriental communities. While the students from the Ashkenazic communities score higher on closeness to Jews of the same communal origin, the positions are reversed in regard to Jews of a different communal origin (see table 67A). Here there is a sharper fall among Ashkenazic students than among Oriental students in the number who declare themselves "very close," and the students from the Oriental sector score higher. This is probably a reflection of the tendency on the part of students in the Oriental communities to reduce the distance between themselves and what is regarded by them as the dominant, more privileged, Ashkenazic sector.

If we now reintroduce the religious observance variable into the picture, we observe that there are hardly any differences between the religious students in the two sectors (Ashkenazic and Oriental) in regard to their feeling of closeness to Jews of the same communal origin— they both score high. The differences we have noted above are to be found among the traditionalist and the non-religious students in the two sectors. In regard to closeness to Jews of different communal origin, the differences exist among the religious and traditionalist students in the two sectors, but not among the non-religious students who in both sectors have low scores of approximately equal size (see table 68A).

CHAPTER 8

The Gentile World and Anti-Semitism

Unlike Jewish minorities in the Diaspora, Israeli youth have grown up in their own majority environment without the need for constant reference to what Gentiles may or may not think about them. But they know that the history of the Jewish people has been set across a long stretch of centuries in a Gentile world, that the greater proportion of Jews still dwell as minorities in this world, and many have been told by their own parents of their experience of life with Gentiles. Simmering at the back of their minds is also the consciousness of the Holocaust which, though not as vivid a memory for them as for their parents, continues to exercise a profound and pervasive influence on their perception of Jew-Gentile relationships. They do not place much reliance on Gentile goodwill, although they have less of a distrust of them than have their parents.

They tend to speak of Gentiles in general terms as a broad, universal category from which they are marked off as Jews. At the same time there is also, when occasion demands, a differential evaluation of different parts of this world. Among the factors which determine this evalu-

ation an important part is played by the treatment accorded in a particular country to the Jewish minority—
during the period of the Holocaust as well as at the present time. Thus, in a study conducted shortly after the
Eichmann trial, students accorded the highest esteem to
the Danish people;[1] the story—highlighted during the
trial—of how the Danes had rescued the Jews of Denmark
from annihilation by the Nazis had engraved itself on their
minds. The associations which go with the word "Ger-
mans" still arouse considerable antipathy, although some
of the students distinguish between Nazis and such liberal
elements as have emerged in Germany. The people of
Russia rank low in the esteem of the students who see
the U.S.S.R. not only as inimical to Israel but as currently
discriminating against its Jewish citizens. The people of
Western democracies, such as the United States and
Britain, are positively evaluated (see table 69A). While
the students are sensitive to attitudes toward Jews in the
Gentile world, their knowledge of the nature of this world
and of its religions was found in the interviews to be very
sparse indeed.

When an Israeli Meets a Non-Jew

The majority of the students have looked at the Gentile
world from afar only. If they were to go abroad and meet
Gentiles, how would they present themselves or wish to
be seen by these "others"? In presenting a "visiting card"
as an Israeli to non-Jews the Israeli is in fact presenting
himself and is being seen as someone who is also a Jew.
But is there an inclination to emphasize one component
in their identity and to underplay the other?

The students were asked to indicate their reaction
to the following hypothetical situation abroad: "If a non-
Jew from abroad were to meet you abroad and mistake
you for a non-Israeli non-Jew, would you correct his mis-

take and tell him that (a) you are a Jew (b) you are an Israeli?" The students—except for a very small minority—indicate that they would correct the mistake in regard to both components of their identity (see table 70Ai). Even if the other party is an anti-Semite, the students would still identify themselves as Jews and Israelis (see table 70Aii). There is no disinclination to appear either as a Jew or as an Israeli although the majority responding with an unqualified "yes" is greater in regard to presentation of themselves as Israelis than as Jews.

It is clear that Israelis view with distaste any attempt to efface or hide an identity—it is seen as an act unbefitting a self-respecting person. At the same time they hold the view that Israeli Jews enjoy higher repute among non-Jews than do Diaspora Jews. Whether this view is correct or not, it seems reasonable to assume that there is likely to be less ambiguity, and consequently less tension, in the relationship between the Israeli and the non-Jew. The meeting is more clearly on an equal status level without the undertones which enter into a majority-minority member relationship. The Israeli is seen by the non-Jew as a Jew but not necessarily as a member of the local Jewish community, and the non-Jew is probably less apprehensive of "sensitive spots" in the Israeli which may result in unexpected reactions to anything he may say, even in good faith, about Jews.

The Perception of Anti-Semitism

"Anti-Semitism" is a familiar word to all the students although many of them have never encountered anti-Semites or personally experienced anti-Semitism. What is their perception of anti-Semitism and of anti-Semites?

They do not absolve the non-Jewish world of anti-Semitism, but they do not regard the greater proportion

Table 71 The extent of anti-Semitism
"Are non-Jews anti-Semites?"

	All Respondents		Religious		Traditionalist		Non-Religious	
	Parents	Students	Parents	Students	Parents	Students	Parents	Students
1. Yes, almost all	15	3	26	6	9	3	8	1
2. A large section	32	11	29	21	37	12	31	6
3. Some of them	42	56	34	55	37	54	57	58
4. Only a small section	11	30	11	18	17	31	4	35
Total %	100	100	100	100	100	100	100	100
N	252	1438	87	346	93	451	72	641

of non-Jews as anti-Semitic. The parents see the non-Jewish world as more extensively anti-Semitic than do the students (see table 71). The religious students, who throughout reveal the stronger in-group feelings, are at the same time the most wary about the Gentile out-group. Twenty-seven percent feel that "almost all" or "a large section" of Gentiles are anti-Semitic whereas this is the feeling of only 7 percent of the non-religious students.

The majority believe that a common factor runs through anti-Semitism everywhere. But they do understand that there are differences in depth and extent in various countries. In a substudy almost half of the students (47 percent) did not see prospects for the eradication of anti-Semitism anywhere in the foreseeable future; 13 percent believed it could be eradicated in a few countries only. Optimistic about its eradication in all countries were 16 percent, and another 24 percent believed it could be eradicated in most countries (see table 12B).

What is seen as the main factor in the development of anti-Semitism? The students were asked to choose

from three sets of factors (see table 72). The majority
choice—55 percent—is "the position of Jews as a minority
among non-Jews." A typical remark in the interviews:

"Anti-Semitism exists because we exist, but we did not stir it
up."

"The characteristics of the non-Jews" is a factor chosen
by a small number (12 percent) only. Non-religious students in particular refrain from attaching any blame to
Gentiles—only 8 percent endorse this factor—but 25 percent of the religious students give this response. This is
a difference which does not appear among the three
categories of parents. Twenty-one percent of the non-
religious parents and an almost equal percentage (22) of
religious parents see in the characteristics of the non-
Jews a main cause of anti-Semitism.

About a third of the students (and of the parents)
choose "the characteristics of the Jews abroad"—more
than choose "the characteristics of the non-Jews." When

Table 72 Causes of Anti-Semitism
"What, in your view, is the main cause of anti-Semitism?"

	All Respondents		Religious		Traditionalist		Non-Religious	
	Parents	Students	Parents	Students	Parents	Students	Parents	Students
1. The characteristics of the non-Jews	23	12	22	25	26	10	21	8
2. The situation of the Jews abroad as a minority	45	55	45	44	43	54	48	61
3. The characteristics of the Jews abroad	32	33	33	31	31	36	31	31
Total %	100	100	100	100	100	100	100	100
N	247	1425	85	347	91	447	71	631

the question did not relate to the *main* cause but asked whether the characteristics or behavior of Jews contributed to the spread of anti-Semitism, 80 percent in a sub-study answered affirmatively (see table 13B). Some of these students speak with a sense of shame of the behavior and characteristics of Jews in the Diaspora and in particular criticize some of the occupations in which they believe Jews are to be found in large numbers. One of the more extreme examples was a student who echoed the prejudices about Jews held by anti-Semites and accused Jews engaged in commerce for causing anti-Semitism by their dishonest practices.

"To blame for it is the Jewish character which countenances dishonesty for the sake of economic gain."

On the part of some of the others—mainly religious students—who endorse the category "the characteristics of the Jews," a different approach is apparent. They speak in terms of Jewish characteristics which, though they "irritate the Gentiles," or "arouse their jealousy," are regarded by the students as far from shameful; indeed they take pride in them. They refer to the uniqueness of the Jews as a "Chosen People," their attachment to their peculiar religion, their reluctance to renounce their customs.

A relationship exists between the attribution of the cause of anti-Semitism to the characteristics of Jews or to the characteristics of non-Jews on the one hand, and attractiveness of the Jewish identity on the other. The tendency to attribute anti-Semitism to "the characteristics of the Jews abroad" is associated with a lesser attractiveness of the Jewish identity. Thus, while 53 percent of those non-religious students who attribute anti-Semitism to non-Jews would wish to be born as Jews if they had to live abroad, only 34 percent of those who attribute it to the characteristics of Jews would so wish to be born (see table 72Ai).

What the students write in the questionnaires and tell in the interviews reflects the considerable confusion that exists in their minds about the causes of anti-Semitism, and in particular about the contribution of the "behavior" and "characteristics" of Jews to the growth of anti-Semitism.

CHAPTER 9

The Religious Factor

The degree of religious observance is the crucial variable in the study of Jewish identity. Significant differences consistently appear on Jewish identity items between religious, traditionalist and non-religious students. The Jewish identity of the religious student is much stronger than that of the traditionalist and non-religious student; the Jewish identity of the traditionalist is stronger than that of the non-religious student. On all questions relating to Jewishness, the Jewish people or Jews abroad the sequence is: I. religious; II. traditionalist; and III. non-religious. Not only do the religious students feel more Jewish and value their Jewishness more under all circumstances, but they feel closer to, and have a greater sense of identification with, Jews everywhere.

In the case of the religious students, home, school and youth movement mutually reinforce one another and there is a closely integrated outlook on Jews and Jewishness, a set of values and an accompanying code of behavior which pervade almost every sphere of their lives.[1] Their replies to any question generally cluster around a particular response category while those of the traditionalist and non-religious students are more widely distributed. In contrast to this relative homogeneity of outlook within the religious sector,[2] the traditionalist and non-religious categories are classifications embracing widely differing subcategories. Generalizations about these categories have to be made with due reservation.

The three categories of students are close together on most items of Israeli identity, on which they all score high. While the religious students score highest on Jewish identity items, they do not fall below the others on questions of Israeli identity (where it is not counterposed to their Jewishness).

Role of Religious Observance among Parents and among Students

The differences between religious, traditionalist and non-religious reappear consistently among the parents, but the gap between religious and non-religious parents is not as wide as it is between religious and non-religious students. The parents are more strongly Jewish than the students.

While the religious students are close to the attitudes of the religious parents, a considerable gap appears between traditionalist parents and traditionalist students, and the gap widens between the non-religious parents and non-religious students.

The Jewishness of the non-religious parents, who are mostly from Eastern Europe, seems to have been shaped by the Jewish folk culture which prevailed in the milieu in which they grew up.[3] The fact that they lived part of their lives as a Jewish minority—specifically designated as such—has apparently also left its imprint on their Jewish identity.

Religious observance is called upon to play a more important role in relation to the Jewish identity of the students than it does in relation to the Jewishness of their parents which was buttressed by other factors in the milieu in which their socialization took place. The effects of the absence of the factor of religious observance are accordingly more pronounced among students than among their parents.

The existence of this sharper difference among the students also becomes apparent from a glance at the measures of association between religious observance and the key items of Jewish identity (see table 73A). The relations between religious observance and intensity of Jewish identity are considerably higher for the students than for their parents.

The Position of the Traditionalists

Standing somewhere between the religious and non-religious on most issues which pertain to the Jewish identity are the traditionalists. Their position merits some attention.

They see themselves outside the religious camp in Israel. More of them indicate that they feel themselves "very close" to non-religious Jews in Israel than the number who feel "very close" to religious Jews in Israel (see table 64 sup.). On the other hand, while their lives are not strictly governed by a religious code of behavior as in the case of the religious students, their general orientation towards the Jewish religion is positive. Thus, while the majority of religious students feel that it is "very desirable" that the Jewish religion play an important part in the public life of Israel, the response of the majority of traditionalists, though less emphatic, is yet positive (see table 84 infra.).

The Jewish identity of the traditionalists is considerably stronger than that of the non-religious students but appreciably less so than that of the religious students. Thus, on the Israeli-Jewish continuum the mean position is near the midpoint but inclining somewhat to the Israeli side of the scale (see tables 10 and 11, sup.). The three clusters—around the midpoint, on the Israeli side and on the Jewish side—reflect the alignments of three subcategories of traditionalists:

(i) Traditionalists who are close to the outlook of the religious students; it would seem that they tend to come from religious homes and/or attend religious schools.

(ii) Those who are generally closer to the non-religious; they would appear to be students in whose homes Jewish traditional practice is more limited, who attend secular schools, participate in secular youth movements, and consort with non-religious friends.

(iii) A residual subcategory who take up the midway position between the religious and non-religious students.

Like the other categories of students the traditionalists are generally high on all items relating to the Israeli identity. A substantial majority see the Israeli and Jewish subidentities as overlapping and consonant—they are higher on these questions than the non-religious but lower than the religious students (see tables 1 and 2, sup.). While in the interviews the religious students speak of their Israeliness as an extension of their Jewishness, the integration of the two subidentities on the part of a number of the traditionalists does not seem to be as close-knit. At the same time their endorsement of consonance between the subidentities is an expression of the harmonious equilibrium they have established between the two.

The majority of traditionalist students attend secular schools, a minority go to religious schools. Does the type of school make a difference? We sought to compare traditionalist students in the two types of schools, holding constant the home background.

The comparison between traditionalist students from traditionalist homes attending *religious* schools with traditionalist students from traditionalist homes in *secular* schools shows that the former score higher on key Jewish identity items (see tables 74A, 75A, 76A). This would seem to indicate that—in regard to the traditionalist students from traditionalist homes—the two types of schools, and the social milieu associated with them, exercise a differential influence. We cannot, however, be sure that there is not a selective factor at work—the traditionalist parents who send their children to religious schools may be more religious than those who choose the secular schools.

In regard to the Israeli subidentity (when it is not juxtaposed with the Jewish subidentity), the two types of schools do not seem to exercise this differential effect (see table 77A).

Religious Students in Religious and in Secular Schools

Of the religious students responding on the questionnaires containing the key identity items, 599 were studying in religious schools and 82 attended secular schools. The position of the religious students in the secular schools remains close to that of their religious peers in the religious schools. The only significant differences are (1) while for both groups their Jewishness is highly central, it is somewhat more so for students in the religious schools, and (2) while both are on the Jewish side of the Israeli-Jewish scale, there is a tendency on the part of the students in the secular schools to move to the midpoint on the scale (see tables 78A to 83A).

It seems that, while they do not remain altogether uninfluenced by the school environment, no basic change takes place in the attitudes of the religious students in the secular schools. It would appear reasonable to suppose that because of the clearly crystallized outlook and practices acquired in, and continuously buttressed by, the religious home, the religious students are less susceptible to contrary influences than are the traditionalist students from traditionalist homes. (Several of those religious students indicated in the interviews that their religious convictions were deepened by the need to defend and uphold them in the encounter with unobservant peers.)

Secular Views on the Role of Religion in Israel and in the Diaspora

The great majority (74 percent) of non-religious students believe that it is either "undesirable" or "very undesirable" that the Jewish religion should play an important part in the public life of Israel (see table 84). A majority, somewhat reduced (57 percent), also feel this way about the role of religion in the private lives of Jews in Israel (see table 85).

When, however, the question relates to the role of religion in the lives of Jews abroad, as many as 88 percent of the non-religious students view this positively (see table 86). In the interviews it becomes evident that in regard to Jewish life abroad religious practices are seen by the students as an expression of Jewish identification and as fulfilling the function of preserving Jewish identity. When they refer to Jews abroad the students—of all the categories—tend to think in terms of their belonging-

Table 84 Role of Religion in Public Life of Israel
"Is it desirable that the Jewish religion should play an important part in the public life of the State of Israel?"

	All Respondents	Religious	Traditionalist	Non-Religious
1. Very desirable	18	62	12	3
2. Desirable	37	36	57	23
3. Undesirable	32	1	30	48
4. Very undesirable	13	1	1	26
Total %	100	100	100	100
N	767	168	247	352

Table 85 Role of Religion in Life of Individual Jew in Israel
"Is it desirable that the Jewish religion should play an important part in the life of the individual Jew in Israel?"

	All Respondents	Religious	Traditionalist	Non-Religious
1. Very desirable	18	61	12	3
2. Desirable	47	39	63	40
3. Undesirable	27	-	23	42
4. Very undesirable	8	-	2	15
Total %	100	100	100	100
N	767	168	247	352

Table 86 The Role of Religion in the Diaspora
"Is it desirable that the Jewish religion should play an important part in the lives of Jews abroad?"

	All Respondents	Religious	Traditionalist	Non-Religious
1. Very desirable	54	72	58	42
2. Desirable	38	26	36	46
3. Undesirable	6	2	5	9
4. Very desirable	2	-	1	3
Total %	100	100	100	100
N	767	168	247	352

ness to a Jewish people rather than in terms of their affiliation with either of two, at times warring, camps of religious and non-religious Jews as in Israel.

The Decline in Religious Observance —
Students, Parents, Grandparents

The students were not only asked to indicate whether they themselves were religious, traditionalist or non-religious, but also to indicate the position of their parents on the scale of religious observance.

Of the students from religious homes, 74 percent classified themselves as religious, 23 percent as traditionalist
and 3 percent as non-religious. Among the students from
traditionalist homes, 66 percent indicated that they themselves were traditionalist, 5 percent were religious and 29
percent non-religious. The students who described their
parents as non-religious also classified themselves as
such except for 3 percent who stated that they were
traditionalist (see table 87).

Table 87 Classification by students of their own religious behavior and that
of their parents

Parents Students	Religious	Traditionalist	Non-Religious
Religious	74	5	-
Traditionalist	23	66	3
Non-Religious	3	29	97
Total %	100	100	100
N	1142	1340	1146

When there is a breakdown according to communal
origin it is seen that in the religious homes of the Oriental
communities there is a greater movement on the part
of students away towards a traditionalist position (see
table 88). Thus, 85 percent of the Ashkenazic students
who describe their parents as being religious remain religious themselves, while this position is maintained by only
62 percent of the Oriental students. In both cases the veering away is towards a traditionalist position (14 percent
of the Ashkenazic students and 33 percent of the Oriental
students), whereas only a small fraction moves to a non-
religious position.

In regard to traditionalist homes the movement towards
a non-religious position is closely similar on the part of
Ashkenazic and Oriental students—31 percent and 25
percent respectively have become non-religious.

Table 88 Communal origin and religious classification by students of themselves and their parents

Parents	Religious		Traditionalist		Non-Religious	
Students	Ashk.	Orient.	Ashk.	Orient.	Ashk.	Orient.
Religious	85	62	3	7		2
Traditionalist	14	33	66	68	3	10
Non-Religious	1	5	31	25	97	88
Total %	100	100	100	100	100	100
N	587	547	865	464	1030	103

Only a small number of Oriental subjects come from non-religious homes, and they have remained, with few exceptions, non-religious. The Ashkenazic sons and daughters of non-religious homes have also—with even fewer exceptions—maintained a non-religious course.

In a further question the students were asked to compare their position in regard to religious observance with that of their parents—were they "more religious," "as religious," or "less religious." The parents were asked an identical question about their religious behavior in

Table 89 Comparison of religious observance of students and parents with that of their respective parents

	All Respondents		Religious		Traditionalist		Non-Religious	
	Students	Parents	Students	Parents	Students	Parents	Students	Parents
More religious than parents	7	5	16	10	7	3	2	-
As religious as parents	51	32	55	50	48	21	51	27
Less religious than parents	42	63	29	40	45	76	47	73
Total %	100	100	100	100	100	100	100	100
N	3626	423	911	144	1183	162	1532	117

relation to that of *their* parents, i.e., the grandparents of the students (see table 89).

The parents in all three categories indicate a decline—of greater magnitude than among the students—in their own religious observance as compared with that of their parents. The standards of comparison of the two generations are, of course, likely to be different, yet the contrast in the two sets of figures is noteworthy. Forty percent of religious parents say they are less religious (as compared with 29 percent of religious students who say so); 76 percent of traditionalist parents (45 percent of students); 73 percent of non-religious parents (47 percent of students). Only 7 percent of the students and 5 percent of the parents report that they are more religious than their parents.

The majority of religious students, however, do not see themselves as less religious than their parents. Sixteen percent see themselves as more religious, another 55 percent assert they are "as religious" as their parents, and only 29 percent regard themselves as less religious.

If we now proceed to break the sample down into its Ashkenazic and Oriental components (see table 90A), we find that more of the Oriental students (48 percent) report a decline in their religious observance as compared with that of their parents than do Ashkenazic students (37 percent). This holds true for all three categories of students—religious, traditionalist and non-religious. With the parents the position is the reverse. More Ashkenazic parents (71 percent) report a relative decrease in their religious observance compared with their parents than do Oriental parents (48 percent).

This breakdown also enables us to see that the sharper decline reported by parents (in relation to their parents) is actually limited to the Ashkenazic sector. In the Oriental sector the decline reported by the students is equal to that of the parents. The heterogeneous background of the communities comprised in the classification "Oriental" demands caution in regard to any generalization, but it would seem that, at any rate, in some of these communities the cleavage between the religiously patterned life of the generation of parents and the practice of the students is sharper than it is among the Ashkenazic sector.

Is the decline more marked among the sons than the daughters? In the Ashkenazic sector 44 percent of the sons report a decline relative to their parents as compared with 31 percent of the daughters (see tables 91A and 92A). In the Oriental sector the decline is reported by 52 percent of the sons as compared with 44 percent of the daughters. (Again there may be differences within the communities which comprise these sectors.) The differences between sons and daughters apply to the traditionalist and non-religious students in the two sectors but not to the religious students.

CHAPTER 10

Divisions Within
the Jewish Community

A. Ashkenazic and Oriental Jews

One of the broad divisions of Israel's Jewish population is between Ashkenazic (Jews from Europe) and Oriental (Jews from Asia—mainly the Middle East—and North Africa). We have referred to differences between the two sectors on specific issues (such as the Holocaust) and it remains for us to determine whether any differences exist between the communities in regard to the strength of their Jewish identity.

The small Jewish population which lived in Palestine before the beginning of modern Jewish settlement in the 1880's included a number of Jews of Sephardic (Spanish) origin. (Some of these Sephardic families, who are classified as falling within the Oriental sector, are now part of Israel's elite.) The Zionist movement had its origins in Europe and the pioneers of the first (1882–1903) and second (1904–1914) *aliyot* were mainly from Eastern Europe. The *aliyot* which came after World War I during the period of the British Mandate were largely composed of European immigrants (almost ninety percent of the total) although they also included Oriental immigrants from countries such as Yemen and Aden, Iran and Tur-

key.[1] It was as part of the large-scale immigration which
followed the establishment of the State in 1948 that Israel
received (in addition to the survivors of the European
Holocaust) an appreciable accession of Oriental Jews.
The exodus from Yemen (the "Magic Carpet Operation"),
from Iraq and Libya, and (later, after the Sinai Campaign)
from Egypt, was almost complete, and substantial numbers also came from Iran, Turkey, Morocco, Tunisia and
Algeria. As a result the proportions of Oriental and European Jews in the population are now approaching equality.

Coming as they did, for the most part, from countries
still lagging far behind in technological development,
Oriental immigrants have entered the lower socio-economic strata of an Israeli society, the political, social
and economic patterns of which were determined by the
European settlers. Illiteracy is much higher among Oriental than it is among European immigrants. The number
of children of Oriental immigrants who enter secondary
school is considerably below their proportion in the population, and the disproportion is even greater in the field
of higher education. At the same time the disproportion
may be expected to decrease as a result of the special
efforts of the educational authorities to stimulate the
progress of children of the Oriental communities.[2]

There is considerable heterogeneity within the Oriental
sector. Although many of them are in the lower socio-
economic strata, there are at the same time wide differences in socio-economic status and educational background between immigrants from the different countries,
and also, for example, between those from urban and
rural regions within a particular country. There are Oriental immigrants who came from peasant societies untouched by any technological development; others had
already been influenced by the stirrings of modernization
before they left their countries of origin. But while these
differences exist, the Oriental communities on the whole

tend to regard themselves as an underprivileged community—with the psychology attendant on such feeling—as compared with the Ashkenazic community which is seen as the dominant sector.[3] The fact of communal belongingness is accordingly more central in the consciousness of members of the Oriental communities than it is among the Ashkenazic groups. At the same time there are factors which are reducing the sense of difference. The period of service in the army provides occasion for equal status contact. The constant threat from the surrounding Arab countries enhances the sense of interdependence and makes them feel Israelis and Jews rather than members of separate subgroups. There appears to be an increasing tendency to view the cause of the differences which exist as primarily socio-economic and educational and to avoid attributing them to communal discrimination.

The Oriental immigrants brought with them traditional patterns of Jewish life which had been relatively unaffected by ideological currents such as those which had swept through European Jewry. This means that in the new environment the children face social challenges to which their parents had been oblivious.

In the fact of their Jewishness the Oriental Jews see the common bond with their prestigious Ashkenazic brethren and the key to their acceptance into Israeli society. They are accordingly likely to stress their Jewishness for this, and for yet another reason—coming as they do from the Arab countries they are anxious to be marked off as different from the Arabs.[4]

Who is more "Jewish"?

Turning now to the data of the study (see tables 93, 94A–96A) a first glance would indicate that the Oriental communities are the more "Jewish." But a further examination shows that these differences are largely due to the fact that in the Oriental communities the religious and traditionalist students greatly outnumber the non-religious whereas in the Ashkenazic sector the non-religious students are the preponderant group (see table 97). The more strongly religious and traditionalist composition of the Oriental sector is in itself a fact of importance in any description of the Jewish character of that sector. If, however, we proceed further and break down the responses in the two sectors according to religious, traditionalist and non-religious categories, we find that the differences between Ashkenazic and Oriental subjects within a given category are greatly reduced and on some questions almost disappear. Thus, for example, on the question whether they would wish to be born Jews under the conditions of life outside of Israel, 64 percent of the Oriental subjects answer in the affirmative as against 52 percent of the Ashkenazic students (see table 93). But the further breakdown reveals that among the religious students of Ashkenazic and Oriental origin there are no differences

Table 93 Valence of Jewishness: According to communal origin
"If you were to live abroad, would you wish to be born a Jew?"

	All Respondents		Religious		Traditionalist		Non-Religious	
	Oriental	Ashkenazic	Oriental	Ashkenazic	Oriental	Ashkenazic	Oriental	Ashkenazic
1. I would wish to be born a Jew	64	52	85	84	57	56	43	37
2. It makes no difference	19	26	6	6	22	25	34	34
3. I would not wish to be born a Jew	17	22	9	10	21	19	23	29
Total %	100	100	100	100	100	100	100	100
N	376	1055	131	215	162	285	83	555

Table 97 Religious Distribution of Students in Ashkenazic and Oriental Communities

	Oriental	Ashkenazic
Religious	34	22
Traditionalist	44	27
Non-Religious	22	51
Total %	100	100
N	1121	2498

(84 percent and 85 percent respectively in the affirmative) nor among the traditionalists (56 and 57 percent respectively) and only a small, statistically non-significant, difference among the non-religious (37 and 43 percent respectively). The original overall difference arose from the fact that in the Ashkenazic sector the non-religious are a substantial majority whereas in the Oriental sector they are a small minority.

When the factor of communal origin (Ashkenazic or Oriental) is kept constant, the relationship between category of religious observance and Jewish identity is still maintained. There is a close correspondence in the measures of association when for each sector separately we relate religious observance to some of the relevant variables (see table 98A).

Within the Oriental sector—which, as we have noted, is a broad classification embracing a variety of groups—there may conceivably be differences in strength of Jewish identity between students who differ in regard to the country of origin of their families. Even among students from one particular country there may be differences related, for example, to the peculiar conditions of the subregion from which they hail. Thus, among immigrants from Iraq, differences are likely to exist between Kurdish Jews and the other Arab-speaking Jews.

Within some of these communities the differences may be traceable in greater or lesser measure to varied degrees of adherence to, or departure from, traditional patterns of life. This again means that religious observance is the crucial variable. The data of our study permitted a breakdown of the Oriental sector into students of families whose country of origin is (1) North Africa (mainly Morocco), (2) Yemen and Aden, and (3) other countries of the Middle East (Iraq, Iran, Egypt, Syria, Lebanon). A glance at the religious composition of the three subgroups shows the greater ratio of religious students among the "Yemenites" than among the other communities. Among the Yemenite students in our sample, 63 percent classified themselves as religious, 31 percent as traditionalists and only 6 percent as non-religious (see table 99A). Next in order—in terms of the proportion of the religious students—come the Jews of families from North Africa (mainly Morocco) of whom 44 percent are religious, 41 percent traditionalists and 15 percent non-religious. A considerable falling off in the proportion of religious students is noticeable in the third bloc of Middle Eastern countries—only 21 percent classify themselves as such; in this bloc the traditionalists are a preponderant group (53 percent) and 26 percent classify themselves as non-religious.

On key identity items the Yemenites score highest, with the North Africans following closely (the difference is non-significant statistically), while the students from the other countries score significantly lower (see tables 100A and 101A). When in a further breakdown, however, the factor of religious observance is controlled, the differences between the communities narrow. The religious students are particularly close to one another, whatever be the country of origin (see tables 102A and 103A). The differences that still appear to exist between traditionalist students and their counterparts and between non-religious students and their counterparts are statistically non-significant. (The small number of Yemenites in these categories makes comparison with them difficult.)

B. Veteran Settlers and New Immigrants

Are there differences in the Jewish identity of veteran
settlers (in Hebrew, *vatikim*) and of new immigrants (in
Hebrew, *olim chadashim*)? How does length of residence
in Israel influence the quality of a Jewish identity?

An answer to this question would require a developmental study of individuals across time or an examination
of homogeneous groups of immigrants who have come
at different periods of time from a relatively unchanging
background. The data of our study do not allow for the
adequate disentanglement of the complex set of factors
which need to be taken into account in an analysis of this
kind. There have been so many differences in the moti-
vational background and composition of the immigration
waves, and so many changes in the social climate in the
countries from which the immigrant families come (e.g.,
the non-religiousness of the more recent immigration
from Eastern Europe, the differing degrees of stability
in traditional patterns in the countries of the Middle East)
that comparisons cannot easily be made on the basis of
the questionnaire data.[5]

If we divide our student sample into three blocs—local-
born, members of families who arrived between 1948 and
1953, and those who arrived between 1954 and 1965—we
observe the different proportions of students from the
Ashkenazic and Oriental sectors and also the different
proportions within each sector of religious, traditionalist,
and non-religious students (see table 104).

It will be noted that while among local-born students
the ratio of Ashkenazic to Oriental students is 5 : 1, among
the immigrants the ratio is 2 : 1. In regard to religious
observance in the Ashkenazic sector, only 17 percent of
the local-born and 15 percent of the 1954–1965 immigrants declare themselves to be religious; the proportion
for the 1948–1953 bloc is considerably higher—27 per-

Table 104 Religious Observance Among Local-born and Immigrants in the Ashkenazic and Oriental Communities

	Local-born		Immigrated 1948–1953		Immigrated 1954–1965	
	Ashkenazic	Oriental	Ashkenazic	Oriental	Ashkenazic	Oriental
Religious	17	22	27	35	15	39
Traditionalist	24	41	32	47	28	43
Non-Religious	59	37	41	18	57	18
Total %	100	100	100	100	100	100
N	1110	207	630	346	330	170

cent. In the Oriental sector the proportion of religious students in both immigrant blocs (39 and 35 percent) is higher than among the local-born (22 percent). While among the local-born students an appreciable difference in religious and traditionalist composition between the Ashkenazic and Oriental communities still prevails, a strong secularizing trend among the Oriental local-born students has narrowed the gap. At the same time it is noteworthy that the difference between the two sectors has been particularly wide in regard to the most recent—1954–1965—immigration wave which contained a large non-religious proportion among the immigrants from Eastern Europe.

The religious composition of the immigrant and local-born blocs is a major factor affecting the relative strength of their Jewish identity. Thus, the 1948–1953 immigrant bloc is the most "Jewish" among Ashkenazic students on a question such as readiness to be born a Jew abroad. Sixty-two percent of this bloc answer this question in the affirmative, as against only 39 percent of the local-born and 45 percent of the 1954–1965 bloc (see table 105A). When the breakdown into religious categories is carried out it is seen that the differences are largely due to the greater proportion of religious students among the Ashkenazic sector in the 1948–1953 bloc. The more appreciable differences are between religious, traditionalist and non-religious students rather than between local-born and immigrants. Religious observance is again the crucial variable (see tables 106A and 107A).

The "Yemenites"

The Yemenite Jews are a group who have come from what has been a relatively unchanging background. We accordingly sought to examine the question about the influence of length of residence in relation to this group. In our sample there were seventy local-born Yemenite students and 102 in the 1948–1953 immigrant bloc and a mere seven in the more recent 1954–1965 bloc (ruling out a comparison with them). Comparing the religious distribution of the local-born Yemenites with those in the 1948–1953 bloc, we again see evidence of the secularizing trend (although even the local-born Yemenites remain a highly religious-traditionalist group as compared with the local-born in other sections of the population).[6] There is only one student in the 1948–1953 bloc who classified himself as non-religious while 15 percent among the local-born do so classify themselves (see table 108). Since even the Yemenite students of the 1948–1953 immigration have—like their local-born peers—received their education in Israel, the difference may conceivably be sought in the greater measure of secularization within the families of the local-born.

Since—like the rest of our sample—only a proportion of the Yemenite students appear as respondents on a particular questionnaire, the numbers are not sufficiently large to permit a meaningful breakdown according to religious categories on the various questions. An examina-

Table 108 Religious distribution of local-born and immigrant Yemenite students

	Local-born	1948–1953 Immigrants
Religious	49	73
Traditionalist	36	26
Non-Religious	15	1
Total %	100	100
N	70	102

tion of the responses on two key questions—on valence of Jewishness and on the Jewish–"private individual" scale (see tables 109A and 110A)—show the expected tendency, i.e., the less secularized immigrant group have a somewhat stronger Jewish orientation than the local-born (although the differences are non-significant).

Second-Generation Israelis

In our sample, there were 174 students who were second-generation Israelis, i.e., sons and daughters of local-born parents. The great majority of their grandparents came from Europe; only 16 percent of the grandparents born outside of Israel came from countries of the Orient. There was a somewhat greater proportion of non-religious students among these second-generation Israelis than among their local-born parents—an indication of the continued decline in religious observance in the second generation (see table 111A).

We matched these students one by one with an equal number of their peers who had been brought to Israel by immigrant parents. The matching was on the basis of country of origin óf grandparents, own religiosity, religiosity of parents, and sex.

The comparison of the matched pairs showed no appreciable differences between them on the key Jewish identity items (see tables 112A–118A). The immigrants, however, have a stronger Jewish orientation on the Jewish-"private individual" scale (see table 119A); but there is no significant difference on the Israeli-"private individual" scale (see table 120A). When confronted with the choice on the Jewish-Israeli scale, both groups veer more to the Israeli side, but the immigrant group less pronouncedly so (see table 121A).

On specific issues which reflect experience of life in the Diaspora, some differences predictably exist. Thus, more of the immigrants see the Gentile world as anti-Semitic (see table 122A). There is a greater tendency on the part of the immigrants to believe that the behavior of Jews is a cause of anti-Semitism, but the difference between the two groups on the subject is not significant (see table 123A).

CHAPTER 11

The Students and Their Teachers

There have been differing views about the nature and extent of the influence of the school on the values of its pupils, and the findings of research on the subject are by no means conclusive.[1] The school is, of course, part of the wider social milieu. A school system may be closely integrated into one segment of the larger society rather than into another, but the society (or part of it) invariably constitutes a background setting which overlaps a particular school situation and determines the limits as well as the direction of its influence. Indeed, it has been asserted that "it seems to be easier for society to change education than for education to change society."[2]

The teacher is just one element in the school situation in which other factors, such as the general atmosphere prevailing at the school and the informal peer groups, also play their part. But after comparing the attitudes of the students with those of their parents, it seemed of interest to extend the comparison to include the attitudes of their teachers (see Appendix 1). The material presented by the teachers in courses such as Bible, Talmud, Jewish history and Hebrew literature has a bearing on problems of Jewish identity. Moreover, the teachers are aware of the policy of the Ministry of Education which requires schools to strengthen the "Jewish consciousness" of the pupils. We did not go beyond the comparison of attitudes and enter upon the difficult task of analyzing the influence of the teachers on their pupils, although there is some reference to such influence in the four case studies which follow in the next chapter.

We assumed that religious observance would be the most important variable differentiating between teachers—as it had been found to be in the study of the students and their parents. It was apparent that the religious teachers are a relatively homogeneous group on the issues which are the subject of this research, whereas a variety of secular ideologies affect the attitudes of the other teachers.

While in the original research report a detailed comparison was carried out between the attitudes of the teachers and the responses of the students and parents on a number of subjects, we shall in this chapter limit the discussion to questions of overlap and valence, and then will briefly summarize the positions of the teachers on other issues.[3] We shall also enquire how the teachers appraise the identity of their students.

Comparing the Teachers with Students and Parents

The great majority of teachers in all three categories perceive Israeliness and Jewishness as overlapping (see tables 124 and 125); they score even higher than the parents. In comments added to their responses a number of teachers give emphatic expression to their view.

"There should be no separation of the concepts Jew and Israeli. It is necessary to emphasize the common past and the common destiny of the entire Jewish people."

"Why treat the two separately? A good Jewish education is also a good Israeli education."

While the attitude of the religious teachers is closely approximated by religious students, the number of traditionalist and non-religious students who perceive overlap is considerably lower than the corresponding categories of teachers.

Some of the non-religious teachers differentiate in their responses to the questions in tables 124 and 125. When these teachers feel more Jewish, they also feel more Israeli, but when they feel more Israeli, they do not feel more Jewish. The percentage who see no relationship rises from 13 percent (see table 124) to 24 percent (see table 125). They see their Jewishness as strengthening their Israeliness, but they feel that there is much in their Israeliness which is unrelated to their Jewishness.

Like the parents and students, hardly any teachers (a mere 2 percent) perceive any incompatibility between feeling Israeli and feeling Jewish.

Table 124 Teachers: Overlap and Consonance (Jewishness-Israeliness)
When I feel more Jewish:

	All Respondents			Religious			Traditionalist			Non-Religious		
	P	T	S	P	T	S	P	T	S	P	T	S
I also feel more Israeli	83	88	70	81	89	82	88	95	76	76	85	62
There is no relationship between my feeling Jewish and my feeling Israeli	17	10	27	19	8	15	12	5	22	24	13	36
I feel less Israeli	-	2	3	-	3	2	-	-	2	-	2	2
Total %	100	100	100	100	100	100	100	100	100	100	100	100
N	434	225	2980	147	83	680	165	42	942	122	100	1358

P = Parents; T = Teachers; S = Students

Table 125 Teachers: Overlap and Consonance (Israeliness-Jewishness)
When I feel more Israeli:

	All Respondents			Religious			Traditionalist			Non-Religious	
	P	T	S	P	T	S	P	T	S	P	T
1. I also feel more Jewish	84	82	67	84	88	87	85	90	72	79	74
2. There is no relationship between my feeling Israeli and my feeling Jewish	15	16	29	16	10	10	13	10	24	18	24
3. I feel less Jewish	1	2	4	-	2	3	2	-	4	3	2
Total %	100	100	100	100	100	100	100	100	100	100	100 1
N	434	224	2980	147	82	680	165	41	942	122	101 13

P = Parents;   T = Teachers;   S = Students

The religious and traditionalist teachers are almost unanimous (97 and 93 percent) in the desire to be born again as Jews (see table 126). In this respect, again, religious students (94 percent) closely resemble the religious teachers, but a gap begins to appear between traditionalist teachers and traditionalist students (75 percent).

Only 54 percent of non-religious teachers would wish to be born again as Jews; to 38 percent it would make no difference and 8 percent would not wish to be born Jews. The figures for the non-religious students are almost identical.

If they have to live abroad, religious teachers (94 percent) would still wish to be born Jews. The responses of the religious students are close to those of the teachers (see table 127). The number of traditionalist teachers who would wish to be born Jews in such circumstances drops to 68 percent; 24 percent would in this case not wish to be born Jews (the figures for traditionalist students were 57 and 20 percent respectively). The attitude of the non-religious teachers is similar to that of the

Table 126 Teachers: Valence of Jewishness
"If you were to be born all over again, would you wish to be born a Jew?"

	All Respondents			Religious			Traditionalist			Non-Religious		
	P	T	S	P	T	S	P	T	S	P	T	S
Yes	80	78	70	97	97	94	82	93	76	61	54	54
It makes no difference to me	16	18	28	-	1	6	18	5	22	27	38	43
No	4	4	2	3	1	-	-	2	2	12	8	3
Total %	100	100	100	100	100	100	100	100	100	100	100	100
N	434	213	2980	147	80	680	165	42	942	122	91	1358

=Parents;   T =Teachers;   S =Students

Table 127 Teachers: Valence of Jewishness (in life abroad)
"If you were to live abroad, would you wish to be born a Jew?"

	All Respondents			Religious			Traditionalist			Non-Religious		
	P	T	S	P	T	S	P	T	S	P	T	S
Yes	73	64	54	86	94	84	71	68	57	58	37	37
It makes no difference to me	9	12	25	4	-	8	12	8	23	12	23	34
No	18	24	21	10	6	8	17	24	20	30	40	29
Total %	100	100	100	100	100	100	100	100	100	100	100	100
N	434	211	2980	147	80	680	165	41	942	122	90	1358

=Parents;   T =Teachers;   S =Students

non-religious students (rather than to that of the non-religious parents). Only 37 percent of these teachers would—if they have to live their lives abroad—wish to be born Jews; for 23 percent it is a matter of indifference, and 40 percent would not wish to be born Jews.

The teachers, like the parents and the students, would wish to be born Israelis if they were to be born again (see table 128).

Table 128 Teachers: Valence of Israeliness
"If you were to be born again, would you wish to be born an Israeli?"

	All Respondents			Religious			Traditionalist			Non-Religious	
	P	T	S	P	T	S	P	T	S	P	T
1. Yes	89	80	81	86	83	79	93	85	78	82	74
2. It makes no difference to me	10	18	17	10	16	17	7	13	18	18	21
3. No	1	3	2	4	1	4	-	2	4	-	4
Total %	100	100	100	100	100	100	100	100	100	100	100 1
N	434	204	2980	147	75	680	165	40	942	122	89 1:

P = Parents; T = Teachers; S = Students

The religious and traditionalist teachers are high both in their desire to be born Jews and to be born Israelis, although the percentage of those who desire to be born Jews is somewhat higher. In the case of the non-religious teachers, however, there is a marked difference; 74 percent favor being born Israelis as against 54 percent who express the wish to be born Jews.

On other Jewish identity items the differences noted between the three categories among students and parents are reflected among teachers as well.[4] Religious teachers score highest; they are followed by the traditionalists, and lowest are the non-religious teachers. Generally, on questions of Jewish identity the religious teachers and students are closer to one another than are the non-religious teachers and non-religious students to one another.

On questions of Israeli identity the teachers, though scoring high, generally score lower than parents and at times lower than students. The religious teachers in particular are appreciably lower than religious parents and students on questions of Israeli identity.

When the Israeli and Jewish elements are juxtaposed on the Israeli-Jewish continuum, the religious teachers are to be found very strongly on the Jewish side of the scale—more so than either of the corresponding cate-gories of students and parents. A considerable percentage of traditionalist teachers cluster round the midpoint but incline more to the Jewish than to the Israeli side, whereas traditionalist parents and students inclined to the Israeli side. The non-religious teachers choose the Israeli side and occupy a position similar to the non-religious parents but less strongly on the Israeli side than the non-religious students.

When the teachers are presented with two separate scales—Israeli-"private individual," and Jewish-"private individual"—there is hardly any difference between the three categories of teachers on the Israeli scale, but con-siderable difference on the Jewish scale. The Jewish orien-tation of the religious teachers is particularly pronounced, more so than that of the religious parents or students. Their Israeli orientation is less pronounced than that of the students, much less than that of the parents. The traditionalist teachers take up closely similar positions on the two scales. The non-religious teachers have a stronger Israeli than Jewish orientation.

The pride of the teachers in a number of periods from the Jewish past is more emphatic than that of the students. The teachers show less shame than do the students for the period of the Jewish *shtetl* in Eastern Europe. At the same time the religious teachers show greater pride in this period than do the non-religious teachers. There is close similarity between the views of teachers and of students about the behavior of Jews during the Holocaust. The great majority have feelings of pride. Among the non-religious teachers, however, 27 percent have feelings of shame (as have 25 percent of the non-religious students). As with the students there is a unanimous expression of pride in the period of Jewish settlement in Eretz Israel and the establishment of the State of Israel.

The teachers are more demanding than the students in what should be the activities required of a good Jew.

On the part of the teachers—as with the students—
there is a sharp difference in the feeling of closeness for
Jews who support Israel and those who do not. When
there is expression of distance from any group of Jews,
the teachers generally indicate less distance than the
corresponding category of students.

The great majority of the teachers see the main reason
for anti-Semitism in the situation of Jews as a minority.
This emphasis is much stronger with teachers (in particular the traditionalist and non-religious teachers) than with
parents or students. "The characteristics of the Jews
abroad" as a reason for anti-Semitism is endorsed by only
a small percentage (9 percent) of the teachers as con-
trasted with 32 percent of parents and 32 percent of students. Little weight is attached to "the characteristics of
the non-Jews," except by the religious teachers, of whom
31 percent endorsed this response category.

There are no significant differences in terms of Jewish
identity between the younger and older religious teachers—between the generations of teachers. Such differences do, however, exist among the non-religious teachers. Most strongly Jewish among them are the older teachers, forty-eight and above. The otherwise wide gap that
exists between religious and non-religious narrows somewhat between the non-religious teachers of this older
generation and the religious teachers. It may be noted
too that these older teachers belong to the same generation as the parents.

In regard to Israeli identity no significant differences
are found between older and younger teachers.

The Students through the Eyes of the Teachers

How do the teachers appraise the identity of the students? The majority of teachers (65 percent) feel that
the Jewish identity of their students is positive but weak;

25 percent feel it is strongly positive; only 10 percent report indifference.[5] None of the teachers report negative feelings on the part of their students toward their Jewish identity. As was to be expected religious teachers more frequently found a strongly positive identity among their pupils.

In their appraisals of the Israeli component in the identity, the majority of teachers (61 percent) regard the Israeli identity of their students as strongly positive, 37 percent describe it as positive but weak, and only 2 percent report indifference. More non-religious teachers rate the Israeliness of their students as strongly positive than do the two other categories of teachers. Actually—as the data on the students indicate—there are no significant discrepancies between the Israeli identity of the three categories of students (in all three categories it is high).

There is widespread agreement among teachers that the Jewish identity needs to be strengthened. Since the Israeli component in the identity of their students was regarded by them as strongly positive, it was to be expected that the teachers would see less need for special efforts to strengthen that subidentity. The religious teachers are the most emphatic about the need to strengthen both the Jewish and the Israeli components in the identity of the students. Among all categories of teachers, including the non-religious, more stress the need to strengthen the Jewish identity than stress the need to strengthen the Israeli identity.

When asked to rank a list of six facets of identity in order of their importance in actually determining the quality of the Jewish identity of their students, the teachers rank "pride in being a Jew" first, "faith in the future of the Jewish people" second, and "sense of common fate with Jews throughout the world" third. While the faith of the students in the future was rated high, their relation to the Jewish past in the Diaspora was ranked low.

When asked to rank a parallel list of facets determining the Israeli identity of their students, "pride in being an Israeli" was ranked highest, "the sense of common fate with Israel" second, and "faith in the future of Israel" third. Again, "faith in the future" was seen as in practice determining the Israeli identity more importantly than the tity need to be strengthened, the traditionalist and non-Israel" which was ranked low.

When asked which facets relating to the Jewish identity need to be strengthened, the traditionalist and non-religious teachers placed first "the sense of a common fate with Jews throughout the world." "Pride in being a Jew" was placed first by the religious teachers who, however, rate the "sense of common fate" second. The non-religious teachers see the need for strengthening the attitude of their students to the Jewish past in the Diaspora as second in order of importance.

In regard to the Israeli subidentity, "sense of common fate with Israel" is seen by all categories as the facet that needs most to be strengthened. Afterward follow the facets relating to "the history of the *Yishuv* and the State of Israel" and "belief in the future of Israel."

In assessing the sources of influence in the formation of the Jewish identity, all categories of teachers place "home and family" first, school second, and youth movements third. In rating the influence on the Israeli subidentity the religious and traditionalist teachers still accord pride of place to the home, followed by school and youth movements. The non-religious teachers, however, place the home third; they see the school and youth movements as having greater influence.

Within the school situation the teachers feel that the educational approach of the teacher plays the most important part in the development of both the Jewish and Israeli subidentities. When asked what in the educational approach of the teacher is seen by them to play the most important part, the response is (in order of importance):

(i) personal example; (ii) informal talks; and (iii) the subject matter of the studies. A number of the religious teachers take occasion—when stressing the force of personal example—to add their view that only teachers who themselves are observant Jews (practicing the *mitzvot*) will be able to convey to the students a proper feeling for their Jewish heritage.

PART III

Four Profiles

CHAPTER 12

Introduction to the Profile Categories

Three profiles in this chapter were prepared to provide a concrete reflection of the differing backgrounds—more particularly in the home—of the religious, traditionalist, and non-religious students. The fourth profile indicates some of the characteristics deriving from membership in the Yemenite community.

The four sketches have been presented as far as possible in the words of the students with a minimum of explanatory comment. They are largely based on interviews with the four students, here named Reuven, Dan, Rachel and Saadia, but some general features typical of the categories to which the students belong have been grafted onto the material they presented. The emphasis in these sketches is on the differing home background, and limited details have been added about the school and youth movements.

While the home background of the religious students interviewed in our study had, as could be expected, much in common, there were considerable variations in the traditionalist homes, and still greater differences among non-religious households.

The religious and traditionalist students are agreed that the foundations of their Jewishness were laid in the home and they look upon the home as the major formative influence in the Jewish sphere. A number of the non-religious students also tend to attribute to influences in the home the genesis of their attitudes, positive or negative, to their Jewishness.

From interviews with the religious students it was clear that home, religious school and religious youth movement interlocked to produce an intensity of Jewish identity. The traditionalist and non-religious students reported that the secular youth movements to which a number of them belonged strengthened their sense of Israeli identity, but in most cases did not contribute in any appreciable way to the strengthening of their Jewishness.

The students from the secular schools attributed varying degrees of influence by their schools on their Jewish identity; their reports reflect considerable differences in the social climate of these schools. While the school obviously contributed a substantial body of Jewish knowledge, a number of students indicate that it did little to change their orientation to Jewish life. They stress the exceptions, pointing to this or that teacher who exerted a special influence, or naming a student who gave expression to Jewish convictions differing from those of his peers. The students of several schools, on the other hand, provide a more favorable picture of their institutions and some of them tell of the efforts of a principal and teaching staff to create a positive Jewish atmosphere.

Reuven: A Religious Student *(Dati)*

Reuven is almost seventeen years old, the son of a religious family in Jerusalem and a student in the eleventh grade at a Benei Akiva yeshiva high school *(yeshiva tichonit)*. A quiet, pensive lad, he listens carefully and replies with great earnestness to the questions of the interviewer. There is a quality of respectful courtesy in his relationship with the interviewer, as indeed with all with whom he comes into contact. It is to this quality that his father refers when he proudly told the interviewer that Reuven shows *derech eretz* in all his relationships.

In the interview Reuven defined himself as being "national-religious." On the Jewish-Israeli continuum in the questionnaire he indicated that he was rather more Jewish than Israeli. He explained: "I am, in the first place, a Jew who observes the religious precepts *(mitzvot)*. At the same time I am an Israeli: Israel is my country, I am a loyal citizen and I must make my personal contribution to the State."

According to Reuven, it is impossible to separate the "Jew" and the "Israeli." Together they constitute an organic whole. He says: "A Jew and an Israeli, as I understand it, are essentially one and the same thing. A Jew is more completely such in Israel." He believes that Jews should settle in Israel, commenting: "A Jew resident in Israel thereby observes a religious obligation to live in Eretz Israel." At the same time in his response on the questionnaire he stated that he would wish to be reborn a Jew even if he had to live abroad, declaring emphatically: "This is a choice I would make irrespective of the place of birth—even if it be the Golah. A religious Jew always wishes to be a Jew, and I would like to be born a Jew wherever I was born." To the question relating to the centrality of Jewishness in his life he replied that Jewishness was "very important" for him, and he amplified: "My entire way of life is determined by my Jewishness. It influences my way of thinking and conduct. For me it is a natural state. I am a Jew all the time and can't even imagine myself being anything else." "Being an Israeli" he places one degree lower in point of centrality as "important." He maintains that it exercises a lesser influence on his daily conduct, but that at the same time it is a major

factor governing his future. By way of illustration he adds:
"When I finish my studies in the yeshiva high school I
shall have to decide whether to continue religious studies
in a regular yeshiva *(yeshiva gedola)* or enlist in the Army.
As I now feel about it, I think when the time comes I will
enlist."

The Home

Reuven's parents belonged to religious families in the
same provincial town in Poland. While still children they
joined a religious Zionist youth movement, and shortly
after their marriage, in the thirties, they came to Palestine.
Since then they have been living in Jerusalem; they own a
four-room apartment in a large apartment house in the
Rehavia suburb. The father, now a senior government
official, had served in the War of Independence, and had
fought in various actions in Jerusalem and the immediate
vicinity. Reuven is the youngest in the family; he has two
older brothers, one of them a Yeshiva student, and a married sister.

Reuven's father scrupulously observes the religious
precepts. He prays thrice a day and dons *tephillin* (phylacteries) at the morning prayer; he worships regularly at the
Yeshurun synagogue on Sabbaths and Jewish holidays.
A festive spirit always pervades the home on the Sabbath
and holydays. Reuven's eyes glow with delight when he
speaks of the special atmosphere on the eve of Sabbath:
"You feel something special in the air. On Friday afternoon all work comes to an end. Then we go to the synagogue. When we come home we sit down for the Sabbath
meal. The food is specially good. Then we sing the Sabbath hymns *(zemirot)*. We spend the evening at home,
reading and chatting. We talk about all sorts of things—
but mainly of a religious nature, especially when my older
brother, who is a Yeshiva student, is at home. We also

discuss various problems which are of interest to the religious community, and the current news in Israel and the world at large. Then each of us goes to his own corner. My brother usually reads some religious work; my father sits down with *Hatzofe* [a morning newspaper, organ of the National Religious Party]; the others of us share parts of the Friday edition of *Ma'ariv* [a popular afternoon newspaper]."

Reuven maintains that his religious feeling stems primarily from the influences of the home. It was in the home that he became accustomed to the meticulous observance of the religious precepts. The ceremonial washing of hands before partaking of food, grace after meals and other blessings, have become daily habits. *Kashrut* is strictly observed. There is no switching on or off of lights after the coming of the Sabbath, and despite the intense interest in news, the radio is never turned on until the Sabbath has ended.

Reuven claims he was influenced in particular by the example of his father. "When I was small," Reuven relates, "I loved to watch my father putting on his *tephillin*, and I waited for the day when I would be able to do likewise. I used to hurry after him to wash my hands and to recite the blessings. When I was a little older and went together with him to the synagogue on the Sabbath and the festivals, I would note the devotion with which he and other adults said their prayers." He soon learned the prayers and was proud when he could pray together with his father.

The question as to how his home had influenced his religious feelings evokes from Reuven the simple statement: "I grew up with it." At the same time Reuven's father took special care that his son observe the precepts and religious prohibitions. But when he reminded him of some religious duty or reprimanded him for some transgression it was always within the general framework of discipline in the home. Religion did not constitute a special sphere; it belonged pervasively and integrally to the life of the family.

On the Sabbath afternoons his father, after reading a chapter of the Bible with the children, would review a period of Jewish history by choosing an historic figure around whose life he wove the events of that period. The stories around these personages—ranging from Rabbi Akiva to Rabbi Kuk, from Moses and King David to Herzl and Weizmann—have remained engraved in Reuven's memory.

When his mother talked to the children she would often tell about the home of her parents in the Polish town in which she grew up, and would give a graphic picture, tinged with much nostalgia, of the milieu in which she had spent her childhood. One part of the family had immigrated to Palestine before the outbreak of World War II; others had chosen the United States. The unfortunate ones were those who had remained in Poland, and after Hitler's conquest of Poland they were taken to concentration camps, never to return. The only survivor was his mother's brother whose wife and two young children were killed by the Nazis. The uncle had reached Palestine in one of the illegal immigrant boats, and Reuven was enthralled by the story of how they had outwitted the British and slipped ashore one dark night on the beach near Herzlia. The uncle had since remarried; his wife too was a survivor of the concentration camps. A childless couple, they have a special fondness for Reuven and he for them, and he often visits their home in Tel Aviv. He remembers with some feeling of shame the grim fascination with which as a child he would glance at the concentration camp numbers engraved on their arms. As he grew older he developed a sense of compassion for the tragedy which he realized had stalked through the lives of his uncle and aunt.

Through the months of the Eichmann trial the entire family would gather around the radio each evening to hear the special recordings and reviews of the day's proceedings in the Jerusalem court. Reuven's father would visit the courtroom whenever he could find the time, and Reuven would listen spellbound to his account of the testimony given by survivors of the Holocaust who appeared as witnesses for the Prosecution. Reuven remembers his father's remark to the children of the family—"I hope you who have been born in Israel will not forget what happened to us before we had a State of our own. We must never let this happen again."

The entire family participates joyously in the Independence Day celebrations each year. Reuven's father remarks that the celebrations still lack the content and form which characterize the observance of the traditional festivals. About his own grasp of the War of Independence, Reuven observes: "When I was small the War seemed to me to be the sequel to the heroic battles fought by the Jews in ancient times, the wars of King David and the Hasmoneans."

The discussions in his home induced in Reuven a deep consciousness that there was "one Jewish people"; whatever the location of its parts in time and space might be, its essential unity was undisturbed. He explains: "I was conscious of ties with the Jews who had gone out of Egypt, who had lived in this country, had fought in it and had then been exiled from it, and so too with those who lived in the Golah and kept alive the spark of Jewish faith, and who were now returning to the Homeland, which God had promised them in ancient days."

A frequent subject of conversation in the home was the relationship with non-religious Jews in Israel. As far back as he can remember Reuven was aware of the differences between himself and non-religious children in the neighborhood. The latter went to a different school, did not attend synagogue, traveled on the Sabbath. They seemed to belong to a world apart and he would have little truck with them. But his attitude now is mellowing, and in this, as in other respects, he has been influenced by the example of his father who counts many non-religious colleagues among the friends he invites to his home. His father's attitude remained impressed in his mind by an incident when he was a young child: "Once at home I used the word *goyim* when referring contemptuously to the non-religious. I still remember how unusually angry my father became with me; he told me that they were Jews like us." When he grew up arguments ranging around the same subject continued. Reuven's father always insisted upon patience and tolerance "for in the last resort we are all Jews and together we have to build and defend our country." But his father does not conceal his scorn for the anti-religious Canaanites; "a lunatic fringe" he calls them. Nor does he hide his indignation at the behavior of the Netorei Karta whom he describes as "those religious zealots whose acts of intolerance do harm to the cause of religion." In regard to the Netorei Karta he was wont to console himself by saying "their children will have a good Jewish background without the anti-Zionist ideology of their parents."

Reuven's brother, a Yeshiva student, is highly critical of secular trends in Israel. "My brother would have it," says Reuven, "that the country should be governed by Torah laws." The father on the other hand stresses the obligation of the citizen to the State, even if it is secular in character. Reuven, while not as tolerant as his father in respect to non-religious Jews, has absorbed his civic loyalty. Recently he has been engaged in frequent and heated arguments with his brother about enlisting in the Israel Defense Forces. His brother seeks to persuade him to continue his studies in a regular yeshiva *(yeshiva gedola)* when he finishes his high school studies. Reuven's intention to join the Army has his father's support.

Reuven has not personally met non-Jews and has no clear views about the Gentile world. He understands why his uncle is so distrustful of Gentiles. "My uncle tells

me that at times there were opportunities to slip past
Nazi guards in the concentration camps, but those who
succeeded in doing so were often handed back by anti-
Semitic Poles. There were some 'righteous' Gentiles who
helped but they were few in number." His father's view
is that one should distinguish between Gentiles who are
anti-Semitic and those who are not. But he adds: "We
cannot depend upon them. Even the democracies were
indifferent to our plight. The people of Denmark were
among the notable exceptions."

The home not only provided Reuven with religious
norms of conduct but determined with whom he would
associate and made the religious group his main reference
group. Reuven himself ascribes much importance to the
influence of the home in directing him to religious society.
"The fact that I was sent to a religious kindergarten, to a
religious primary school, and then to a yeshiva high
school, that I was encouraged to join a religious youth
movement, and that most of my friends were religious
themselves, all contributed to my remaining religious."

Primary School

Reuven went to a state religious school which reinforced what he had acquired in the home.

In school, even more than at home, the special character of the Jewish people was stressed: "We learned that
we were the chosen people, the eternal people, continuing
to exist notwithstanding all persecutions. All our enemies
were defeated and finally disappeared, with the aid of the
Holy One." Some of the teachers underlined their special
character as a religious group: "They showed me the
superiority of the person who observed the *mitzvot* over
the non-religious person who behaved differently."

In the seventh and eighth grades one of the teachers
exerted a strong influence over him, and it was chiefly

due to him that Reuven resolved to continue in a yeshiva high school. This teacher constantly stressed, Reuven observes, that it was not enough to have faith and to observe the religious precepts; it was also important to understand why one did so. Reuven says: "He explained the significance of the laws of the Torah, the religious precepts and the customs which we observed daily." What Reuven had done up to then practically as a matter of habit now began to take on a deeper significance.

A landmark in his religious development was his *bar mitzvah* which occurred at the end of the seventh grade and which was invested with its due traditional character. The entire event, in particular his being called up to the reading of the Torah, made a powerful impression on him. He waited expectantly for the great day for a long time, and when it came he had the feeling that his life had moved onto a higher plane: "I had the feeling that henceforth I bore a special responsibility as a Jew, particularly in the field of religion."

The Youth Movement

While the youth movement, like the school, guided him in a Jewish direction, its special contribution was in strengthening the Israeli elements in his identity. When he was in the sixth grade Reuven joined a national religious youth movement, the Benei Akiva. The members often prayed together, arranged their celebrations in keeping with religious tradition on the holidays, and were proud of the knitted skullcaps they wore on their heads. Reuven enjoyed the participation in the campfires and scouting games. In the eighth grade they went out for a week to a work camp in a religious kibbutz. Here a new world opened up for Reuven; he was enthused by his contact with the members of the kibbutz who, as he put it, "observed all the religious obligations and at the same time worked the land—this combination of Torah and *Avodah* (Labor)."

Reuven went on frequent *tiyulim* (hiking excursions) into the country with members of Benei Akiva. "We became familiar with places we had learned about in the *Tanach* (the Bible), in stories of the War of Liberation. We learned to love the country more."

In the youth movement public issues, including Israel's political and security problems, were heatedly discussed. In these discussions much attention was given to the role of religion in Israel. "I began to see that it is not enough to observe religious customs; it is also necessary to fight for Judaism's rightful place, mainly by strengthening the status of religion in the State."

The discussions in the movement ranged beyond specific Israeli topics and extended to the condition of Jews in the Diaspora, to anti-Semitism and assimilation. He tells: "We were most concerned about the decline of religion among the Jews of the Golah, which we regarded as the major reason for the inroads of assimilation. This is the danger which faces Jews in a country such as the United States."

Reuven took part in a meeting with religious youth, members of Benei Akiva, who had come to Israel on a tour from the United States. The Israelis and Americans found they had much in common as Orthodox Jews. (Reuven invited one of them to the Friday evening meal and the delighted guest told them how much he felt at home among his hosts.) The Americans agreed about the threat of assimilation and spoke with concern about the growing rate of intermarriage. But they indignantly rejected the contention put forward by Reuven and his friends that anti-Semitism might become a serious danger. "They told us, in no uncertain terms," said Reuven, "that we did not know what we are talking about. The boy who came to us on the Friday evening remarked, 'You think that what happened in Germany may happen in the States. You are wrong, you do not understand how different America is.'" Reuven's summing up of his meeting with the Americans: "These youngsters are good material, and we must do everything to ensure that at least they—if not their parents—come here to settle."

When asked to define Zionism, Reuven says it is "the return of Jews to their ancient homeland." He regards himself as a Zionist, and at the same time is critical of the secularist trends among the non-religious branches of the Zionist movement.

During the past few years, his activity in Benei Akiva has declined as a result of the attention he must devote to his studies. The movement, however, still exercises its influence, although he now turns to it primarily as a means of relaxation after the exertions of his studies in the yeshiva high school. The members of the movement serve as a source of reference when it comes to plans for his immediate future. "Some of the teachers in our yeshiva high school prefer us to continue our studies in a regular, full-time *yeshiva gedola;* the movement wants us to join the *Nachal* and then a kibbutz. I do not propose to join a kibbutz, but I will join the Army, perhaps a *Nachal* unit, together with other members of my movement." (The *Nachal* units in the Army combine military training with agricultural work.)

The Yeshiva High School

When Reuven finished primary school his parents pondered their decision as to where he should continue his education. While it was taken as a matter of course that he would continue in a religious school, the question was whether he would go to an ordinary religious high school or a yeshiva high school *(yeshiva tichonit).* The curriculum of the religious school, based upon half a day of study, does not differ radically from that of the secular high school, although more attention is paid to specifically Jewish studies, and the Bible and Jewish history are, of course, studied from the religious angle. One of Reuven's older brothers went to a school of this type. (This brother is a technician. He does not live with the family and has non-religious friends, and though he has remained religious, he is, according to Reuven, not strictly observant, and his deviations cause pain to his parents.) The other brother, at present a student at a regular yeshiva, was formerly a pupil at a yeshiva high school, and he persuaded Reuven to follow suit despite the strenuous effort required. The brother described in detail what lay ahead of him in the yeshiva high school where studies continue throughout the day. The mornings are given to religious studies, mainly *Gemara,* first in class and then private study in pairs. The afternoons are devoted to the regular secondary school studies. The evenings are set aside for homework and talks, and the pupils are dismissed at eight or nine o'clock. The boys accepted must be very good students, and even then some fall out, as they are not able to maintain the sustained effort required.

Reuven's father was in favor of the proposal that Reuven continue at a yeshiva high school. One of his reasons: "Here Reuven would be kept away from 'negative influences.'" His primary school teacher also supported the idea—he argued that such a school would deepen Reuven's religious consciousness. Only his mother was opposed to his assuming such a heavy burden. Reuven had his doubts and hesitations, but he decided to accept the challenge. In the beginning he found things very difficult. At times he envied those of his friends who had proceeded to an ordinary religious high school and who finished their studies each day at the end of the morning. Now, however, he is mainly conscious of the fact that his Jewish studies are on a superior plane as compared with theirs.

Reuven speaks proudly of the studious atmosphere

which prevails in his yeshiva high school: "There is a
serious atmosphere of devotion to study, principally
religious studies, the other things being considered 'tri-
fling.' I have the feeling now that I am engaged in something that is important and serious." The emphasis is on
the religious studies; the ordinary high school studies are
regarded as of relatively secondary importance, and
'dry,' to use Reuven's term. In regard to these general
studies Reuven remarks: "We study mainly for the examinations." Fortunately he is a good pupil and so he experiences no difficulty in his studies.

The pupils meet their teachers only during the study
periods and Reuven does not regard them as his main
educators. The Rabbis, on the other hand, who teach him
Gemara serve as his mentors and educators, and exercise
a powerful influence over their pupils. They spend long
periods of the day together with their pupils: during the
lessons devoted to religious studies, at the prayer services
which are held thrice daily, and sometimes even during
the evenings.

Reuven pays tribute to the Rabbis and their influence:
"They live in the immediate neighborhood and you can
only have the highest respect for them. They constitute
a personal example, creating an intimate relationship to
Torah and religious observance, intensifying the respect
for religion and for religious study generally. The Head of
the Yeshiva (the *Rosh Yeshiva*) is a man of towering influence. On the eve of the Sabbath, and also when the
Sabbath comes to an end, he regularly gives a talk to the
pupils." The influence of the yeshiva is much strengthened by the fact that the pupils spend the whole day
within its walls. Reuven attempts to describe this influence: "The fact that we live together in what is almost a
sort of island has a powerful effect; we are cut off from
alien influences. You absorb the values and views current
in the yeshiva."

It is clear from the interview with Reuven that the yeshiva's influence pervades many spheres of his life and that it has fostered a religious outlook on a wide variety of problems. On the other hand, Reuven points to the fact that general fields of human culture, such as literature and art, are neglected, as they are regarded as marginal. Nor does the yeshiva pay much attention to matters affecting life in Israel today.

Reuven says: "The stress put on study and religion in the yeshiva has estranged me recently from practically all other interests. I have hardly any time to read a book or even a newspaper." Interest in sports serves to relieve some of the tension for Reuven and his fellow-students, though the Rabbis regard this sort of thing as "fools' play." His participation in the activities of the youth movement and in events in and around Jerusalem is much less than what it used to be.

Reuven hopes that ultimately he will find the necessary measure of equilibrium. He will join the Army and on the completion of his service will begin studies at the University. In his view: "The yeshiva gives me an important spiritual grounding, enabling me to hold my own in all situations, to withstand external influences, and to continue in the path of religion."

Dan: A Non-Religious Student *(Lo-Dati)*

Dan, aged seventeen, grew up in a non-religious home in Haifa and is at present studying in a municipal school in that city. He is in the eleventh grade, an excellent student in the natural sciences, but rather less proficient in the humanities.

His blunt and outspoken manner of speech on occasion gives an impression of brusqueness, though not of discourtesy. His answers to questions are brief and to the

point; he has an obvious distaste for any show of rhetoric.
There were occasions in the interview when he began
speaking with some enthusiasm, but when he became
aware that his words were flowing more freely than usual
he would pull himself up somewhat shamefacedly. Sun-
tanned, of muscular build, dressed in open-necked shirt,
khaki shorts and sandals, he corresponds very much to
the stereotyped picture of the young sabra. He loves the
outdoor life and is noted for his prowess on the sports-
field.

On the Israeli-Jewish scale Dan located himself close to
the Israeli end of the continuum. He says he feels first and
foremost an Israeli. He takes an interest in all problems
of the State, and has his own opinions on many subjects.
He is enthusiastic about the Israel Defense Army and
takes a close interest in security problems and in every
border clash. He explains with warmth: "I am waiting
for the day when I will enlist. I consider service in the
Israel Defense Army an opportunity for every young person to prove himself and to make his contribution towards
the State."

In contrast to his enthusiasm about Israeli affairs, he
confesses that things Jewish have no special interest for
him. He says: "I think very rarely about Jewish affairs,
mainly only when something happens to the Jews abroad,
like now that there is so much talk about anti-Semitism
in Russia, and also at the time of the holydays." He regards certain Jewish customs, like the Passover Seder,
the lighting of Hanukah candles, and even the Sabbath,
as being "very fine." And he proceeds to explain: "These
customs in effect have become Israeli customs, observed
in practically every home with no connection to religion.
In our house, too, we enjoy the happy atmosphere, have a
festive meal, but it has hardly any connection with Judaism." On the other hand he is not prepared to fast on
Yom Kippur (the Day of Atonement); Tisha Be'av (The
Ninth Day of Av) has even less significance for him. On

this point he says: "We have re-established a Jewish State, so why mourn the destruction which took place two thousand years ago?" He finds it difficult to understand religious people, how they can live in keeping with laws formulated "so many centuries ago," but he adds: "Let them live as they like. Faith is the private affair of every individual." In keeping with this view, he favors separation of religion from the State.

Dan regards the Jews as both a religious group and a people. When he speaks of Jewishness in Israel, it is clear that he has the religious aspect mainly in mind; in regard to ties with Jews abroad, the national factor takes precedence.

When he was questioned further about his attitude to Jews of the Diaspora his replies indicated that what interested him was the possibility of their *aliyah.* "It is a pity that the Jews living in the affluent countries do not come to Israel, but ultimately I believe that anti-Semitism will persuade them to do so." In the meantime Israel must concern itself about them in the cultural and spiritual fields, in order to ensure that they do not become assimilated, and "when the time comes, they will settle in this country." Israel, for Dan, is the center of World Jewry, and it is incumbent upon her to help them. And he enlarges as follows: "Israel must help them mainly in the spiritual sphere, and they must help Israel to become economically consolidated, for it can serve as their refuge in times of trouble."

He reiterates, however, that he does not concern himself much with these problems. Occasionally they are discussed in the school and in the youth movement, but according to him, the first time he gave any serious thought to some of the matters raised was during the interview. He pointed out in response to the questions on centrality that Jewishness had little importance for him, while Israeliness possessed great importance.

In reply to a question Dan defines Zionism as "the

upbuilding of the State of Israel." Asked whether he regards himself a Zionist, Dan hesitates, and then replies "I dislike 'Zionist' speechifying. But if Zionism is what I have just now defined it to be, I suppose I am a sort of Zionist, although I don't call myself that."

The Home

Dan's father was born in Germany. He comes from an assimilated home, and until the date of Hitler's seizure of power he had little awareness of his Jewishness. He came to Israel (then Palestine) in 1938 with Youth Aliyah and was placed in a kibbutz. His parents remained in Germany and lost their lives in the European Holocaust.

Dan's mother grew up in a religious home in a Hungarian country town. The family subsequently moved to a city at which time she joined a Zionist youth movement and later came to Israel. She settled in the same kibbutz as Dan's father, and at some stage became completely estranged from religion.

The parents made each other's acquaintance in the kibbutz, were both active in the *Haganah,* the father fighting in the War of Independence, in the course of which he was wounded.

Dan's mother's parents survived the European Holocaust, and came to Israel. It was shortly before they arrived that, for a variety of reasons, Dan's parents left the kibbutz, and his father obtained a post as an electrical engineer with a Haifa firm.

Dan's father remains alien to Judaism; at the same time he is proud of being Israeli. He located himself on the extreme Israeli edge of the Israeli-Jewish continuum. His Israeliness he states to be "important" and his Jewishness "of little importance." The mother located herself closer to the midpoint of the continuum, inclining nevertheless more to the Israeli side.

In Dan's home there are now practically no signs of Jewish tradition. When his mother's parents arrived she had introduced a few Jewish customs to make them feel a little more comfortable. She herself had missed this atmosphere from her childhood and had wished to give her children a little *Yidishkayt.* Of his father's reaction Dan has the following to relate: "My father was not enthusiastic. He is indifferent to Judaism. But he did not interfere when Mother tried to bring us a little closer to tradition." The mother had begun to observe Sabbath and holiday ceremonies, even keeping *kashrut* for the sake of her parents. She took Dan and his sister to the synagogue on Rosh Hashana (the New Year) and Yom Kippur. Dan sums up this period: "Mother did not succeed in her efforts at the time. Some of the customs I liked, but without any relation to religion. The world of religion had no attraction for me. In this respect I am more like my father in my views."

Later, after the death of the grandparents, the family discontinued the observance of most of the customs. Dan recalls: "Mother stopped observing *kashrut* shortly after the death of Grandfather. Today we no longer build a *succah,* and I do not go to the synagogue on Rosh Hashana and Yom Kippur. My little sister sometimes accompanies Mother. In fact only the lighting of the Sabbath candles and the family Seder have remained."

Dan, like almost all other boys in his school, duly celebrated his *bar mitzvah.* Although the religious aspects of the ceremony had little meaning for him, he did not want to be an exception by not celebrating. There was a lavish reception for friends of the family, and Dan treasures the many presents he received. The young man, a graduate of a yeshiva, who prepared him for the reading of the *Haftorah,* also taught him to don *tephillin,* but Dan never does so nor does he have recourse to prayer.

Jewish subjects are not much spoken about in the home except when they are given prominence in the daily newspaper, *Ha-aretz,* which members of the household read. Dan's father has a critical attitude towards the religious sector, the *dati'im* as he—and also Dan—refers to them. Dan observes: "My father is sometimes angry about what he regards as manifestations of religious coercion—although life in Haifa has a more secular character than in most other cities. The *dati'im* certainly are not as strong here as in Jerusalem or in Benei Brak. Although my father is critical, he is tolerant and says that they must allow us to live as we wish and that they in turn can live according to their beliefs." Dan holds views similar to his father on these questions. When asked what comes to mind when he hears the word *dati'im,* he says "I tend to think of a man with a beard, long earlocks *(peyot),* with black hat and long black coat." He adds, "I do not see so many of them here in Haifa. But when I spent my vacation in Jerusalem I would go down to Mea Shearim on a Friday evening, looking in for a few minutes at some of the many synagogues in that section of the city. When I walked through the streets of Mea Shearim during weekdays I was amused to see little boys with skullcaps and long earlocks playing marbles and other games and addressing one another in Yiddish."

There was a tense atmosphere in the home at the time of the Eichmann trial. Dan describes it as follows: "At the time of the Eichmann trial I remember that there was a lot of tension in the house. We never failed to listen to broadcasts of the trial on *Kol Yisrael* (the Voice of Israel). But Mother asked us not to speak about the subject with Father." The mother tried to explain to the children something of what had taken place, but as Dan says: "I found it difficult to understand why so many Jews allowed themselves to be murdered without putting up a fight." It seems that the point that aroused his enthusiasm was the action of the Israeli Security Services in capturing Eichmann and the fact that Israel had succeeded in meting out punishment to a murderer of Jews. "I was proud that Israel had done all this."

National issues are often discussed in the home. In regard to the past Dan likes to hear his father's reminiscences about the illegal immigration and the struggle with the British and the Arabs. He says: "This active heroism seems to be real to me; on the other hand I find it difficult to understand the concept of passive courage which my mother tried to explain to me in connection with the conduct of Jews during the European Holocaust."

Dan likes to hear his parents tell of the period they spent in the kibbutz. He is planning with some of his high-school friends to join a kibbutz after their service in the Army.

The home plays an important part in providing Dan with a general cultural background. Dan says: "Father wants to give us a broad cultural education. We visit concerts and exhibitions a lot. We have many records of classical music at home and my sister is learning to play the piano." His mother reads widely and encourages the children to do likewise. Dan likes reading. Some of the books he has read are on Jewish subjects but they have not influenced him to any extent. His mother is very fond of modern Hebrew literature and has transmitted this love to Dan.

Dan sums up the influence of the home in the following terms: "Our home influenced me mainly in the direction of a strong Israeliness and towards general culture. I absorbed practically no Jewishness though I am tolerant towards the religious Jews."

The Primary School

Dan recalls with some pleasure the celebration of the festivals by the children in the secular primary school he attended. He recollects especially how the last lesson on Fridays took the form of a ceremony for the reception of the Sabbath *(Kabbalat Shabbat),* and how it was "sweetened" for them by candy supplied by each of the

pupils in turn. Dan says: "The celebrations were signposts
recalling that the holidays had come round." But from
what he has to tell it is apparent that the resemblance
of one celebration to the next blurred the special character of the various festivals.

In the course of the lessons the Jewish aspect was not
stressed. According to Dan: "One of the teachers tried to
inculcate some *toda'ah yehudit* (Jewish consciousness)
in us by explaining various Jewish customs. But I don't
think any of us took these things seriously."

Summing up the influence of the primary school on his
Jewishness, Dan states: "It gave me quite a good knowledge of the *Tanach* (Bible), I learned some Jewish history and something about Jewish traditional observances
but the outlook on Jewish matters I acquired in my home
underwent hardly any change."

The Youth Movement

At first Dan was a member of the Scout movement;
later he joined the Noar Oved ("Working Youth" Movement) which seemed to him to be more pioneering in
character. Today he is a member of a *garin* (nucleus of a
settlement group), together with whom he is thinking of
joining the *Nachal,* and later perhaps a kibbutz. His
madrich, a member of a kibbutz, is "quite a guy," and has
a powerful influence on Dan. He took his group to a work
camp in a kibbutz, arranged for them to meet youngsters
of the kibbutz and also the veteran settlers, who told them
about the early days of the settlement.

The *madrich* also takes them on frequent *tiyulim* (excursions) about which Dan speaks enthusiastically. "Our
madrich could tell us about every place we came to, especially about the battles fought there during the War
of Independence." The *madrich* himself had been an
officer in the Army, had fought in the Sinai Campaign;

Dan admires him and hopes that he, too, will be an officer in the Army.

About Jewish activities he says: "There was no Jewish
atmosphere in the movement. In the *Tsofim* (Scouts),
when we were still children, they held celebrations on the
festivals and had talks about Jewish history. But there
too later we hardly spoke about these subjects."

The High School

The high school which Dan attends is secular in character,
but the principal and some of the teachers are interested in the strengthening of the Jewish identity of the
students. When asked to describe the "Jewish activities"
at the school, Dan refers to the morning assembly at
which the "Verse of the Day," a passage from the Bible, is
read out, and to the special ceremonies on holidays and
anniversaries. But he notes that in their informal circles
the students rarely discuss matters of specific Jewish interest. "We discuss the current Israeli issues featured in the
newspapers, and are particularly excited by any action by
the Israel Defense Forces on the border."

Israeli patriotism also finds expression in the realm of
sport, which is the subject of much talk during the inter-
vals among the boys. Dan relates: "We follow all matches
Israelis play abroad, and also the matches played by visiting teams from other countries in Israel. We rejoice over
every Israeli victory and are sad about defeats."

Dan thinks that he himself has been influenced but
little in the Jewish sphere. He knows that there are pupils
who have been influenced to a greater extent. He says:
"Some of them did not know what Judaism was at all, and
here at school they have at least learned something about
it. They may even have come to like it." In his class there
is one pupil whose parents are non-religious, but who
has acquired religious convictions since his *bar mitzvah.*

About this pupil Dan has the following to tell: "He loves to argue with the other pupils on the subject of Judaism, and sometimes some of the things he has to say even convince me." But discussions between the students about Jewish problems are the exception rather than the rule, and such influence as is exercised is by teachers. According to Dan: "There are some teachers who have influence, such as the Principal who teaches *Tanach* (Bible) and is an inspiring personality. He often connects up what we are learning in the Bible with a discussion of current problems. The history teacher likes to talk to the pupils even outside the classroom and he is respected by many of us." Dan thinks there are pupils who admire one or another of the teachers and as a result benefit more from their lessons. In regard to himself he says: "I do not think that I have been influenced to any major extent, or that my attitudes towards Judaism or Israel have been affected in school."

Despite this general statement, however, it appears from other remarks that the teachers did exercise some influence on his views. Thus, for example, he comments: "The Bible lessons at one time did not interest me at all; I like them now that the Principal has shown that the problems are of universal significance and still exist today. This increased my appreciation towards this Book and I have understood what its contribution has been to world culture."

In the course of the history lessons his image of the Jews of the Golah has improved. According to him: "From the books I read I got the idea that the Jews who lived in this country in ancient times lived robust lives, worked hard and fought hard. On the other hand I regarded the Jews of the Golah as pitifully weak beings who could be trampled upon and would not even fight for their lives." Dan recalls how impressed he was when the history teacher showed them that, compared with their non-Jewish neighbors in the Middle Ages, the Jews possessed a high degree of culture. He sums up: "Today, it is true, I still do not feel any great attachment to those Jews in the medieval ghettos or in the East European villages, but I do not despise them as I did previously."

They devoted some lessons in history to a discussion of the problems of anti-Semitism. Dan has modified, but has not completely changed, his views on the causes of anti-Semitism. As he himself says: "At one time I thought that the Jews themselves were to blame for the fact that they are hated. Many of my classmates held the same opinion. Today it seems to me that the conditions under which they lived in the Golah were such as to compel them to concentrate in the occupations which caused them to be hated." He believes that anti-Semitism will continue as long as Jews live in the Diaspora, and the only solution is *kibbutz galuyot*—the in-gathering of Jews from the lands of the Dispersion.

They also had discussions in class about the European Holocaust and the teacher took them on a visit to the "Holocaust and Resistance" exhibition in Kibbutz Lochmei Hagetaot (a kibbutz in Western Galilee founded by former partisan fighters). In this respect, too, there has been some change in his views: "I am less critical now than I was of the conduct of the Jews in Europe and do not regard all of them as having been passive and submissive. Nevertheless, it is difficult for me to understand how so many people demonstrated practically no resistance." On this count he feels himself different from them, and he thinks that he and sabras like himself would not wait idly until they were killed. He expresses indignation at the callousness of those other countries which extended no aid to the Jews in their plight and sees in their indifference confirmation of his view "that the Jewish people and Israel must help themselves, for in times of trouble the other nations will leave them in the lurch."

In the course of their form master's lesson, too, they had a number of talks on topics such as "Who is a Jew?"

"State and Religion," and the relations between Israel and the Golah. Dan maintains that he has not substantially changed his position on these subjects, and explains: "I still think that Religion and State should be separate. I believe the Jews of the Golah should settle in Israel." But he has moderated his views to some extent. So, for example, he says: "I do not think that the introduction of civil marriage in Israel is as simple as I used to believe. I have been especially influenced by the arguments of the religious boy in my form who showed to what a cleavage in the Jewish people such a thing could lead." He is also prepared to concede that "not all Jews in the Golah can be expected to settle in Israel immediately." A strong impression was made on him by a symposium on the subject together with members of American Young Judaea who visited Israel and by his subsequent conversations with them. He comments: "In the meantime it is important to strengthen ties with the Golah and to enable the Jews there to remain attached to Judaism so that in the future they will settle here." He no longer thinks that the aid given by the Jews abroad is just a sop to their consciences, but that some of them, at least, have a real interest in the State and what comes to pass within it. He stresses that: "What is important, in my view, is to try and persuade the younger generation to settle in Israel."

Dan received very little in the way of Jewishness from his home, but under the impact of his school something has moved. His relationships to Jews abroad has become more positive.

Although he has no feeling of closeness to religious Jews in Israel, whom he regards as so unlike himself, and although he still looks upon Jews abroad in terms mainly of their contribution to the State of Israel as potential immigrants, he is more conscious than he was of the interdependence between Jews everywhere and has a deeper sense of the mutual responsibility between Israel and the other Jewish communities. Although he finds it difficult to identify with much in the Jewish past, he is less contemptuous of the Jews of those periods.

Dan recently watched new immigrants arrive at Haifa port, and was deeply stirred by what he saw. "When I looked at their troubled, bewildered faces, I asked myself if there was anything I could do to help." He subsequently visited some of the immigrants in their new homes and learned about their problems of adjustment; he was taken aback when he saw how meager were the belongings they had been allowed to take out with them from the country from which they had come. He had participated in and out of the classroom in discussions about new immigrants, but he had never previously given the matter serious thought. He has now volunteered to teach new immigrants Hebrew.

Rachel: A Traditionalist Student *(Mesoratit)*

Rachel is a girl of seventeen who describes herself and her family as being *mesoratit* (traditionalist). She is a pupil in the eleventh grade in a secular Tel Aviv school and is considered a middling student. A smiling, cheerful, seemingly carefree girl, her replies to questions in the interview came in rapid, unpunctuated sentences with little attention to the niceties of diction. The interviewer was at times obliged to ask her to repeat her reply which she readily did with no hint of condescension.

Rachel considers herself as definitely not belonging to "the religious camp," as she terms it, and takes no special interest in the problems that engage this sector of the community. She is fond of the traditional customs observed by her family, but she has no deep religious faith, and disregards many of the religious precepts. She says: "What is important is to feel oneself Jewish, to consider oneself part and parcel of the people, and to observe at least some of the Jewish customs which symbolize the

special character of the Jewish people." She emphasizes that as far as she is concerned Judaism is not only a
religion, and adds: "I admire Jewish culture and like the
Jewish types in the East European townlets described by
the author, I. L. Peretz. I like learning Jewish history
although I do not identify myself with everything that is
in it. I consider myself to be a link in that chain of Jewish
life which has remained unbroken through so many vicissitudes. This is reflected in my observance of traditional
customs." Rachel fondly recalls moments of elevation in
the family's observance of tradition. At the same time,
in her daily life, among her friends in school, questions
of Jewish import rarely come to the fore, and she views
most events taking place around her in much the same
way as these non-religious friends. Even in her home—
apart from *kashrut*—the observance of Jewish religious
practice is limited, being felt mainly on the Sabbath and
the Jewish holidays.

Because of the nature of her daily interests and practice Rachel explains she stated in the questionnaire that
her Israeliness was "very important" for her while her
Jewishness was only "important." But when she was required to locate her position on the Israeli-Jewish continuum, she chose the midpoint. She explains that, after
much inner debate with herself, she has achieved "a certain equilibrium between Jewishness and Israeliness; they
are not quite the same thing for me, although often I
really don't distinguish between them." She maintains that
her Jewishness pertains more to the traditions of the home
and to what she terms her "spiritual world," while her
Israeliness belongs more to her social life and her interest
in her country's development.

When asked to define "Zionism" she replies that it
means "support of Israel," and she adds, "or better still,
aliyah." She states that since she lives in Israel she does
not have to be a Zionist.

The Home

Rachel's father, a successful building contractor, comes from a religious family in Poland and in his childhood went to a *heder*. He came to Israel prior to the outbreak of World War II. His parents and a younger brother remained in Poland and lost their lives in the European Holocaust. When he came to this country he became estranged from religion, but the calamity which overtook his family brought about a renewal of his religious feeling. Now he is observant, but not strictly so. He does not engage in prayer during weekdays but goes to the synagogue on Sabbaths and holidays.

Rachel's mother was born in this country to parents who had come from Lithuania. The home atmosphere was traditionalist, but Rachel's mother went to a non-religious school and was for a time a member of Hashomer Hatzair, a left-wing youth movement. She helps in maintaining the traditionalist atmosphere of the home, but of this Rachel says: "I believe she does so because she married Father and wants to please him, more than out of any religious consciousness."

The difference between the parents is also reflected in their replies to the questionnaire. The father defined himself as being in the middle of the Israeli-Jewish continuum, and regards both subidentities as being "very important." The mother defined herself as being a little more Israeli, regarding the Jewish subidentity as only "important." Rachel noted: "I am traditionalist like Mother, but both of us are less religious than Father."

Rachel says that she feels herself closer to her mother, but her brother, Ya'akov, who is two years her junior, is closer in spirit to their father and has a stronger tendency towards religion. Rachel is conscious of a certain distance between herself and her father, and she thinks that she was influenced less by him than by the general traditional atmosphere in the home. She says: "I grew fond of the traditional customs of the family and I think that I shall try and observe in my own home, too, when I grow up." At the same time she points out that they are not as observant in their home as are the *dati'im.* "On the Sabbath we switch lights on and off, we listen to the radio, and Mother heats food in the oven."

The traditional observances in the home are described by Rachel in the following terms: "My mother prepares the traditional dishes on each festival. We have a big family Seder, we build a *succah,* light the Hanukah candles. On Friday nights, of course, candles are lit, *Kiddush* is made over the wine, and all the family sits down to the table together." Rachel indicates that she greatly enjoys the festive atmosphere of the home on the Sabbath evenings and the festivals.

Rachel's father, however, complains about her. He says that Rachel has become overly lax in regard to religious observance since she has come into "bad company," where the young people "seek the pleasures of the fleeting moment." They organize dance parties on Sabbath evenings, and sometimes Rachel misses the Sabbath meals or leaves the table early and comes home late at night. He expresses his sorrow at this state of affairs: "She has been swept up in the general current. With the exception of her home, every place she visits is far from Judaism. She seems to think that she will miss the pleasures of living if she observes the religious precepts."

Rachel herself admits that this is the case, but explains: "I consider it hypocrisy to observe precepts which I do not believe in. When I was a child I did believe and then I was more strict in observance. Today I try mainly not to offend Father, and I do nothing that is prohibited in his presence."

She recalls that until the seventh or the eighth grade she observed a number of the precepts and the prohibitions. She did not write on the Sabbath and did not go for outings by car or on bicycle rides with her friends. She took care to participate in the Friday evening meals, even if it meant missing a date with her friends or coming late. Now she often goes for outings in cars together with her friends on the Sabbath, and if she has much homework she writes on the Sabbath, although, as she herself says: "It seems a little strange to write on the Sabbath, as I have not been accustomed to do so for so many years." She does so in her own room in order not to hurt her father's feelings. At one time Rachel used to accompany her father when he went to the synagogue on the Sabbath and the holidays. Today Rachel goes to the synagogue only on the New Year and Yom Kippur.

It seems that the decline in observance is not only due to the influence of the social environment outside the home; it is also apparently connected with estrangement from her father, who, she says, is "becoming more and more strict in the observance of the *mitzvot,*" and, on the other hand, with the growing laxity of her mother in this respect.

The mother's influence is exercised more directly and more positively on the Israeli component in Rachel's identity and Rachel is conscious of the example her mother sets. "My mother, before she got married, hiked a lot in Israel and she loves to talk about the places she visited. She has transmitted to me her love for every place in this country."

Both father and mother were members of the *Haganah* and the father fought in the War of Liberation. The children love to hear tales about this period. So too today they are excited by every action in which the Israel Defense Forces are involved, and applaud every success.

Rachel's maternal grandmother is still alive and often visits them. She loves to tell about the home in which she grew up in Kovno. From her grandmother Rachel has heard about the relatives they have in the United States and Canada; some of them she met when they

visited Israel. The grandmother intersperses Yiddish with
her Hebrew, and Rachel has, in consequence, learned
a little Yiddish. "How can a Jew not know Yiddish?"
her grandmother is wont to ask wistfully.

The European Holocaust used to be discussed only
when the father was not present. But things have changed
since the Eichmann trial. The trial had a cathartic effect
on the father, who formerly had avoided any discussion
of the Holocaust. He began speaking freely to members
of the family about his home in Poland, about the parents
and brother he had left behind and never saw again, the
synagogues and the schools which had been destroyed.

Rachel herself followed the Eichmann trial with intense
interest. "I asked myself why all this had happened. I
could not find an answer. But there was a second question—how to prevent it happening again. Here the answer
seemed to me to be to bring as many Jews as possible to
Israel and to do all we can to make the State strong."

Primary School

When she reached schoolgoing age Rachel was sent
to a secular primary school close to her home, in North
Tel Aviv. There had been an argument between her parents about the school to which she should go. Rachel
recalls: "My father wanted me to go to a religious primary
school, because he was afraid that a secular school would
estrange me from tradition. I did not want to do so, for
in our neighborhood there were hardly any religious
families at all, and I wanted to go to the same school as
most of the friends I had known since my childhood. My
mother supported me, and the upshot was that I went
to a secular school. My younger brother was sent to a
State religious school, in keeping with my father's wishes."

Rachel's teacher had a traditionalist outlook with a
decidedly positive orientation to religion and to Jewish
issues generally. The teacher won the young girl's admiration. "Our teacher arranged ceremonies on the holidays

in keeping with the customs, telling us about the background of the festivals. She tried to instill in us a Jewish
consciousness, even in the pupils coming from non-religious homes. She could always reply to the questions the
pupils put to her about Jewish matters, and I respected
her for it." Rachel excelled in these lessons and loved the
holiday ceremonial, being more familiar with the customs
than the other pupils. She adds: "I was very fond of the
Bible lessons, the tales told about the ancient heroes, and
also of the explanations we were given about the Torah
laws. At home I was acquainted mainly with the practi-
cal side of the customs. Now I learned about their historical background." Many aspects of Judaism about which
she had heard in her home now became much clearer
for her. It was only in the higher class at school, when
an analysis of the Bible was undertaken, that she was
conscious of any clash with the conception she had developed at home.

Rachel maintains that through her school she has
gained a fair knowledge of both Jewish and Israeli subjects. The direction given by the primary school, generally
speaking, dovetailed into the influence exerted by her
home. At the same time, perhaps precisely because of the
resemblance to the home influence, she contends that the
primary school exercised no special influence on her
Jewish development.

The Youth Movement

When she was in the fifth grade Rachel joined the Scout
movement *(Tsofim)* together with many other children
in her class. Rachel describes her classmates in the following terms: "We were all born in this country and accept
our being Israelis as a natural fact. We went to the same
school and now most of us belong to the same youth
movement." Rachel indicates that in the discussions
in the movement the stress was on "Israeli rather than
Jewish issues." She elaborates: "We argued about topical

issues, such as the problem of *yerida,* to which many of
the boys and girls, myself included, expressed strong
opposition."

Her enthusiasm was especially aroused by the *tiyulim.*
"We went out on trips to all parts of the country, and
we learned to love it." Later they went out to work camps
in the settlements, and plans for joining a kibbutz began
to take shape. The movement, however, gave them,
Rachel asserts, practically no Jewish content.

A problem emerged regarding her participation in
activities arranged for Friday nights, the Sabbaths and the
festivals. At one time, notwithstanding the fact that non-
participation affected her integration in her social group,
she used to forego the outings if traveling by car was
involved. Sometimes she did not go to the functions held
on Friday nights. But later, when she was in high school,
the conflict became more acute, and the importance of
the age-group was enhanced and the home influence
declined. Rachel was interested in being accepted by her
friends and allowed herself to make certain concessions
in the sphere of tradition. She began to prefer movement
activities to the family Friday evening meal.

In the tenth grade, when they had more homework to
do, many of Rachel's classmates left the movement, and
she did likewise. Today she says, resignedly: "I have such
a lot of homework and so little leisure. But on Saturday
nights I go to parties where we dance and chat." Rachel
has become estranged from the ideals the movement tried
to inculcate, and though she wants to join the Army,
she is not thinking of going to a kibbutz.

The High School

Rachel continues her secondary school studies in a
secular school. This particular school did not help the
home in imbuing Rachel with any desire to continue to
observe Jewish traditions. Little stress was put on Jewish,

or for that matter, on Israeli values. Rachel remarks sarcastically: "The only thing that is important in school is good marks and success in examinations in the various subjects." Even the form master's period which is, at least formally, an opportunity to discuss various subjects and topical issues in Israel and the world at large, is "wasted," for, as Rachel says: "The form master does not raise any questions about what is happening in Israel, nor are the students encouraged to bring up such subjects for discussion. The period is wasted on various school arrangements and discussion of problems of discipline." Neither Rachel, nor—so she says—her friends, think highly of their teachers.

Insofar as Rachel has been influenced at all by her school, she believes it is by the subject matter of her lessons and not by her teachers. She explains as follows: "In the literature period, for example, in tales dealing with Jewish life in the Golah the teacher stresses the literary aspect. I, however, am interested particularly in accounts of how Jews lived there, the various characters and types, which remind me of the tales told me by Grandmother. For example, I was very much impressed by *Tuvia the Milkman,* a virile, alert Jew, full of humor, alive, who works and does not depend on other people's charity." She is particularly fond of Shalom Aleichem, who describes "the bright side of Jewish life in the Golah." But she recalls: "I did not like *The Travels of Benjamin the Third* who portrays Jewish life in the Golah negatively, and I believe, incorrectly."

She also likes the Bible studies. On the other hand, this year her interest in the history lessons has declined, and she explains: "Previously we had an excellent history teacher, and I liked both Jewish and general history. This year we have a poor teacher. We are studying the period of the Jewish Middle Ages. She transmits the material in a very dry manner, showing only the negative aspects of Jewish life at the time."

Rachel is an avid reader. She is impressionable and identifies herself with the characters in the books she reads, as she says: "It is easier for me to identify myself with literary characters in literature than living people."

She has read much about the European Holocaust, apparently under the impact of the tragedy which overtook her father's family and also in the wake of the Eichmann trial. But what especially aroused her interest in the books on this period was the "adoption" by her class in school (as part of a country-wide project) of one of the communities that had been destroyed in the Holocaust. The class project involved gathering all the material they could about the community they had adopted, its history, the special character of its life and the personalities prominent in it. Rachel has also read all she could find about the Jewish Brigade which came from Palestine in World War II and the rescue work it carried out among the surviving Jews after Europe was liberated. Her imagination had been kindled in particular by the stories of the volunteers from Eretz Israel who were parachuted behind enemy lines in Europe in order to establish contact with the Jewish communities. High on her list of heroes are two of the parachutists, Hannah Czenes and Enzo Sereni (both of whom were killed by the Nazis).

Recently the family had as its guest a cousin of Rachel's from New York, Barry, who, along with his parents, belongs to a Conservative congregation. Barry's interest in Israel had been aroused by his participation in one of the Ramah summer camps. He was taken aback by Rachel's laxity in observance, and at the same time found the service in the synagogue to which her father took him less to his taste than that in the Conservative synagogue in which he worshipped in New York.

Together with Rachel and Ya'akov, Barry spent a Sabbath in a religious kibbutz, Sde Eliyahu in the Beisan

Valley, where an uncle lived. Barry was enthralled by his contact with the kibbutz members and by the religious life they lived. "When I heard about the *dati'im* back in New York what came to mind were the religious zealots who stoned passing cars on the Sabbath. I never really gave thought to the fact that among *dati'im* should also be counted people of the caliber I found over here in this kibbutz." Ya'akov, who is at a religious school and has become more traditionally observant, also found the life of the kibbutz most congenial. Rachel was duly impressed, but felt that this was not the life she could readily undertake to live.

At present Rachel is moving closer to her non-religious friends, but she still underlines the value and importance of tradition, which she regards with affection even though she is not religiously observant.

Saadia: A Yemenite Student

Saadia, a young Yemenite Jew, studies at a religious high school *(yeshiva tichonit).* He is never without his knitted *kipah* (skullcap) but wears no other headgear. Although somewhat bashful, he replies with quiet conviction to the questions raised by the interviewer. The answers are in accomplished Hebrew with due accentuation of the gutterals. He frequently quotes from religious writings in support of his statements: "As our sages of blessed memory have said . . ."

Like Reuven he is nearer to the Jewish than to the Israeli edge of the Jewish-Israeli continuum. He comments: "I am Jewish all day, every day of my life. My feeling of being an Israeli is stronger in times of crisis— as when there is a threat on the borders." He adds: "In Israel, the Jewish religion is in its natural environment and can find its full and proper expression. And here a

Jew can fulfill all the *mitzvot.* He can be more completely Jewish here than in the Golah." If he had to live
his life outside of Israel, he would still wish to be born
a Jew. "I would certainly not wish to live in any part of
the Golah. I would be looked down upon and in some
countries persecuted as a Jew. But if it was my bitter
fate to live in any one of these countries, I would still
wish to be a Jew." Saadia regards the Jews as "the Chosen
People" but makes it clear that it is not in the sense of a
"Herrenvolk" that he uses the term. "Far be it from me so
to think." They have been chosen "to carry out God's
bidding and live by the light of the Torah."

The Home

Saadia's parents lived in a village in Yemen until 1949.
The father had a small foundry which had been be-
queathed to him by his father. When news reached him
of the establishment of the State of Israel, the father was
jubilant—verily, "the days of the Messiah" had come.
The family—together with a number of others—trekked
to Aden where they waited in one of the transit camps
for the plane which took them ("on the wings of eagles,"
as they saw it) to Israel, in what was known as the Magic
Carpet Operation.

The first winter in the immigrant camp was difficult.
The demands of the Yemenite families were more modest
than those of some of the other immigrants, and the
feeling of religious bliss at being in the Promised Land
helped them to bear the hardships uncomplainingly.
Later, the family, along with others, settled in a *moshav*
(smallholders' village).

The father, whose education was based wholly on the
religious writings, is a strictly observant Jew, careful
not to commit any religious transgression. Saadia, while

traditionally observant, is not quite as meticulous. He notes that his father is not prepared to subject any of his religious tenets or observances to critical scrutiny, whereas he, Saadia, is prepared to undertake a rational analysis. It appears that he has become a little ashamed of some of his father's practices which he regards as based on superstitious beliefs.

Saadia nonetheless attributes his religious attitudes to the home and describes how even as a child he would accompany his father to the synagogue and would repeat the prayers as they were intoned aloud. The father personally supervised his Jewish education and inducted him into the religious practices. He remembers his father's pride and his own sense of "growing up" when, at the age of seven, he was called to the reading of the Torah. Saadia observed that the *bar mitzvah* ceremony held at the age of thirteen for boys in other communities was not common among the Jews of Yemen, although lately in Israel the Yemenite community has tended to adopt it as well.

Saadia speaks with a sense of delight of the celebration of the *Shabbat* and the festivals in his home. He is particularly fond of the Seder evening on Passover when all branches of the family gather for the reading of the *Hagaddah* in the version popular among Yemenite Jews.

Although he has developed a taste for European foods, he still relishes the richly-spiced dishes prepared by his mother and by his paternal grandmother who lives with the family in the *moshav*. Saadia describes gratefully the loving care bestowed on him by both his mother and grandmother, but adds that they had but little in the way of educational background and that he owes his Jewish training to his father.

Saadia is the youngest of five in the family. His sister is married to a member of the *moshav*, and she and her husband frequently join the rest of the family for meals and are present at all festive occasions. The eldest brother is majoring in Hebrew language and literature at Bar Ilan, the religious university near Tel Aviv. Another brother works in the offices of a printing press. Saadia sorrowfully remarks that this brother is the least religious member of the family, and he attributes his defection to the influence of the brother's secular fellow-workmen. "When he discarded his *kipah* I saw in it a sign that other deviations would follow." But when the brother comes to the parents' home and is under the stern eye of the father, he, too, dons a *kipah*. The third brother is presently doing his army service, and when he comes home on leave and tells of his experiences, he finds an eager listener in Saadia who will enter the Army on matriculation.

Saadia has due filial love and respect for his father and will often discuss with him questions of religious observance. But he reconciles himself to the fact that many of the things in Israeli society which now interest him are outside his father's ken. These are matters he and his brothers discuss among themselves.

Both father and son are proud of their membership in the Yemenite community. Although they agree that the Yemenites can be subsumed under the general classification of *edoth hamizrach* (Oriental communities), they prefer to regard themselves as an independent entity which has made its own special contribution to Jewish culture.

The father recalls the persecution to which he was subjected in Yemen and has a deep distrust of Arabs—although he speaks with gratitude of the protection accorded to his Jewish subjects by a benevolent Imam (Yemeni ruler). Saadia has had little occasion to meet Arabs but is not uninfluenced by his father's attitude of distrust. At the same time he asserts: "There dare not be any discrimination against Arabs who are loyal citizens of Israel." He adds: "I think that any realistic view tells us that it's going to be very difficult to achieve peace with

Arab countries who are in such a belligerent mood. But
we must never cease striving to attain this peace. They
on their part will only come to terms with us if they realize
we are strong and are here to stay."

He is wary about the Gentile world. While he remembers how as a child he listened sorrowfully to stories
of the sufferings of Jews in Yemen and other Arab countries, Saadia does not recall any discussion in the home
about the European Holocaust. But the Eichmann trial
and what he has read and heard at school have made a
deep impression. "We dare not ever forget. They were
slaughtered simply because they were Jews."

Saadia sees the Bible as "the title-deeds of the Jews
to Israel." He views Jewish history as a continuity of which
the State of Israel is a part. So, too, he regards the centuries of Diaspora existence as part of that continuity.
"I cannot share the negative attitudes of some people
to Jewish life in the Golah." Although he has no knowledge of Yiddish, he asserts that his attitude to it is positive
for he sees it as one of the cultural expressions of Jewish
life "at a certain time and place in our history." To his
father, Yiddish is a strange tongue "spoken by the Ash-
kenazim."

While Saadia refrains from expressing any negative
attitudes toward Jews in the Diaspora, he is critical of
Jews who can, but do not, immigrate to Israel. "To me,
this is a paradox. I participated with some American
students in a synagogue service. They all prayed 'may
our eyes witness your return to Zion. . .' and yet very few
of them thought of settling in Israel."

He defines Zionism as the age-old yearning of Jews
for Zion, and stresses the religious motif. This is the way
his father thinks of Zionism as well. When the family
lived in Yemen, political Zionism passed them by, and
to this day his father is unacquainted with the ideologies
which were the warp and woof of the modern Zionist
movement.

School and Youth Movement

The primary schools Saadia attended and the *yeshiva
tichonit* at which he now is are both similar to the schools
discussed in the case of Reuven. But while the transition
for Reuven from home to school was relatively easy, the
little Yemenite boy found himself alongside children of
Ashkenazic families in a world very different from that
of the home. Saadia struggled hard to adjust himself to
his new environment and leaned for encouragement on
his brothers rather than on the parents. When he joined
Benei Akiva, the religious youth movement, he again
encountered ideas with which the other children had
become familiar in their homes but which had never been
the subject of discussion between him and his parents.
Listening to the *madrich* of the group speak on subjects
such as the ideology of the kibbutz and *chalutziut* (pioneering), he often had difficulty in integrating the concepts into his own frame of thought.

Gradually, however, he adopted the norms of his
Ashkenazic peers. Their influence became apparent in
the *yeshiva tichonit,* and when asked directly how he
differed in terms of religious observance from the other
youths in his class, he could point to no substantial difference. His model—although he is not always conscious
of it—is the Eastern European-Israeli prototype of the
religious student. His views, now, are very similar to those
of Reuven.

He attributes the influence of the *yeshiva tichonit* on
him very largely to the fact that he is now part of a com-
pact group whose members are in constant interaction
with one another and which constitutes a very distinctive
religious environment. At the same time he is critical of
the fact that this group is almost hermetically sealed off
from the surrounding environment, and that some of the

older Rabbis who have come from Eastern Europe are not in the position to discuss with their pupils the challenges which await them in the wider world, but rather do what they can to keep the students away from it and its temptations.

PART IV

*The Future of
Jewish Identity*

CHAPTER 13

Review and Prospect

Israelis are not—as some observers have claimed and as some Israelis would have it be—an entirely new people. The majority of the Israelis in this study see themselves linked to the Jewish people and to its past. The thread of historic continuity has not been snapped; it still runs strongly through the new forms of Jewishness made possible by the return of a people to its ancient homeland.

The new molds of Jewish life in Israel have not yet been firmly nor finally cast. But into the making of Israeli society there enter a number of ingredients which remain essentially Jewish even if in the new context they inevitably undergo transformation. The festivals of Israel are the ancient Jewish festivals, the day of rest the Jewish Sabbath, the language Hebrew, the raison d'être of the State is conceived—in the Declaration of Israel's Independence, in the statutes of the Knesset and in the minds of the people—as inherent in its function as a Jewish homeland, gathering in its sons and daughters from the lands of Dispersion. While it lays no claim to the civic allegiance of Jews who are the citizens of other states, Israel sees itself both entitled and obliged—in its role of

Jewish State—to act as the representative of the Jewish people. It was as such that it brought Eichmann to trial in Jerusalem, and in this capacity, too, insistently draws attention—in the councils of nations and before the bar of public opinion—to the plight of Jews in Soviet Russia and in the Arab countries. At the same time, however, the radical difference between the Jewish present in Israel and the Jewish past in the Diaspora, between the position of Jews living as a majority in their own land and that of Jewish minorities continuously subject to the influences of the majorities among whom they dwell, adds to the complexity of problems which would in any case arise in regard to the relationship between parts of a people located in diverse environments. Moreover, for the unity of any people the weakening of a major bond common to all its parts would have had serious consequences, but for a people in whose case religion and ethnicity are inextricably linked, a decline in religious observance has even more far-reaching implications.

Religion and Ethnicity

Let us turn first to the decline in religious observance referred to in some detail in the earlier pages of this volume. We have noted that in the case of many of the non-religious parents—particularly the parents from Eastern Europe—the defection from religion did not always seriously impair their sense of Jewish identity which was fortified by other forces in the cultural climate in which they lived. A greater void is created by the absence of the religious factor in sections of the youth growing up in Israel. At a time when this factor is called upon to play an increasingly crucial role in Jewish identity, a large number of students report a decline in their religious observance compared to that of their parents. This decline is particularly marked among students from the Oriental communities who have hitherto had a preponderance of religious members but are now being caught up in the trend towards secularization. They are moving in a traditionalist and, in some cases, a non-religious direction. (For those among them who reach a secular position the break with the established family patterns is particularly sharp; no new Jewish values take the place of the old, and they are left without anchor or rudder.) In the Ashkenazic communities the non-religious students already constitute a majority. The decline is not arrested in the second generation.

The interviews and case-studies in the present study show the home to be a main vehicle for the transmission of Jewish attachment. The indications are that the homes many of the students will set up will have less of a Jewish atmosphere than those of their parents.

The religious decline poses the question as to what can be the strength and durability of a secular Jewish identity. Religion and ethnicity are so closely interwoven in the Jewish identity that any tendency toward their separation raises serious problems.

In a society composed of ethno-cultural groups, clearly delineated as such—as in some countries of Eastern Europe in the years before World War II—a basis may conceivably have existed for the maintenance of a secular identity.[1] On the other hand, in a society such as that of the United States, where religion is the recognized and acceptable criterion of group distinctiveness, the prospects for the preservation of a secularized Jewish identity are far from clear.[2] What course the development of the Jewish identity will take in the Jewish majority society of Israel still remains to be seen. Where the Jewish training is based on religious foundations a Jewish-conscious youth is growing up who may be expected to constitute the hard Jewish core of this society. The problem exists acutely in regard to the wide circles among whom religious observance has declined and some of whom can no longer accept a religious orientation for themselves or for their children. Accordingly, there is need to open up paths to an intensified Jewishness—in keeping with the historic Jewish tradition—which can be followed by members of these circles as well. Given the common traditional core it would seem feasible to develop diversified expressions of Jewish living around it.

Continuity does not necessarily mean the maintenance of the traditions of the past as static and unchanging. Indeed what has been regarded as "Jewish" has been changing across the centuries in response to the varying circumstances of Jewish life—although a certain measure of essential sameness has throughout been preserved. There has been an understandable tendency on the part of religious authorities under the exposed conditions of Diaspora minority existence to hedge in, and to view change with apprehension. In Israel this tendency persists, despite the fact that in a majority Jewish society changes may be effected without fear of the intrusion of alien influences. If these changes are to be acceptable, they will have to originate within the indigenous Israeli society, and it is unlikely that they can—as some would believe—be successfully imported from the outside. We would suggest that they can best come from circles who are themselves rooted in Jewish tradition and are determined to preserve continuity while fostering change.

The religious decline cannot easily be stemmed, but the attitudes of the younger generation are uncomplicated by the ideological revolt against religion which characterized a section of the older generation who came from Europe in the early years of the century. Religious influences, however, do not easily permeate the non-religious circles in Israel even when the latter are in search of new spiritual paths. There is, first of all, an absence of a popular religious leadership which conceives of its function as embracing guidance to the non-religious and not only to the religiously committed. Moreover, the prominence achieved by the actions of extremist religious elements seems to have produced a distorted image about the nature of religious groups, the *dati'im,* in Israel. Even the traditionalist students, who on the whole have a positive orientation to religious observance, gave expression to a sense of distance from religious Jews in Israel—greater than from religious Jews abroad. They see themselves outside "the religious camp," and, together with the non-religious students, speak critically in the interviews conducted with them about acts of intolerance on the part of religious zealots in Israel.

These zealots are a minority in the religious sector and their actions are very often not representative of the wider religious circles, including, for example, the religious kibbutzim. (So too is the strident anti-religious minority unrepresentative of the non-religious circles.) The religious students in our study are from schools within the orbit of the Israel Ministry of Education; their orientation is "national-religious," as a number of them proudly term it, and they dissociate themselves from the Netorei Karta and other extremist factions. These religious students feel less of a distance between themselves and non-religious Jews in Israel than the distance perceived by the non-religious students between themselves and religious Jews. There may be a wider basis than is usually imagined for cooperation between religious and non-religious elements in working out a common cultural future. In any event, the social cleavage would seem to be reducible despite the differences in religious values and observance. Furthermore, religious and secular young Israelis after matriculation meet during their three years of army service under conditions of equal status contact and in situations which underline their interdependence.

Although there has been no systematic study of the influence of this contact, it would be reasonable to assume that it contributes to mutual understanding and draws these young Israelis closer together.

Israeli Jews and Jewish Israelis

In an analysis of the strengths and weaknesses in the Jewish identity of Israeli youth special attention has to be given to the finding that for so many of the non-religious students—and the non-religious are the preponderant category numerically—the valence, or attractiveness, of being Jewish is low. Only a bare majority of these students would wish to be reborn Jews, and they are reduced to a minority when the question relates to the wish to be reborn Jews if they had to live abroad. There are thus serious limits to the value these students attach to their being Jewish. While some of them have no wish at all to be reborn Jews, for others the readiness to be Jewish is predicated on life in Israel.

Differing widely from them are the great majority of religious students, a fair majority of traditionalists and a minority of non-religious students, for whom the valence of their Jewishness is such that they declare their readiness to opt again for a Jewish birthright even under the conditions of Diaspora minority existence.

It follows that the relative potency or strength of the two subidentities varies markedly among segments of Israel's population. There are Israeli *Jews* for whom the Jewish element is primary, and Jewish *Israelis* with whom the Israeli component is dominant. In the case of the former it is in the Jewish context that their Israeliness finds its meaning; in the case of the latter their Jewishness is mainly a differentiating feature within the Israeli context.

These emphases tend to have implications in regard to the attitude to Jews abroad. With the Israeli Jews the stress is on the Jewish people of which Jews in Israel are seen as an integral part. On the part of the Jewish Israelis the point of departure is an Israeli community which may have links of varying strength with Jews and Jewish communities abroad.

The Jewish Past in the Diaspora

A further source of weakness in the Jewish identity of a not insignificant minority of students is their relationship to facets of the Jewish past. The teachers in our study comment on the difficulty which their students encounter in linking their present as a majority in Israel with the Jewish past as a minority in the Diaspora, and they stress the need for attention to this area in the education of Israel's youth.

The students in question do not view their Jewish affiliation in the broad perspective of Jewish history, as representing the continuity of the Jewish people and its cultural heritage. An Israeliness such as theirs which is not anchored in the Jewish past would seem to be a shallow nationalism lacking the dimension of cultural and spiritual depth which a Jewish perspective gives; it is invariably accompanied by a weakening of the links with the Jewish communities of the Diaspora.

With the religious students the problem does not arise. It is an integral part of their outlook to view Jewish history as an unbroken chain. It is when we consider what course the development of the Israeli-Jewish identity of the secular students will take that this question of historical time perspective—how they will relate themselves to the Jewish past in the Diaspora—becomes an important touchstone of their attitudes.

Of particular significance in the orientation to the past is the attitude to the period of the Holocaust, the nature of the identification with the tragedy of European Jewry.

There is every reason why young Israelis should be given a realistic view of the Holocaust. It has been suggested, indeed, that Israeli prowess in battle has been so clearly demonstrated that Israelis now possess the self-esteem which can enable them to analyze unflinchingly all features of the tragedy of European Jewry with compassion and understanding and without shame.[3] But if the consciousness of the Holocaust merely expresses itself in hatred for the Nazi perpetrators of the crimes or in admiration for the acts of resistance, it cannot play its full part in the development of the Jewish identity. The more important question is whether Jews of this generation come to see themselves *as if* they were survivors of the Holocaust; to the extent they so see themselves they are the readier to undertake their share of the responsibility for the continued existence of a Jewish people. It is when the study of the Holocaust leads to this sense of responsibility that it gives added purpose and intensity to the Jewish identity of our times.[4]

Israeliness and Jewishness as Mutually Reinforcing

In the majority Jewish society of Israel a large measure of overlap exists between the Jewish and Israeli subidentities, and, where this is so, they are mutually reinforcing. Where, however, they are separated and compartmentalized, the result is a weaker Jewishness and a less rooted Israeliness.

The patriotic attachment which young Israelis have to their homeland is strengthened and deepened when it is given a Jewish perspective. An Israeliness divorced from Jewishness has dangers for a country which wishes to be a land of immigration and not of emigration. Thus, Israel is facing the problem experienced by many other countries that a number of its students do not return after the completion of studies overseas—more particularly in the

United States. There are many factors which are likely to enter into the choice between Israel and the more affluent parts of the world with their educational and professional opportunities and other allurements. But the direction of the choice will be determined, in part at any rate, by whether in making it their Israeli loyalties are reinforced by a consciousness of what Israel means to them *as Jews.*

Understanding Jewish Life in the Western World

While the students can understand the plight of a Jewry facing grave discrimination and feel themselves close to the Jews who are so attacked, they cannot easily comprehend the problems of Jewish communities living in freedom. What was conspicuously absent in the interviews with them was insight into the subtler predicaments and dilemmas faced by Jews in a free society, a compassionate feeling for the Jewish strivings and the Jewish unease peculiar to these communities. In a parallel study of American Jewish students visiting Israel, the American students indicated how disconcerted they were at the absence of a sympathetic insight on the part of the Israeli students they met into the problems of American Jewish life.[5] Some of the Israeli students based themselves on the European experience of the Jewish people in predicting what lay in store for the future of the American Jewish community—an approach which evoked indignant dissent from the visiting American students.

These are the communities the students will meet when they journey abroad; they are ill-equipped to understand what they find. There is likely to be a lack of rapport and a failure to establish adequate contact with the Jewish community in whose midst they reside. In addition, if they are Israelis in whose identity the Jewish component is weak, they will often be undiscerning in regard to the not always obvious, but yet crucial, differences between

the life of a Jew in a Jewish society and his life in even
the friendliest non-Jewish environment. And while they
would not willingly surrender their own Jewish identity
and while they would not wish it to be extinguished in
other Jews, some of them are not sufficiently aware of the
corrosive effects of the less blatant forms of assimilation
nor do they appreciate the threat to Jewish survival which
out-marriage constitutes.

A Confrontation with Non-Jews
Based on Mutual Understanding

Just as the students are ill-equipped for their meeting
with Jewish life in the Western world, so too they are
unprepared for any confrontation with Gentiles in that
world. They know little about the fundamental differences
that have existed, and still exist, between Judaism and
Christian civilization, nor are they acquainted with the
developments that have taken place across the years in
the direction of a more cordial relationship between
them. Israel provides the Jew with an equality of status
in his meeting with others; this encounter can lead to
cooperation on a realistic basis, if he as well as the others
is aware of what constitutes common ground between
them and on what they differ.[6]

Jewish Behavior and Anti-Semitism

Considerable confusion exists in the minds of the students about the responsibility of Jewish behavior for the
growth of anti-Semitism. Social research has indicated
that anti-Semitism—like other ethnic prejudices—is
primarily a function of the prejudiced group and not of
the behavior of the Jews against whom it is directed.[7]

What then brings Israeli students to attribute so much importance to the behavior or characteristics of Jews in the context of anti-Semitism?

Such confusion is understandable among Jews living as a minority in the Diaspora—particularly among those Jews on the periphery of their group—and in some cases it is associated with Jewish self-hatred.[8] When the phenomenon appears in the Diaspora there are two possible ways of looking at it. One explanation points to the fact that for some Jews the balance of forces is on the side of leaving their minority group rather than remaining in it, but there are barriers in the way of crossing into the majority. The resulting frustration produces aggression directed not outward against the majority which erects the barriers but inward against the Jewish group which is seen as the obstacle in their path. Self-hating Jews will blame "Jewish behavior" or "foreign Jews" for their ills. An alternative explanation bases itself on the "looking glass image" of the minority group member. The majority culture in which they are socialized views Jews with a certain derogation, more pronouncedly so in some cultures, more subtly so in others.[9] The Jews begin to see themselves in the distorted mirror held up by the majority (although the image may be modified somewhat through the prism of their own Jewish subculture). They develop feelings of inferiority about their Jewishness and in some cases fully accept the hateful image of themselves.

When what resembles self-hatred appears among Israeli youth living as a majority in their own Jewish society the sources are different. From the interviews with the students it would appear that their notions about Jewish characteristics have been derived—in part, at any rate— from a Hebrew literature which has been critical of the Galuth to the point of contempt of the Jews who live under such conditions.[10] They have been seeing these Jews in what is in a sense a distorted Jewish mirror. The Jews thus mirrored are seen as contributing to anti-Semitism because of their concentration in certain occupations, because of "bad behavior."

A further factor may possibly enter. Israeli youth as members of a majority may conceivably tend more readily to a view that a minority is responsible for some of the ills which beset it.

The Jewish "self-hatred" of Israeli youth would seem to be more amenable to change by an appropriate educational approach than that of Jews in the Diaspora, which is inherent in the minority situation they occupy with its resultant psychological marginality. The subject of anti-Semitism needs to receive more systematic attention in any study program than it seems to have been given.

The Sense of a Common Fate

The sense of interdependence rather than similarity is the basis of Jewish cohesiveness in the world of today. Despite the growing dissimilarities between Israelis and Jews of the Diaspora, there is strikingly present in the majority of students a sense of Jewish interdependence and this is invoked in particular when Jews anywhere are under attack *qua* Jews. (In recent years they have been deeply stirred by the plight of Jews in Soviet Russia and in the Arab countries.) Hand in hand with this feeling of solidarity goes a wide acceptance of the mutual responsibility which exists between Israel and the Jewish communities of the Diaspora.

The students are interested in the maintenance of the Jewish identity by Jews everywhere. They would also not deny their own Jewish identity; such denial is seen as a shameful act even by those for whom their Jewishness has little attraction.

In any assessment of the strengths and weaknesses of

the Jewish identity of the Israeli, the recognition of the common destiny of Jews and the interest in the preservation of a Jewish identity represent a source of strength. This is a reservoir of Jewish feeling from which a program for strengthening the Jewishness of Israelis can draw.

Knowledge and Values

Whatever the shortcomings of Israeli schools, the curriculum of studies permits them to impart—and they do, in fact, impart—a body of Jewish knowledge equaled by only a tiny fraction of the children in any other Jewish community. The possession of the requisite body of knowledge, however, does not always in itself ensure the desired values although there is some relation between knowledge and values. It is precisely the values which are the essence of the problem.

In any effort to strengthen the Jewish identity through the school the teachers would need to play a key role. The teachers in our study are aware of the need to strengthen the Jewish subidentity of their students. (They indicate that the position in regard to the Israeli subidentity is more satisfactory.) Some of the non-religious teachers, however, share the weaknesses of their students in regard to their Jewish identity—in particular, the valence of their Jewishness is low. This means that the teachers themselves would need to be the object of attention in any program to strengthen Jewish identity through the school.

CHAPTER 14

The Six Day War and After

There were few facets of the life of Israel which were left untouched by the Six Day War and the events preceding and following it. The events of this period dramatically emphasized the Jewish dimension in Israel's existence. "This was a Jewish war and not just an Israeli war," is a refrain running through the utterances of many Israelis.

Inside Israel the external dangers heightened the cohesiveness of the community and produced a slurring over of differences between religious and non-religious, Ashkenazic and Oriental, immigrant and veteran. In the face of the danger all sections became more intensely aware of both the Israeliness and Jewishness they shared. During the years that have followed the Six Day War they have stood together in constant, never-relaxing vigil, and the ties which unite them have been further cemented.

The extraordinary revelations of world Jewish solidarity with Israel were an expression of the sense of interdependence, of a common destiny experienced more keenly in the hours of crisis than in normal times. Israeli youth was witness to the support, unstinted and unconditional, extended by all sections of the Jewish people. As not only material support but volunteers poured in, Israelis recognized more than ever before that Jews everywhere deeply identified with them, sharing a common cause and a mutual responsibility. The indications are that they drew nearer to Jews in the Diaspora.

The Six Day War not only elicited manifestations of world Jewish support for Israel. It reflected the common Jewish fate in yet another way familiar through the centuries. In Poland the Six Day War became the occasion to step up an anti-Semitic campaign against the Jewish community—a small remnant of twenty thousand Jews of the three million who once lived there; in France anti-Israel and anti-Jewish feelings at times became indistinguishable; in Egypt, Syria, and Iraq vengeance for the defeat of the Arab armies was wreaked on the Jews still remaining in those countries. It became evident once more how the destiny of one Jewish community was interlocked with that of others; in this case with that of Israel.

The Memory of the Holocaust Reactivated

Despite the fact that the Israeli War of Independence was fought only a few years after the Holocaust, and the Six Day War twenty years later, the indications are that the consciousness of the Holocaust was even more strongly present in 1967 than it was in 1948, conceivably because of the directness of the threat of destruction posed by the Arab states. It would seem that in the face of this threat the memory of the Holocaust moved before the Israelis as "a pillar of fire" and steeled their determination when they joined battle with the Arab armies in the Six Day War. In the interviews carried out with soldiers, members of kibbutzim, after the War there are numerous references to the profound influence of the memory of the

Holocaust as a background factor in their reaction to the threats of the enemy.[1] Into the minds of many of them came the thought that an Arab victory would mean another Holocaust. "We saw it [the Holocaust] as a picture of the enemy's victory which we must prevent."[2] But they were not only determined to prevent a recurrence of that tragedy. The sense of indignation at the humiliation to which defenseless Jews had been subjected spurred their resolve to show their mettle as free Jews in their homeland hurling back an enemy bent on their destruction. This theme runs through a number of the interviews with the soldiers and finds poignant expression in a letter written by a paratrooper, Ofer Feninger, who later fell in the battle for Jerusalem. He describes graphically how after a visit to the Museum of the Holocaust at Kibbutz Lochmei Hagetaot he was haunted by the picture of inmates of a concentration camp, "those abysmal eyes behind the electrified fence," and he concludes with the resolve that Jews must be "strong and proud, never to be led again to slaughter."[3]

The memory of Jewish suffering also seems to have been a factor influencing humane treatment of Arab families fleeing from the scene of battle. "We knew what the destruction of a people means—those who were witness to the Holocaust and those who were born after it. The world which does not understand this will not understand us: they will not understand the courage and they will not understand the hesitations and the moral doubtings at the time of the war and afterwards . . . the slogan "Pardon us, we won" was not a piece of irony, it truly reflected our feelings."[4]

What the Holocaust still means to Jews was reflected not only in the reactions of the Israelis. A study of American Jewish students who were in Israel during the Six Day War shows how the crisis reactivated for them the memory of the Holocaust; at the same time these students were impressed by the contrast between the position of a beleaguered, but self-reliant, State and a powerless European Jewry.[5] The consciousness of the Holocaust also accounts in no small measure for the swiftness and spontaneity of the unprecedented aid extended by World Jewry when danger threatened Israel. Indeed, Arab threats aroused greater anxiety among Jews outside of Israel than among Israelis who were on the whole confident of their capacity to resist.

The Western Wall and Historical Time Perspective

Peculiarly revealing were the reactions of Israelis, soldiers and civilians, old and young, religious and non-religious, to the liberation of the Old City of Jerusalem, and in particular the Western Wall. It was a dramatic illustration of the relationship between an ethnic identity and an historical time perspective. By some, the Western Wall may have been perceived as a monument reflecting Israel's past as do a number of the archaeological discoveries, but for many others it symbolized the relation of the Jewish people through the centuries to the Land of Israel. And so a soldier observes: "When we heard over the transistor the report of the victory in Jerusalem, there was not a single soldier in my company who did not shed tears, including myself. I then sensed for the first time not the Israeliness but the Jewishness of the people. The paratroopers bursting into tears when they reached the Wall became the symbols of the historic meaning of the victory."[6] Observes another soldier: "The paratrooper stood not only before the Western Wall—he stood before 2000 years of exile, he stood before the history of the Jewish people."[7] In a memorable address at a ceremony of the Hebrew University on Mount Scopus at the end of June 1967, the Commander of Israel's Defense Forces, Yitschak Rabin, described the feelings the soldiers had experienced just a few weeks before.

"The entire nation was exalted and many wept when they heard of the capture of the Old City. Our Sabra youth, and most certainly our soldiers, do not tend to be sentimental and they shrink from any public show of feeling. But the strain of battle, the anxiety which preceded it, and the sense of salvation and of direct confrontation with Jewish history itself cracked the shell of hardness and shyness and released wellsprings of emotion and stirrings of the spirit. The paratroopers who conquered the Western Wall leaned on its stones and wept—in its symbolism an act so rare as to be almost unparalleled in human history. Rhetorical phrases and cliches are not common in our Army, but this scene on the Temple Mount, beyond the power of words to describe, revealed as though by a flash of lightning truths that were deeply hidden." [8]

In some secular circles the War has had profound spiritual implications. It has intensified the search for a closer relationship with Jewish tradition; at the same time these circles are earnestly seeking to clarify to themselves what substance a Jewish tradition can have for them if it is not accompanied by religious faith. [9]

The Call for Jews to Settle in Israel

The War resulted in a considerable extension of the territory and with it an appreciable increase in the Arab population under Israeli sway. Whatever the nature of a future peace settlement it is clear that Israel will never consent to a return to the insecure borders of May 1967. In the new situation now prevailing there is an increased eagerness and readiness on the part of Israelis to receive Jews from the Diaspora as immigrants into their midst. In the minds of some the need for additional Jewish manpower through immigration is bound up with the continued external threat posed by belligerent Arab countries with their populations of many millions. What is dominant in the minds of others is the need to counterbalance the increase in the Israeli Arab population (demographers have also drawn attention to the higher birth-rate of the Arab population) and to ensure that Jews remain the majority and preserve the "Jewish character" of the State. The call for *aliyah* from the free countries, sounded across the years, has now received additional urgency. At almost every conference, in numerous statements by Israeli leaders, in discussions in press and on radio, the problem of *aliyah* has been presented as crucial for Israel's future.

Jews everywhere have recognized as never before the importance of such *aliyah* but, although there has been some response to the call, the stream of immigrants is only slowly gathering momentum.[10] A decision to immigrate from one of the free countries to Israel is the culmination of a gradual process and is dependent not only on the "pull" or attraction of Israel but on the existence of a "push," a dissatisfaction with conditions in the country of present residence.[11] Although many Jews experience an "unease" which is associated with their Jewish identity in a non-Jewish environment, the "push" is in most cases not sufficiently strong to impel them to uproot themselves. And so, while in the hour of Israel's danger thousands unhesitatingly volunteered for service and were prepared to die in its defense, a movement of only limited dimensions has so far developed for permanent settlement in Israel.

Even this limited response, however, seems to have reduced the ambivalence which was previously discernible in the attitudes of some Israeli circles to Jews of the Diaspora. It has also led to a certain amount of self-examination, even self-castigation, as Israelis have begun asking themselves how far the call for *aliyah* has been accompanied by a readiness among the Israeli public to do everything possible to make the newcomer feel welcome and facilitate his social adjustment to the country.

On the whole, it would seem that a new equilibrium in Israeli attitudes to Jews of the Diaspora has been established because of the psychological forces stimulated by the events of June 1967. And as they anxiously watch the vagaries in the policies of governments and the vicissitudes in public opinion in the Gentile world, Israelis lean more than ever toward a closer association with Jews of the Diaspora. In the fourth year after the Six Day War Israelis still have reason to feel themselves a beleaguered people, and the sense they have of "standing alone" would be bitterly acute were it not for their deep conviction that they can count on the unfaltering support of Jews the world over.

A New Psychological Climate

While the Six Day War emphasized the Jewish dimension in Israel's struggle, the problems of the emerging Israeli-Jewish identity discussed in our study remain basically unchanged. There is still need to face up to the problem of a weakening in the Jewish identity which comes with the decline in religious observance, to the fact of the low attractiveness of their Jewishness for a considerable minority of young Israelis, to the consequences which flow from a sundering of the Israeli and Jewish subidentities, to the tendency to adopt a conception of the Jewish past in which periods of Jewish life in the Diaspora are obscured, to the failure to understand the peculiar problems of Jewish existence in the free countries of the West. But while the basic attitudes have not been fundamentally changed, the events of this period have created a psychological climate which can facilitate the development of a program designed to strengthen the Jewish identity of the Israeli.

Appendices and Tables

APPENDIX I

The Sample, the Methods and Procedures

I. The Population of High School Students

It would have been desirable to sample from the entire high school population. This did not turn out to be a practicable enterprise with the means at the disposal of the research project and certain limitations were accordingly introduced into the design.

The eleventh-graders—the 16–17-year-old group—were selected after it was discovered in the pre-tests that the younger pupils did not always respond adequately to the questionnaire; furthermore the older students, the matriculating class, were heavily preoccupied with preparations for the examinations. The choice thus fell on the penultimate class.

The population studied was further restricted to students registered in high schools under the supervision of the Israel Ministry of Education. A project of the dimensions of the present study was practicable only if there was easy access to the schools; indeed the implementation of the study on the scale it was conducted was feasible only because of the ready cooperation of the Ministry of Education. (A small number of schools fall outside the direct orbit of the Ministry; they are mainly those which belong to the independent system controlled by the extreme traditionally religious, non-Zionist party, Agudath Israel.)

Education in Israel is not compulsory beyond the primary school level, and a considerable number of children do not enter the high schools. It is estimated that of the approximately 46,000 young persons in the 16-17 age group in the 1964/65 school year when the study was undertaken 22,000 (48 percent) were enrolled in the schools supervised by the Ministry of Education. These were the students who constituted the population of our study.

II. Sampling

The sample was thus designed to be representative of the schoolgoing youth attending schools under the supervision of the Ministry of Education; it does not extend to youngsters who do not attend high school. Among the non-schoolgoing youth of this age group the proportion of youngsters from the Oriental communities (families from Asia and Africa) is particularly large—for socioeconomic and other reasons.

A sample of 3679 high school students in 117 schools was selected by drawing classes from lists of the Bureau of Statistics checked against the detailed *Guide to Secondary Schools* published by the Ministry of Education. Classes were sampled on a stratified basis according to four criteria:

1. Type of school: academic; vocational; yeshiva; agricultural; collective settlement (kibbutz).

2. Religious status: secular or religious. The Ministry of Education supervises both state secular and state religious schools.

3. Recency of immigration: A school was considered to be populated by new immigrants if Bureau of Statistics

Table 129 Composition of school sample by strata

Sampling Strata	N Schools	N Classes	N Pupils	% Pupils
1. Academic, Secular, Veteran, Ashkenazic	13	22	681	19
2. Evening, Secular, Veteran, Oriental	9	11	228	6
3. Academic + Seminary, Religious, Veteran, Oriental	8	12	303	8
4. Academic + Vocational, Religious, Veteran, Oriental	6	6	170	5
5. Academic + Vocational, Religious, Immigrant, Ashkenazic	2	4	97	3
6. Academic, Religious, Immigrant, Oriental	5	5	67	1
7. Religious, Boarding Schools (Acad. + Vocational)	4	5	139	4
8. Academic, Vocational, Secular, Immigrant, Ashkenazic	8	10	272	7
9. Academic + Vocational, Secular, Immigrant, Oriental	6	7	118	3
10. Hakibbutz Hameuchad*	4	5	98	3
11. Ichud Hakibbutzim Vehakvutzot* Organization	8	8	174	5
12. Hakibbutz Haartzi* Organization	6	6	150	4
13. Vocational, Secular, Veteran, Ashk.	10	14	354	10
14. Vocational, Religious, Veteran +Immigrant, Oriental	6	9	161	4
15. Vocational, Secular, Veteran, Oriental	6	9	161	4
16. Agricultural, Secular, Veteran, Ashkenazic	4	8	195	5
17. Agricultural Boarding + Vocational, Secular, Oriental	6	8	137	4
18. Agricultural Boarding + Vocational, Religious, Oriental	6	8	212	6
	117	155	3679	100%

Note: Certain schools were combined whenever the number of pupils in separate categories was too small. Efforts were made never to combine schools across communities (Ashkenazic-Oriental) or extent of religious observance.

*These are three federations of collective settlements affiliated to different parties within the Labor movement. The reference is to the schools at these settlements.

records showed that more than 50 percent of the population in the school attendance area had reached the country since 1948.

4. Communal origin: A school in which 60 percent or more of its pupils were from families originating from Europe was considered "Ashkenazic." This cut-off point was selected when it became clear that few secondary schools could be considered "Oriental" by choosing the 50 percent cut-off point.

A variety of combinations of the four criteria yielded the eighteen strata described in table 129. Each stratum is represented in the sample according to its proportion in the population, with the ratio of sample to population about 1 : 5.

III. Administration of Questionnaire

In view of their large number, the questions were distributed across three questionnaires. There were questions which overlapped from questionnaire to questionnaire, but in addition each questionnaire contained a number of questions which were specifically limited to it. The student, of course, had to answer one questionnaire only; the distribution of questionnaires was organized in a way which maintained the reliability of the sample.

The N in the tables depends upon whether the particular question appears in one, two, or all three of the questionnaires. It should be noted that: (1) The number of non-respondents to a question was not considered in response totals. (There were very few such non-respondents on any particular question); (2) In some tables the category subtotals do not sum to the total N. (This is because of imcomplete information in reference to the classification of some of the respondents in the subcategories.)

Members of the research team visited the schools in

pairs and were responsible for the administration of the questionnaire in the classrooms during the two hours which were set aside for the purpose (by the permission of the Ministry of Education). The 117 schools were located in towns and settlements throughout Israel; this part of the project, which involved considerable organization and took a number of weeks, was effectively completed because of the cooperation of the principals and other teachers in the schools. The teachers were asked not to be present in the classroom during administration of the questionnaire.

At a later stage—after the completion of the fieldwork—a substudy obtained data from students in two schools on a few specific questions not covered in the main study.

At the beginning of 1968 a series of supplementary substudies were carried out which encompassed 255 students in seven schools in Jerusalem and Haifa.

IV. Interviews and Other Sources of Data

A series of detailed, focused interviews were carried out with 128 eleventh-graders who had previously completed questionnaires. The interviewees were drawn from both religious and secular schools. Schools were chosen on the basis of accessibility for detailed interviewing of students by the research team. This led to a concentration of interviews in Jerusalem and Haifa (respective headquarters of two interviewing teams) but interviews were also held with students from schools in various other parts of the country.

A main purpose of the interviews was to obtain amplifications of the responses of the students to key questions in the questionnaire.

Available to the study also were autobiographical sketches about the development of their attitudes to their

Jewishness, prepared according to an outline guide, by sixty students in a Social Psychology class at the Hebrew University. Reference was made to these sketches as a source of background material.

After the Six Day War, further background material was obtained from University students who provided—as part of a psychology class assignment—data on their reactions, and on those of their friends, to the Six Day War.

At a few points in the present study reference is made for comparative purposes to data of another study conducted by the author on American students in Israel.[1]

V. The Parent Sample

The desire to compare the attitudes of two generations led to the selection of a sample of 539 parents. The parents were chosen from lists of students. To ensure comparability parents were included from each of the classes in which the students had been interviewed.

With selection based on students' questionnaires it was possible to match the sex of the parent to that of the pupil and also maintain a 1 : 1 ratio of fathers to mothers.

The parents, who were located in all parts of the country, were visited personally by our interviewers. This proved to be a more complicated task than the administration of the questionnaire in the schools. Addresses had to be checked and rechecked; a number of the parents were illiterate, or could not read Hebrew. The team of interviewers was trained to meet all contingencies, which they successfully did, and responses were obtained from 443 parents, i.e., a return of 82 percent.

To test the comparability of student and parent samples the distribution of the responses of the subsample students whose parents were selected was compared with those of the entire sample of students on several of the key questions. The distributions corresponded within the limits of random fluctuation (see tables 130A, 131A, 132A).

VI. Tests of Statistical Significance

The statistic mainly employed to estimate the significance of differences between the response distributions of criterion groups is *gamma,* a measure of predictive association between sets of ordered classes.[2] This is actually a measure of relation, but when properly interpreted permits inferences about differences between response distributions. In certain instances we used tests of significance of difference between proportions and means. Most of the differences reported in the present study are significant at the .05 level, and whenever they are not, attention is duly drawn to the fact.

VII. Characteristics of the Student and Parent Samples

Four characteristics were of particular relevance in describing our sample: religious observance, communal origin, country of birth, and recency of immigration.

I. Religious Observance

Table 133 shows that 25 percent of the student sample described themselves as religious *(dati'im)*; 32 percent as traditionalists *(mesorati'im)* and 42 percent as non-religious *(lo-dati'im)*; with 1 percent unclassified. The religious category does not include the extreme orthodox fringe of the population which is not within the framework of the educational system supervised by the Ministry of Education.

Among the non-religious there were 293 students (i.e., 19 percent of this category) who classified themselves as anti-religious. Among the religious students there were 102 (11 percent of this category) who classified themselves as "very religious."

Among the parents, 33 percent classify themselves as

religious, 37 percent as traditionalists and 27 percent as non-religious (3 percent unclassified). Since the parent and student samples may be considered to represent a parent-child population this is a reflection of the secularizing trend from one generation to the other; this aspect was explored more fully on the basis of other data in the study (see Chapter 8).

Table 133 The sample, as classified by religious observance

	Students		Parents	
	N	%	N	%
Religious	908	(25)	145	(33)
Traditionalist	1,188	(32)	164	(37)
Non-religious	1,456	(42)	121	(27)
Unclassified	37	(1)	13	(3)
Total	3,679	(100)	443	(100)

II. Communal Origin

Table 134 shows a breakdown of the student and parent samples by communal origin. The sample is about two-thirds Ashkenazic, one-third Oriental. As previously indicated, the Oriental sector is underrepresented among high school youth in proportion to its numerical strength in the population, in which over half the children are from that sector.

Table 134 The sample, classified by communal origin

	Students		Parents	
	N	%	N	%
Ashkenazic	2,498	(68)	293	(66)
Oriental	1,121	(30)	147	(33)
Unclassified	60	(2)	3	(1)
Total	3,679	(100)	443	(100)

III. *Country of Birth*

A breakdown according to country of birth in table 135 shows that about half of the students in the sample are local-born; 28 percent are from countries of Europe, 23 percent from Asia and Africa and a small number from other parts of the world.

Half of the parents immigrated from Eastern Europe, close to a third from countries of Asia and Africa.

Table 135 Sample, classified by country of birth

Country of birth	Students N	%	Parents N	%
Local-born	1,714	(47)	18	(4)
E. Europe (Poland, Rumania, Hungary, U.S.S.R.)	653	(18)	223	(50)
Central Europe	270	(7)	44	(10)
Western Europe	96	(3)	5	(1)
North Africa (Morocco, Tunisia, Algeria, Lybia)	322	(9)	43	(10)
Yemen, Aden	110	(3)	22	(5)
Other Middle East (Iraq, Iran, Syria, Lebanon, Egypt)	394	(11)	67	(15)
Balkan countries	51	(1)	16	(4)
Anglo-American countries	28	(1)	2	(1)
Total	3,638	(100)	441	(100)
Unclassified	41		2	

IV. *Recency of Immigration*

Almost a third of the students immigrated during the first years after the establishment of the State, between 1948–53. They received all of their schooling in Israel. If they are different from the local-born who constitute close to half of the sample, the difference should conceivably be traced to the home. Thirteen percent of the students arrived between 1954–60, mainly from Morocco and Rumania. The remaining 7 percent immigrated since 1961 and are the real newcomers (Table 136).

Among parents the majority are immigrants who arrived in the years following the establishment of the State in 1948. Thirty-eight percent arrived during 1948–53; 14 percent arrived between 1954–60 and 7 percent are very recent immigrants. Forty-one percent of the parents were in the country before 1948.

Table 136 Sample, according to year of immigration

Period of Immigration	Students		Parents	
	N	%	N	%
Local-born	1,714	(47)	19	(3)
Immigrated until end of 1932	-	-	33	(8)
Immigrated 1933–1939	-	-	73	(17)
Immigrated 1940–1947	43	(1)	55	(13)
Immigrated 1948–1953	1,195	(32)	165	(38)
Immigrated 1954–1960	476	(13)	62	(14)
Immigrated 1961–1965	247	(7)	31	(7)
Total	3,675	(100)	438	(100)

VIII. The Teachers

It was thought of interest to explore how the students compared on key identity items not only with their parents but also with their teachers. At the same time an enquiry was made into the teachers' evaluation of the identity of their students.

A questionnaire was distributed among the teachers of the eleventh-graders in the schools in the sample. These were the Form teachers (in general charge of the education of the eleventh grade classes), and also the special teachers of Jewish and General History, Hebrew Literature, Talmud and Bible.

Completed questionnaires were obtained from 231 of

the 399 teachers (i.e., 58 percent of the total) to whom questionnaires had been distributed. It is conceivable that the respondents were the teachers with the greater involvement in Jewish matters, and they accordingly may score somewhat higher on Jewish identity items than would the non-respondents. It should also be borne in mind that the special teachers are instructing in subjects which are likely to be taught by teachers with a stronger Jewish identity than colleagues teaching other subjects.

Ninety percent of the teachers belonged to the Ashkenazic communities, and 10 percent were members of Oriental communities. Table 137 indicates the breakdown according to communal origin and religious category.

Table 137 Teachers: According to communal origin and religious observance

	All Teachers	Religious	Traditionalist	Non-Religious
Ashkenazic	90	87	88	93
Oriental	10	13	12	7
Total %	100	100	100	100
N	228	83	42	102

Of the small number (42) of traditionalist teachers, 5 (i.e., 12 percent) teach in religious schools, and 37 (i.e., 88 percent) in secular schools.

* * *

The student and parent samples, we submit, are representative of the population of eleventh-graders in the State-supervised schools and their parents, respectively. Statements about the samples should be generalizable to these larger populations. Although the same cannot be said with any confidence about the teacher respondents, some idea may yet be gained of where at least those teachers who responded stand on the key items and how they view the ethnic identity of their students.

Age Trends in Jewish Identity

In the study of ethnic identity among adolescent youth the question arises whether there are any systematic changes with age. While our country-wide study explored attitudes in the eleventh grade only, two substudies (carried out by colleagues using our questionnaire) permit age comparisons.[1] One of these studies surveyed a city school population of over 400 pupils from the eighth to the twelfth grades; the other obtained data from ninth and eleventh graders in an agricultural secondary school. In spite of the many differences between purpose, curriculum and student population, results from the two schools yielded consistent returns. (It should at the same time be mentioned that both were secular schools with a population of preponderantly non-religious students.)

Table 138 lists mean scores obtained at the urban school. The means refer to answers given by pupils of the various grades to key questions of the study. Each such question attempts to capture some aspect of ethnic identity. The questions have been given elsewhere (Chapter 4 sup.). Here we shall merely report the labels by which we identify these aspects. In the column marked "scoring," the key for mean values is given; for example, high centrality (the assignment of great importance to being a Jew or Israeli), is scored 1; low centrality, 4. In general, low scores indicate strong identity.

Table 138 Comparison of mean scores by grades eight to twelve in an urban secular school

Variable	Scoring	Grade					
		8	9	10	11	12	All Respondents
Israeli-Jewish continuum	Isr: 1 Jew: 7	3.1	2.7	3.2	2.9	2.6	2.9
Jewish v Private Indiv.	Jew: 1 Pvt. Indiv. 7	3.4	4.0	4.1	4.8	5.1	4.2
Israeli v Private Indiv.	Isr: 1 Pvt. Indiv. 7	2.6	3.0	2.9	3.4	4.4	3.1
Jewish Centrality	Hi: 1 Lo: 4	2.2	2.4	2.4	2.5	2.6	2.4
Israeli Centrality		1.7	1.6	1.6	1.6	1.9	1.6
Valence Jewishness	Hi: 1 Lo: 3	1.5	1.7	1.6	1.6	2.1	1.6
Consonance	Hi: 1 Lo: 3	1.3	1.5	1.3	1.4	1.6	1.4
N		76	142	130	78	35	461

The most definite trend appears on the two scales in which Jew and Israeli respectively have been set opposite "private individual." Pupils here were required to place themselves at the most fitting place on the seven-step continua. A tendency to move toward the "private individual" pole of the band was thought to show a weakening of ethnic identification. It will be noted that there is a definite (and statistically significant) trend toward the option of private status. This is true for both the Jewish and Israeli subidentities though the Israeli position is always stronger than the Jewish one. At any age pupils may feel more strongly about being Israelis than about being Jews, but both of these lose ground to being a "private individual" as pupils move through adolescence to maturity.

None of the other trends are significant in a statistical sense, but changes in the values of means from the lower to the higher grades suggest a weakening of, at least, the Jewish identity throughout.

The relative strength of the Israeli and Jewish subidentities has been measured by placing Israeli (1) and Jew (7) at opposite ends of a seven-step scale. Throughout, mean ratings favor the Israeli side, but it is only after the tenth grade that Israeliness gains further momentum.

Table 139 lists mean scores for 63 ninth graders and 125 eleventh graders at a school combining a high school curriculum and agricultural training. Several differences between the two schools may be noted. The urban school prepares all the pupils for academic matriculation, places major emphasis on study, and releases its students after the day's classes. The agricultural school prepares all of its pupils for general studies and agricultural skills and some of them for agricultural matriculation, attempts to impart both habits of study and physical work, and boards its students on a 24-hour-a-day basis. In spite of these and other differences age trends in the two schools are consistent. Table 139 reveals a decline in strength of Jewish identity between the ninth and eleventh grades. The first comparison, between positions on the Israeli-Jew seven-step scale, reveals eleventh graders to be significantly more on the Israeli side than ninth graders. Again, as before, the older pupils think of themselves as less Jewish and Israeli and more as "private individuals." Again, as before, centrality of Jewishness declines. Furthermore, to eleventh graders the Jewish and Israeli subidentities appear less overlapping and consonant than

Table 139 Mean scores and standard deviations in agricultural school

Variable	Grades		Comparison		
	9	11	Diff.	t	Signif.
Israeli-Jew	M 3.13	2.73	.40	1.70	p>.05
(1) (7)	SD(1.33)	(1.78)			
Jew-Private Person	M 3.69	4.38	.69	2.46	p<.05
(1) (7)	SD(1.96)	(1.71)			
Israeli-Private Person	M 2.39	3.10	.71	2.81	p<.01
(1) (7)	SD(1.52)	(1.67)			
Centrality of Jewishness	M 2.30	2.47	.17	1.04	p>.05
Hi: 1 Lo: 4	SD(.85)	(1.10)			
Centrality of Israeliness	M 1.52	1.62	.10	-	-
Hi: 1 Lo: 4	SD(.65)	(.75)			
Consonance	M 1.34	1.52	.18	2.00	p<.05
Hi: 1 Lo: 3					
N	63	125			

they do to ninth graders. (A question testing valence of Jewishness unfortunately did not appear in the questionnaire used in this study.)

The evidence of the two studies points to a decline in strength of Jewish identity with increase in age during the high school years among non-religious students.

John Hofman, who carried out the study in the urban school, interviewed teachers and students in order to ascertain their explanation for the decline. He sums up the interviews as follows:

"Teachers acknowledge this [decline] and have explanations to account for it. One feels that older pupils turn inward and become more preoccupied with their own future and their own problems. Another reason given is that the heavy stress on the emotional and sentimental appeal in teaching for national values backfires in the upper grades. If the appeal were more rational, he thinks, it would stand a better chance against the developing sense of criticism. These and similar lines of thought see attitudes toward the Israeli and Jewish self in the context of adolescent development.

"Pupils, who also acknowledge that a decline in ethnic identity checks with their observations, more often than teachers point to curricular content as the central cause. As far as they recall, elementary school stressed the Jewish heritage much more than does the secondary school. They note the widening sweep of subject matter which must of needs leave ethnic values in more limited perspective. Here then we have an explanation in terms of what the school does or does not do. Future studies might test hypotheses on changes in ethnic identity derived from theories of adolescent development or curricular content, or some combination of both.[2]"

(It should be noted that recently the Ministry of Education has given attention to the question of curricular content by introducing a course dealing with developments in Jewish life in the modern period.)

APPENDIX III

Sex Differences

THE data of our study do not indicate any sharp differences between the sexes on questions of ethnic identity. Thus, when the positions of the two sexes are compared in regard to the valence of Jewishness and of Israeliness, a close correspondence is found (see tables 140A and 141A). On the Jewish–private individual and Israeli–private individual continua, however, the girls have the more "individualistic" orientation (see tables 142A and 143A).

TABLES

Supplement A

The tables in this supplement are referred to but not inserted in the text of the study. (In the reference in the text the letter A is suffixed to the number of each of these tables.) They relate to the student sample, and also, in regard to a number of questions, to the parents of the subsample. The exceptions are tables 3 and 4 (which are taken from a separate study on American-Jewish students in Israel) and tables 17 and 18 (which are based on a limited substudy).

Since questions were distributed over three questionnaires, the N (number of respondents) varies according to whether a particular question appeared in one or more of these questionnaires.

Table 3 American-Jewish: Overlap and Consonance as perceived by a group of American-Jewish students (N = 79)

When I feel more American:	per cent
1. I also feel more Jewish	14
2. There is no relationship between my feeling Jewish and my feeling American	68
3. I feel less Jewish	18

Table 4 Jewish–American: Overlap and Consonance as perceived by a group of American-Jewish students (N = 79)

When I feel more Jewish:	per cent
1. I also feel more American	13
2. There is no relationship between my feeling Jewish and my feeling American	61
3. I feel less American	26

Table 14 A comparison between "compatibles" and "separatists": Israeli–Jewish Continuum

	All Respondents		Religious		Traditionalist		Non-Religious	
	Comp.	Sep.	Comp.	Sep.	Comp.	Sep.	Comp.	Sep.
Israeli 1–3	35	67	8	6	36	50	56	83
Midpoint 4	38	19	35	22	39	30	39	15
Jew 5–7	27	24	57	72	25	20	5	2
Total %	100	100	100	100	100	100	100	100
N	964	402	303	36	327	108	344	258

Table 15 A comparison between "compatibles" and "separatists": Centrality of Jewishness
"Does the fact that you are Jewish play an important part in your life?"

	All Respondents		Religious		Traditionalist		Non-Religious	
	Comp.	Sep.	Comp.	Sep.	Comp.	Sep.	Comp.	Sep.
1. A very important part	29	10	59	56	21	12	10	4
2. An important part	51	33	38	42	62	53	52	23
3. Of little importance	17	42	1	2	15	25	33	54
4. It plays no part	3	15	2	-	2	10	5	19
Total %	100	100	100	100	100	100	100	100
N	978	402	305	36	328	108	345	258

Table 16 A comparison between "compatibles" and "separatists": Valence of Jewishness
"If you were to live abroad, would you wish to be born a Jew?"

	Comp.	Sep.	Comp.	Sep.	Comp.	Sep.	Comp.	Sep.
1. Would wish to be born a Jew	64	36	85	75	60	47	49	25
2. It makes no difference	18	39	5	14	21	31	26	45
3. I would not want to be born a Jew	18	25	10	11	19	22	25	30
Total %	100	100	100	100	100	100	100	100
N	971	402	304	36	324	108	343	258

Table 17 The Marking-off group in relation to Jewish identity
"We are Jews but they are ____."

A Substudy

	Ashkenazic (N = 66)	Oriental (N = 39)
Gentiles ("Goyim")	48	59
Non-Jews	8	-
Christians	16	-
Moslems	8	3
Arabs	8	31
Other nations, other religions, others	9	-
Miscellaneous	-	2
No reply	3	5
	100	100

Table 18 The Marking-off group in relation to Israeli identity
"We are Israelis but they are ____."

A Substudy

	Ashkenazic (N = 66)	Oriental (N = 39)
Other nations	36	21
Arabs	32	46
Jews	8	-
Non-Israelis	6	-
Gentiles ("Goyim")	3	23
Miscellaneous	3	8
No reply	12	2
	100	100

Table 21 Sensitivity to insult of Jewish people
"When an important overseas journal insults the Jewish people, do you feel as if it were insulting you?"

	All Respondents		Religious		Traditionalist		Non-Religious	
	Parents	Students	Parents	Students	Parents	Students	Parents	Students
1. Always	84	65	87	81	83	66	82	58
2. Often	11	26	7	16	14	27	9	31
3. Seldom	3	7	3	3	-	6	9	9
4. Never	2	2	3	-	3	1	-	2
Total %	100	100	100	100	100	100	100	100
N	126	767	35	168	59	247	33	352

Table 22 Sensitivity to insult of Jews abroad
"When an important overseas journal insults Jews abroad, do you feel as if it were insulting you?"

	All Respondents		Religious		Traditionalist		Non-Religious	
	Parents	Students	Parents	Students	Parents	Students	Parents	Students
1. Always	74	41	80	59	79	45	58	31
2. Often	18	37	13	31	11	38	33	39
3. Seldom	3	16	-	9	4	14	6	21
4. Never	5	6	7	1	6	3	3	9
Total %	100	100	100	100	100	100	100	100
N	125	767	34	168	59	247	33	352

Table 23 Sensitivity to praise of Jewish people
"When an important overseas journal praises the Jewish people, do you feel as if it were praising you?"

	All Respondents		Religious		Traditionalist		Non-Religious	
	Parents	Students	Parents	Students	Parents	Students	Parents	Students
1. Always	77	52	83	64	72	57	76	43
2. Often	14	36	7	29	19	34	15	40
3. Seldom	4	11	3	5	3	8	6	16
4. Never	5	1	7	2	6	1	3	1
Total %	100	100	100	100	100	100	100	100
N	126	767	35	168	59	247	33	352

Table 24 Sensitivity to praise of Jews abroad
"When an important overseas journal praises Jews abroad, do you feel as if it were praising you?"

	All Respondents		Religious		Traditionalist		Non-Religious	
	Parents	Students	Parents	Students	Parents	Students	Parents	Students
1. Always	61	24	73	31	60	29	48	17
2. Often	21	34	10	40	23	39	30	29
3. Seldom	5	29	6	22	3	26	7	33
4. Never	13	13	11	7	14	6	15	21
Total %	100	100	100	100	100	100	100	100
N	434	767	147	168	165	247	122	352

Table 25 Sensitivity to insult of Israel
"When an important overseas journal insults Israel, do you feel as if it were insulting you?"

	All Respondents		Religious		Traditionalist		Non-Religious	
	Parents	Students	Parents	Students	Parents	Students	Parents	Students
1. Always	87	79	94	71	84	81	88	82
2. Often	11	18	3	24	13	16	12	17
3. Seldom	-	2	-	4	-	2	-	-
4. Never	2	1	3	1	3	1	-	1
Total %	100	100	100	100	100	100	100	100
N	126	767	35	168	59	33	122	352

Table 26 Sensitivity to insult of Israeli Jews
"When an important journal insults Israelis (Jews), do you feel as if you were
personally insulted?"

	All Respondents		Religious		Traditionalist		Non-Religious	
	Parents	Students	Parents	Students	Parents	Students	Parents	Students
1. Always	77	40	91	48	83	44	58	34
2. Often	18	47	6	42	14	45	33	52
3. Seldom	2	10	-	9	-	10	6	10
4. Never	3	3	3	1	3	1	3	4
Total %	100	100	100	100	100	100	100	100
N	127	1439	35	346	59	454	33	639

Table 27 Sensitivity to insult of Israeli non-Jews
"When an important journal insults Israelis (non-Jews), do you feel as if you were
personally insulted?"

	All Respondents		Religious		Traditionalist		Non-Religious	
	Parents	Students	Parents	Students	Parents	Students	Parents	Students
1. Always	16	14	14	12	18	15	15	14
2. Often	20	29	27	24	15	31	22	31
3. Seldom	27	34	18	32	23	35	44	35
4. Never	37	23	41	32	44	19	19	20
Total %	100	100	100	100	100	100	100	100
N	123	1439	34	347	59	453	30	639

Table 28 Interdependence between Israel and American Jewish community
N = 1430
"When the prestige of the American Jewish community is lowered, does this result in detriment to the State of Israel?"
"When the prestige of the State of Israel is lowered, does this result in detriment to the American Jewish community?"

	Lowered prestige of A.J. community affects Israel	Lowered prestige of Israel affects A.J. community
1. Almost always	35	23
2. Often	45	31
3. Seldom	15	31
4. Almost never	5	15
	100 %	100 %

Table 29 Interdependence between Israel and World Jewry
N = 1430
"When the prestige of World Jewry is lowered, does this result in detriment to the State of Israel?"
"When the prestige of the State of Israel is lowered, does this result in detriment to World Jewry?"

	Lowered prestige of World Jewry affects Israel	Lowered prestige of Israel affects World Jewry
1. Almost always		
2. Often	37	38
3. Seldom	38	40
4. Almost never	19	16
	6	6
	100 %	100 %

Table 30 Differential effect on World Jewry of decline in prestige of American Jewish community and in prestige of Israel

N = 1430

"When the prestige of the American Jewish community is lowered, does this result in detriment to World Jewry?"

"When the prestige of the State of Israel is lowered, does this result in detriment to World Jewry?"

	Lowered prestige of A.J. community affects World Jewry	Lowered prestige of Israel affects World Jewry
1. Almost always	9	38
2. Often	33	40
3. Seldom	40	16
4. Almost never	18	6
	100 %	100 %

Table 31 Rise and decline in prestige of Jews

N = 1437

"When the prestige of Jews in the world rises, does this benefit other Jews?"

"When the prestige of Jews in the world declines, does this prejudice other Jews?"

	Decline	Rise
1. Almost always	48	26
2. Often	39	38
3. Seldom	11	30
4. Almost never	2	6
Total	100 %	100 %

Table 35 The Period of the Second Temple

	All Respondents	Religious	Traditionalist	Non-Religious
1. Pride	48	62	53	37
2. Neither pride nor shame	48	32	43	57
3. Shame	2	4	1	3
4. Lack of knowledge	2	2	3	3
Total %	100	100	100	100
N	767	168	247	352

Table 36 "Golden Age" in Spain

	All Respondents	Religious	Traditionalist	Non-Religious
1. Pride	65	78	69	55
2. Neither pride nor shame	30	17	26	40
3. Shame	2	2	2	3
4. Lack of knowledge	3	3	3	2
Total %	100	100	100	100
N	767	168	247	352

Table 37 Entry of Jews into the cultural and social life of Europe

	All Respondents	Religious	Traditionalist	Non-Religious
1. Pride	64	49	68	68
2. Neither pride nor shame	25	24	22	27
3. Shame	10	25	9	4
4. Lack of knowledge	1	2	1	1
Total %	100	100	100	100
N	767	168	247	352

Table 38 The Jewish Shtetl in Eastern Europe

	All Respondents	Religious	Traditionalist	Non-Religious
1. Pride	28	46	29	19
2. Neither pride nor shame	46	35	47	49
3. Shame	18	5	14	27
4. Lack of knowledge	8	14	10	5
Total	100	100	100	100
N	767	168	247	352

Table 39 The Melah (The Jewish "Ghetto" of North Africa)

	All Respondents	Religious	Traditionalist	Non-Religious
1. Pride	16	17	20	11
2. Neither pride nor shame	41	32	38	47
3. Shame	19	20	22	18
4. Lack of knowledge	24	31	20	24
Total %	100	100	100	100
N	766	168	246	352

Table 40 The behavior of Jews in Europe during the Holocaust

	All Respondents	Religious	Traditionalist	Non-Religious
1. Pride	73	77	74	70
2. Neither pride nor shame	5	7	4	5
3. Shame	21	14	20	25
4. Lack of knowledge	1	2	2	-
Total %	100	100	100	100
N	767	168	247	352

Table 41 Attitude to Jewish behavior in Holocaust among students from Ashkenazic and Oriental Communities

	Religious		Traditional		Non-religious	
	Ashk.	Orient.	Ashk.	Orient.	Ashk.	Orient.
1. Pride	86	64	80	59	72	66
2. Neither pride nor shame	3	12	2	10	4	9
3. Shame	11	19	16	29	24	23
4. Lack of knowledge	-	5	2	2	-	2
Total %	100	100	100	100	100	100
N	104	58	152	87	300	35

Table 42 Relationship between attitude to behavior of Jews in Holocaust and valence of Jewishness (being born a Jew abroad)

Attitude to behavior of Jews Valence	Pride	Neither pride nor shame	Shame	Lack of knowledge
Would wish to be born a Jew	58	45	38	44
Makes no difference	23	32	34	23
No	19	23	28	33
Total %	100	100	100	100
N	546	38	155	9

Table 44 Attitude towards Yiddish among Ashkenazic students

	All Respondents	Religious	Traditionalist	Non-Religious
1. Very positive	7	9	9	6
2. Positive	28	47	31	18
3. No particular feeling	52	39	46	60
4. Negative	10	4	13	10
5. Very negative	3	1	1	6
Total %	100	100	100	100
N	577	115	147	315

Table 45 Attitude towards Yiddish among students from Oriental communities

	All Respondents	Religious	Traditionalist	Non-Religious
1. Very positive	1	1	-	-
2. Positive	7	1	10	8
3. No particular feeling	69	84	62	74
4. Negative	10	7	13	5
5. Very negative	13	7	15	13
Total %	100	100	100	100
N	200	46	116	38

Table 46 Anti-Semitism as endangering Jewish communities
"In the foreseeable future is anti-Semitism likely to endanger the existence of the Jewish communities abroad?"

	All Respondents		Religious		Traditionalist		Non-Religious	
	Parents	Students	Parents	Students	Parents	Students	Parents	Students
1. Certain it is	32	13	30	18	32	14	31	12
2. Think it is	46	52	42	50	41	48	56	54
3. Think it is not	19	33	28	30	22	35	10	33
4. Certain it is not	3	2	-	2	5	3	3	1
Total %	100	100	100	100	100	100	100	100
N	127	767	34	168	60	247	33	352

Table 47 Maintenance of their Jewish character by Jewish communities abroad
"In the foreseeable future will the Jewish communities abroad retain their Jewish character?"

	All Respondents		Religious		Traditionalist		Non-Religious	
	Parents	Students	Parents	Students	Parents	Students	Parents	Students
1. Certain they will	26	4	35	8	28	4	12	2
2. Think they will	38	50	41	51	38	54	36	47
3. Think they will not	28	43	24	39	22	39	43	47
4. Certain they will not	8	3	-	2	12	3	9	4
Total %	100	100	100	100	100	100	100	100
N	127	767	34	168	60	247	33	352

Table 48 Retention of Jewish character by State of Israel
"In the foreseeable future will the State of Israel retain its Jewish character?"

	All Respondents		Religious		Traditionalist		Non-Religious	
	Parents	Students	Parents	Students	Parents	Students	Parents	Students
1. Certain it will	55	28	58	35	52	28	58	25
2. Think it will	36	53	38	50	40	56	27	51
3. Think it will not	8	17	4	15	8	15	12	20
4. Certain it will not	1	2	-	-	-	1	3	4
Total %	100	100	100	100	100	100	100	100
N	127	767	34	168	60	247	33	352

Table 49 Continuing independence of Israel
"Do you think that in the foreseeable future the State of Israel will remain independent?"

	All Respondents		Religious		Traditionalist		Non-Religious	
	Parents	Students	Parents	Students	Parents	Students	Parents	Students
1. Certain it will	70	64	70	57	67	64	76	67
2. Think it will	30	34	30	40	33	33	24	32
3. Think it will not	-	2	-	2	-	3	-	1
4. Certain it will not	-	-	-	1	-	-	-	-
Total %	100	100	100	100	100	100	100	100
N	127	767	34	168	60	247	33	352

Table 50 Assimilation or preservation of Jewish identity in Diaspora
"A youth abroad who is not prepared to settle in Israel—what should he do?"

	All Respondents	Religious	Traditionalist	Non-Religious
1. He should maintain his Jewishness abroad	88	99	93	82
2. He should assimilate	12	1	7	18
Total %	100	100	100	100
N	767	166	241	360

Table 51 Out-marriage in Israel
"What is your opinion of a Jew in Israel who marries a non-Jew?"

	All Respondents		Religious		Traditionalist		Non-Religious	
	Parents	Students	Parents	Students	Parents	Students	Parents	Students
Opposed	57	40	91	84	59	41	21	19
Opposed but may understand him	16	21	6	7	12	28	30	24
Each one's private affair	27	37	3	8	29	30	48	55
A positive opinion	-	2	-	-	-	1	-	2
Total %	100	100	100	100	100	100	100	100
N	127	767	34	168	60	247	33	352

Table 52 Out-marriage Abroad
"What is your opinion of a Jew abroad who marries a non-Jew?"

	All Respondents		Religious		Traditionalist		Non-Religious	
	Parents	Students	Parents	Students	Parents	Students	Parents	Students
Opposed	53	34	89	70	50	33	21	16
Opposed but may understand him	20	29	11	21	20	33	30	30
Each one's private affair	27	36	-	9	30	33	49	52
A positive opinion	-	1	-	-	-	1	-	2
Total %	100	100	100	100	100	100	100	100
N	127	767	34	168	60	247	33	352

Table 53 Readiness to marry a non-Jew
"Would you be prepared to marry a non-Jew (ess)?"

	All Respondents	Religious	Traditionalist	Non-Religious
1. I would not agree under any circumstances	38	74	44	16
2. Yes, if he/she converts	35	23	45	34
3. Yes, just as with a Jew/Jewess	27	3	11	50
Total %	100	100	100	100
N	765	168	246	351

Table 54 Conversion Abroad
"What is your opinion of a Jew abroad who converts to another religion?"

	All Respondents		Religious		Traditionalist		Non-Religious	
	Parents	Students	Parents	Students	Parents	Students	Parents	Students
Opposed	58	36	82	65	57	35	36	23
Opposed but may understand him	18	34	15	25	20	37	22	34
Each one's private affair	22	29	3	9	21	26	39	41
A positive opinion	2	1	-	1	2	2	3	2
Total %	100	100	100	100	100	100	100	100
N	127	767	34	168	60	247	33	352

Table 55 Conversion in Israel
"What is your opinion of a Jew in Israel who converts to another religion?"

	All Respondents		Religious		Traditionalist		Non-Religious	
	Parents	Students	Parents	Students	Parents	Students	Parents	Students
Opposed	60	50	79	83	59	51	42	33
Opposed but may understand him	13	18	15	6	14	21	9	23
Each one's private affair	26	32	6	12	27	28	46	43
A positive opinion	1	-	-	-	-	-	3	1
Total %	100	100	100	100	100	100	100	100
N	127	767	34	168	60	247	33	352

Table 56 Emigration from Israel
"What is your opinion of an Israeli who emigrates from Israel?"

	All Respondents		Religious		Traditionalist		Non-Religious	
	Parents	Students	Parents	Students	Parents	Students	Parents	Students
Opposed	74	57	82	56	75	54	69	60
Opposed but may understand him	6	20	3	21	3	19	16	20
Each one's private affair	18	22	15	22	22	26	12	20
A positive opinion	2	1	-	1	-	1	3	-
Total %	100	100	100	100	100	100	100	100
N	127	767	34	168	60	247	33	352

Table 57 Emigration from Israel
"Would you be prepared to emigrate from Israel?"

	All Respondents		Religious		Traditionalist		Non-Religious	
	Parents	Students	Parents	Students	Parents	Students	Parents	Students
I would not be prepared under any circumstances	84	52	86	57	85	50	85	53
I think that I would not be prepared	5	15	-	10	6	17	6	17
Only under very special circumstances	8	20	14	22	5	20	6	18
Perhaps I would be prepared	2	12	-	10	2	13	3	11
I am prepared	1	1	-	1	2	-	-	1
Total %	100	100	100	100	100	100	100	100
N	124	767	34	169	57	246	33	352

Table 61 Evaluation of Jewish communities (mean scores)
$$N = 770$$

Jewish Communities

1. Russia	2.12
2. America	2.65
3. England	2.76
4. Iraq	2.85
5. Argentina	2.97
6. Germany	3.94

Very High = 1; High = 2; Moderate = 3; Low = 4; Very Low = 5.

Table 62 Evaluation of Jewish communities by students from Ashkenazic and Oriental communities (mean scores)

	Ashkenazic	Oriental	
1. Russia	2.08	2.27	Very High $= 1$
2. America	2.69	2.50	High $= 2$
3. England	2.80	2.65	Moderate $= 3$
4. Iraq	2.88	2.79	Low $= 4$
5. Argentina	3.02	2.86	Very Low $= 5$
6. Germany	4.13	3.37	

Table 63 Feeling of closeness to Jews abroad (1) who support and (2) who do not support Israel

	All Respondents		Religious		Traditionalist		Non-Religious	
	Supporters	Non-Supporters	Supporters	Non-Supporters	Supporters	Non-Supporters	Supporters	Non-Supporters
Very close	66	6	83	9	72	7	54	5
Close	25	31	14	42	21	32	31	24
Not so close	9	63	3	49	7	61	15	71
Total %	100	100	100	100	100	100	100	100
N	777	777	166	166	243	243	368	368

Table 66 Feeling of closeness to Jews in Israel of same and different communal origin

	All Respondents		Religious		Traditionalist		Non-Religious	
	Same Origin	Different Origin	Same Origin	Different Origin	Same Origin	Different Origin	Same Origin	Different Origin
Very close	63	37	76	52	65	40	56	27
Close	29	48	20	38	27	51	35	51
Not so close	8	15	4	10	8	9	9	22
Total %	100	100	100	100	100	100	100	100
N	769	772	164	165	242	243	363	364

Table 67 Closeness to Jews in Israel of (1) same and of (2) different communal origins: by students from Ashkenazic and Oriental communities

	Ashkenazic students		Oriental students	
	Same Origin	Different Origin	Same Origin	Different Origin
Very close	65	34	59	45
Close	30	48	27	45
Not so close	5	18	14	10
Total %	100	100	100	100
N	572	576	199	199

Table 68(i) Closeness to Jews in Israel of same communal origin by Ashkenazic and Oriental students of differing degrees of religious observance

	Religious		Traditionalist		Non-Religious	
	Ash.	Orient.	Ash.	Orient.	Ash.	Orient.
Very close	75	78	71	56	58	45
Close	22	14	24	32	35	31
Not so close	3	8	5	12	7	24
Total %	100	100	100	100	100	100
N	113	51	146	96	312	51

Table 68(ii) Closeness to Jews in Israel of different communal origin: by Ashkenazic and Oriental students of differing degrees of religious observance

	Religious		Traditionalist		Non-Religious	
	Ash.	Orient.	Ash.	Orient.	Ash.	Orient.
Very close	47	61	35	48	28	24
Close	39	33	52	47	50	55
Not so close	14	6	13	5	22	21
Total %	100	100	100	100	100	100
N	114	51	147	96	313	51

Table 69 Evaluation of peoples of countries (mean scores)

	N = 770
1. England	2.27
2. America	2.34
3. Russia	3.47
4. Argentina	3.50
5. Iraq	3.86
6. Germany	3.94
(People in Israel	1.96)

Very High = 1   High = 2   Moderate = 3
     Low = 4   Very Low = 5

Table 70(i) Correcting a mistake about identity on the part of a non-Jew
"If a non-Jew from abroad were to meet you abroad and mistake you for a non-Israeli non-Jew, would you correct his mistake and tell him that . . .

A) you are a Jew?"		
1. Yes	74	
2. I am not sure but I think I would	14	
3. I don't know what I would do	8	
4. I am not sure but I think I would not tell him	1	
5. No	3	100%
B) you are an Israeli?"		
1. Yes	84	
2. I am not sure but I think I would	8	
3. I don't know what I would do	5	
4. I am not sure but I think I would not tell him	1	
5. No	2	100%

N = 1430

Table 70(ii) Correcting a mistake about identity on the part of an anti-Semite
"If an anti-Semite were to meet you abroad and mistake you for a non-Israeli non-Jew, would you correct his mistake and tell him that . . .

A) you are a Jew?"
1. Yes	70	
2. I am not sure but I think I would	16	
3. I don't know what I would do	7	
4. I am not sure but I think I would not tell him	2	
5. No	5	100%

B) you are an Israeli?"
1. Yes	81	
2. I am not sure but I think I would	9	
3. I don't know what I would do	6	
4. I am not sure but I think I would not tell him	1	
5. No	3	100%
		N = 1430

Table 72 Relationship between attribution by non-religious students of cause of anti-Semitism and valence of Jewishness (being born a Jew abroad)

Cause of anti-Semitism Valence	Characteristics of non-Jews	The situation of Jews abroad as a minority	Characteristics of Jews
Wish to be born a Jew	53	39	34
Makes no difference	35	34	32
No	12	27	34
Total %	100	100	100
N	51	380	197

Table 73 The relative role of religious observance among students and parents: measure of association (γ) between religious observance and Jewish identity items

	Students	*Parents*
Jewish side of Israeli-Jewish continuum	.61	.30
Jewish-"private individual"	.42	.28
Centrality of Jewishness	.66	.43
Valence of Jewishness	.47	.39

Table 74 Comparison of traditionalists in religious and secular schools on Israeli-Jewish Continuum

		Religious Schools	Secular Schools
Israeli	1–3	15	44
Midpoint	4	42	39
Jewish	5–7	43	17
Total %		100	100
N		86	629

Table 75 Comparison of traditionalists in religious and secular schools on Jewish-"Private Individual" Continuum

		Religious Schools	Secular Schools
Jewish	1–3	62	43
Midpoint	4	18	22
"Private Individual"	5–7	20	35
Total %		100	100
N		86	627

Table 76 Comparison between traditionalists in religious and secular schools in regard to centrality of Jewishness

	Religious Schools	Secular Schools
1. Plays a very important part	26	14
2. An important part	67	60
3. A small part	6	21
4. No part	1	5
Total %	100	100
N	86	629

Table 77 Comparison between traditionalists in religious and secular schools on Israeli-"Private Individual" Continuum

	In Religious Schools	In Secular Schools
Israeli 1–3	65	62
Midpoint 4	20	20
"Private Individual" 5–7	15	18
Total %	100	100
N	86	627

Table 78 Religious students in the two types of schools: The Israeli-Jewish Continuum

	In Religious Schools	In Secular Schools
Israeli 1–3	6	11
Midpoint 4	34	41
Jewish 5–7	60	48
Total %	100	100
N	599	82

Table 79 Religious students in the two types of schools: Valence of Jewishness
"If you were to be born all over again, would you wish to be born a Jew?"

	In Religious Schools	In Secular Schools
1. Yes	94	90
2. It makes no difference to me	6	10
3. No	–	–
Total %	100	100
N	593	82

Table 80 Religious students in the two types of schools: Valence of Jewishness (in life abroad)
"If you were to live abroad, would you wish to be born a Jew?"

	In Religious Schools	In Secular Schools
1. Yes	85	80
2. It makes no difference to me	6	12
3. No	9	8
Total %	100	100
N	449	64

Table 81 Religious students in the two types of schools: Centrality of Jewishness
"Does the fact that you are Jewish play an important part in your life?"

	In Religious Schools	In Secular Schools
1. It plays a very important part	63	46
2. It plays an important part	35	49
3. It is of little importance	1	4
4. It plays no part	1	1
Total %	100	100
N	597	82

Table 82 Religious students in the two types of schools: Overlap and Consonance
"When I feel more Israeli . . .

	In Religious Schools	In Secular Schools
1. I also feel more Jewish."	88	87
2. there is no relationship between my feeling Israeli and my feeling Jewish."	10	11
3. I feel less Jewish."	2	2
Total %	100	100
N	597	82

Table 83 Religious students in the two types of schools: Overlap and Consonance
"When I feel more Jewish . . .

	In Religious Schools	In Secular Schools
1. I also feel more Israeli."	82	84
2. there is no relationship between my feeling Jewish and my feeling Israeli."	15	15
3. I feel less Israeli."	3	1
Total %	100	100
N	599	82

Table 90 Communal origin and comparison of own religious observance by students and parents with that of their respective parents

	All Respondents				Religious				Traditionalist				Non-Religious			
	Students		Parents		Students		Parents		Students		Parents		Students		Parents	
	Ashkenazi	Oriental	Ashkenazi	Oriental	Ashkenazi	Oriental	Ashkenazi	Oriental	Ashkenazi	Oriental	Ashkenazi	Oriental	Ashkenazi	Oriental	Ashkenazi	Oriental
More religious than parents	8	7	3	8	17	14	12	8	9	4	1	10	3	1	1	-
As religious as parents	55	45	26	44	63	50	44	55	55	43	16	31	52	44	24	36
Less religious than parents	37	48	71	48	20	36	44	37	36	53	83	59	45	55	75	64
Total %	100	100	100	100	100	100	100	100	100	100	100	100	100	100	100	100
N	2520	1116	273	147	519	373	68	76	734	499	112	49	1267	244	93	22

Table 91 Decline in religious observance: A comparison between sons and daughters in Ashkenazic communities

	All Respondents		Religious		Traditionalist		Non-Religious	
	Sons	Daughters	Sons	Daughters	Sons	Daughters	Sons	Daughters
More religious than parents	7	9	16	18	8	11	2	5
As religious as parents	49	60	64	64	43	60	48	56
Less religious than parents	44	31	20	18	49	29	50	39
Total %	100	100	100	100	100	100	100	100
N	1259	1178	236	284	334	329	689	565

Table 92 Decline in religious observance: A comparison between sons and daughters in Oriental communities

	All Respondents		Religious		Traditionalist		Non-Religious	
	Sons	Daughters	Sons	Daughters	Sons	Daughters	Sons	Daughters
More religious than parents	6	7	15	12	4	5	2	1
As religious as parents	42	49	50	51	39	45	38	52
Less religious than parents	52	44	35	37	57	50	60	47
Total %	100	100	100	100	100	100	100	100
N	515	562	127	228	241	241	147	93

Table 94 Overlap and Consonance: according to communal origin
"When I feel more Israeli . . .

	All Respondents		Religious		Traditionalist		Non-Religious	
	Oriental	Ashkenazic	Oriental	Ashkenazic	Oriental	Ashkenazic	Oriental	Ashkenazic
1. I feel more Jewish."	74	66	88	88	71	74	59	54
2. there is no relationship . . ."	23	30	10	10	27	22	36	41
3. I feel less Jewish."	3	4	2	2	2	4	5	5
Total %	100	100	100	100	100	100	100	100
N	378	1059	131	216	164	288	83	555

Table 95 Jewish-Israeli continuum: according to communal origin

		All Respondents		Religious		Traditionalist		Non-Religious	
		Oriental	Ashkenazic	Oriental	Ashkenazic	Oriental	Ashkenazic	Oriental	Ashkenazic
Israeli	1–3	30	50	8	6	35	43	55	71
Midpoint	4	35	31	29	36	35	37	40	25
Jewish	5–7	35	19	63	58	30	20	5	4
Total %		100	100	100	100	100	100	100	100
N		376	1057	131	213	163	287	82	557
Means		4.2	3.4	5.3	5.0	3.9	3.6	3.0	2.6

Table 96 Jewish-"Private Individual" continuum: according to communal origin

		All Respondents		Religious		Traditionalist		Non-Religious	
		Oriental	Ashkenazic	Oriental	Ashkenazic	Oriental	Ashkenazic	Oriental	Ashkenazic
Jewish	1–3	58	43	77	75	55	40	33	31
Midpoint	4	16	20	14	16	15	24	21	20
"Private individual"	5–7	26	37	9	9	30	36	46	49
Total %		100	100	100	100	100	100	100	100
N		378	1056	131	214	163	286	84	556

Table 98 Communal Origin, Religious Observance and Jewish Identity Measure of Association (γ) between the religious factor and identity variables in the two communal groups

	Oriental students	Ashkenazic students
Jewish side of Israeli-Jewish scale	.56	.61
Jewish-"private individual"	.43	.39
Israeli-"private individual"	.17	.06
Consonance	.45	.47
Centrality of Jewishness	.60	.67
Centrality of Israeliness	.08	.02
Valence of Jewishness	.46	.46
Valence of Israeliness	—.05	—.03

Table 99 Religious distribution of students of Oriental communities according to family's country of origin

	N. Africa (mainly Morocco)	Yemen and Aden	Other M. E. countries (Iraq, Iran, Egypt, Syria, Lebanon)
Religious	44	63	21
Traditionalist	41	31	53
Non-Religious	15	6	26
Total %	100	100	100
N	334	179	483

Table 100 Valence of Jewishness according to country of origin
"If you were to live abroad, would you wish to be born a Jew?"

	N. Africa	Yemen and Aden	Other M.E. countries
Would wish	69	76	56
Makes no difference	16	18	24
Would not wish	15	6	20
Total %	100	100	100
N	146	62	223

Table 101 Jewish-"Private Individual" continuum: according to country of origin

	N. Africa	Yemen and Aden	Other M.E. countries
Jewish 1–3	67	71	57
Midpoint 4	14	21	13
"Private individual" 5–7	19	8	30
Total %	100	100	100
N	198	77	285

Table 102 Valence of Jewishness: according to countries of origin
"If you were to live abroad, would you wish to be born a Jew?"

	N. Africa			Yemen & Aden			Other M.E. countries		
	Religious	Traditionalist	Non-religious	Religious	Traditionalist	Non-religious	Religious	Traditionalist	Non-religious
1. Would wish to be born a Jew	81	65	43	85	50	-	83	57	32
2. Makes no difference	10	16	38	10	33	100	6	25	36
3. Would not wish to be born a Jew	9	19	19	5	17	-	11	18	32
Total %	100	100	100	100	100	100	100	100	100
N	68	57	21	48	12	2	47	123	53

Table 103 Jewish-"Private Individual" continuum: according to country of origin

		N. Africa			Yemen & Aden			Other M.E. countries		
		Religious	Traditionalist	Non-religious	Religious	Traditionalist	Non-religious	Religious	Traditionalist	Non-religious
Jewish	1–3	76	65	45	77	62	-	79	59	36
Midpoint	4	17	11	16	13	33	100	12	11	16
"Private Individual"	5–7	7	24	39	10	5	-	9	30	48
Total %		100	100	100	100	100	100	100	100	100
N		87	80	31	54	21	2	58	158	69

Table 105 Recency of Immigration and Valence of Jewishness
"If you were to live abroad, would you wish to be born a Jew?"

	All respondents		Local-born		Immigrated 1948–1953		Immigrated 1954–1965	
	Ash.	Orient.	Ash.	Orient.	Ash.	Orient.	Ash.	Orient.
Yes	47	63	39	59	62	64	45	64
It makes no difference	30	21	34	23	26	22	26	18
No	23	15	27	18	12	14	28	18
Total %	100	100	100	100	100	100	100	100
N	1289	523	652	138	406	258	231	127

Table 106 Recency of immigration and valence of Jewishness: Among religious categories in Ashkenazic sector
"If you were to live abroad, would you wish to be born a Jew?"

	Local-born			Immigrated 1948–1953			Immigrated 1954–1965		
	Religious	Traditionalist	Non-religious	Religious	Traditionalist	Non-religious	Religious	Traditionalist	Non-religious
Yes	90	58	36	81	56	44	96	51	32
It makes no difference	4	28	33	6	22	36	4	25	36
No	6	14	31	13	22	20	-	24	32
Total %	100	100	100	100	100	100	100	100	100
N	143	198	485	118	153	173	35	63	139

Table 107 Recency of immigration and valence of Jewishness: Among religious categories in Oriental sector
"If you were to live abroad, would you wish to be born a Jew?"

	Local			Immigrated 1948–1953			Immigrated 1954–1965		
	Religious	Traditionalist	Non-religious	Religious	Traditionalist	Non-religious	Religious	Traditionalist	Non-religious
Yes	95	56	41	88	54	44	74	62	59
It makes no difference	-	22	31	4	26	35	13	16	25
No	5	22	28	8	20	21	13	22	16
Total %	100	100	100	100	100	100	100	100	100
N	36	62	55	95	123	47	50	58	20

Table 109 A comparison between Yemenite local-born and immigrant students: Valence of Jewishness
"If you had to live abroad, would you wish to be born a Jew?"

	Local-born	Immigrants
Yes	70	79
It makes no difference	24	15
No	6	6
Total %	100	100
N	33	53

Table 110 A comparison between Yemenite local-born and immigrant students: Jewish-"Private Individual" scale

	Local-born	Immigrants
Jewish 1–3	60	75
Midpoint 4	17	15
Private Individual 5–7	23	10
Total %	100	100
N	42	68

Table 111 Religious composition of second-generation Israelis and their local-born parents (in percentages)

	Students (second-generation Israelis)	Parents
Religious	14	18
Traditionalist	33	40
Non-Religious	53	42
Total %	100	100
N	174	173

Table 112 Second-generation local-born and new immigrants: Valence of Jewishness
"If you were to be born all over again, would you wish to be born a Jew?"

	Second Generation local-born	New Immigrants
1. Yes	67	70
2. It makes no difference to me	32	28
3. No	1	2
Total %	100	100
N	173	173

Table 113 Local-born and immigrants: Valence of Jewishness (in life abroad)
"If you were to live abroad, would you wish to be born a Jew?"

	Second Generation local-born	New Immigrants
1. Yes	52	49
2. It makes no difference to me	20	20
3. No	28	31
Total %	100	100
N	132	132

Table 114 Local-born and immigrants: Valence of Israeliness
"If you were to be born all over again, would you wish to be born an Israeli?"

	Second Generation local-born	New Immigrants
1. Yes	88	76
2. It makes no difference to me	11	20
3. No	1	4
Total %	100	100
N	134	134

Table 115 Local-born and immigrants: Centrality of Jewishness
"Does the fact that you are Jewish play an important part in your life?"

	Second Generation local-born	New Immigrants
1. It plays a very important part	18	20
2. It plays an important part	40	52
3. It is of little importance	35	23
4. It plays no part	7	5
Total %	100	100
N	174	173

Table 116 Local-born and immigrants: Centrality of Israeliness
"Does the fact that you are an Israeli play an important part in your life?"

	Second Generation local-born	New Immigrants
1. It plays a very important part	39	43
2. It plays an important part	53	50
3. It is of little importance	6	5
4. It plays no part	2	2
Total %	100	100
N	174	174

Table 117 Local-born and immigrants: Overlap and Consonance
"When I feel more Jewish . . .

	Second Generation local-born	New Immigrants
1. I also feel more Israeli."	70	67
2. there is no relationship between my feeling Jewish and my feeling Israeli."	29	30
3. I feel less Israeli."	1	3
Total %	100	100
N	174	174

Table 118 Local-born and immigrants: Overlap and Consonance
"When I feel more Israeli . . .

	Second Generation local-born	New Immigrants
1. I also feel more Jewish."	66	65
2. there is no relationship between my feeling Israeli and my feeling Jewish."	32	30
3. I feel less Jewish."	2	5
Total %	100	100
N	174	174

Table 119 Local-born and immigrants: The Jewish-"Private Individual" continuum

	Second Generation local-born	New Immigrants
Jewish 1–3	35	48
Midpoint 4	21	14
Individual 5–7	44	38
Total %	100	100
N	174	174

Table 120 Local-born and immigrants: The Israeli-"Private Individual" continuum

	Second Generation local-born	New Immigrants
Israeli 1–3	56	61
Midpoint 4	24	18
Individual 5–7	20	21
Total %	100	100
N	172	172

Table 121 Local-born and immigrants: The Israeli-Jewish continuum

	Second Generation local-born	New Immigrants
Israeli 1–3	55	47
Midpoint 4	30	26
Jewish 5–7	15	27
Total %	100	100
N	172	174

Table 122 Local-born and immigrants: The extent of Anti-Semitism "Are non-Jews anti-Semites?"

	Second Generation local-born	New Immigrants
1. Yes, almost all	2	5
2. A large section	6	14
3. Some of them	53	61
4. Only a small section	39	20
Total %	100	100
N	127	127

Table 123 Local-born and immigrants: Causes of Anti-Semitism
"What, in your view, is the main cause of anti-Semitism?"

	Second Generation local-born	New Immigrants
1. The characteristics of the non-Jews	8	9
2. The situation of the Jews abroad as a minority	61	50
3. The characteristics of the Jews abroad	31	41
Total %	100	100
N	125	126

Table 130 Valence of Jewishness: Comparison between students from matched parent-student subsample and entire sample
"If you were to live abroad, would you wish to be born a Jew?"

	Religious		Traditionalist		Non-religious	
	All students	Matched Sample	All students	Matched Sample	All students	Matched Sample
Yes	85	80	71	62	35	35
It makes no difference	10	8	12	17	35	38
No	5	12	17	21	30	27
Total %	100	100	100	100	100	100
N	344	90	452	93	638	72

Table 131 Centrality of Jewishness: Comparison between students from matched parent-student subsample and entire sample
"Does the fact that you are Jewish play an important part in your life?"

	Religious		Traditionalist		Non-religious	
	All students	Matched Sample	All students	Matched Sample	All students	Matched Sample
Very important part	59	53	19	20	7	8
Important part	38	45	59	53	39	39
Little importance	2	-	18	20	42	43
No part	1	2	4	7	12	10
Total %	100	100	100	100	100	100
N	344	90	452	93	638	72

Table 132 Israeli-Jewish Continuum: Comparison between students from matched parent-student subsample and entire sample

		Religious		Traditionalist		Non-religious	
		All students	Matched Sample	All students	Matched Sample	All students	Matched Sample
Israeli	1–3	3	8	40	43	68	67
Midpoint	4	42	34	36	37	28	26
Jewish	5–7	55	58	24	20	4	7
Total %		100	100	100	100	100	100
N		344	90	452	93	638	72

Table 140 Valence of Jewishness (in life abroad): according to sex
"If you were to live abroad, would you wish to be born a Jew?"

	Religious		Traditionalist		Non-religious	
	M	F	M	F	M	F
Yes	86	83	56	58	39	37
It makes no difference to me	6	5	26	22	34	34
No	8	12	18	20	27	29
Total %	100	100	100	100	100	100
N	227	182	357	338	554	434

Table 141 Valence of Israeliness: according to sex
"If you were to be born again, would you wish to be born an Israeli?"

	Religious		Traditionalist		Non-religious	
	M	F	M	F	M	F
Yes	79	79	77	81	79	85
It makes no difference to me	17	17	20	15	19	14
No	4	4	3	4	2	1
Total %	100	100	100	100	100	100
N	227	182	357	338	554	434

Table 142 Jewish-"Private Individual" continuum: according to sex

		Religious		Traditionalist		Non-religious	
		M	F	M	F	M	F
Jew	1–3	84	71	48	43	32	30
Midpoint	4	10	18	30	19	24	16
"Private Individual"	5–7	6	11	22	38	44	54
Total %		100	100	100	100	100	100
N		298	377	485	450	757	598

Table 143 Israeli-"Private Individual" continuum: according to sex

		Religious		Traditionalist		Non-religious	
		M	F	M	F	M	F
Israeli	1–3	72	62	64	57	60	50
Midpoint	4	15	19	20	21	22	25
"Private Individual"	5–7	13	19	16	22	18	25
Total %		100	100	100	100	100	100
N		298	377	485	450	757	598

TABLES

Supplement B

The tables in this supplement relate to a substudy carried out in 1968 in seven schools in Jerusalem and Haifa. They are referred to but not inserted in the text of the study. In the reference in the text the letter B is suffixed to the number of each of these tables.

Table 1 Israelis as a continuity of the Jewish people
"In your opinion, are we in Israel

	All Respondents	Religious	Traditionalist	Non-Religious
1. a continuation of the Jewish people?"	72	94	67	56
2. a new people that has been formed here?"	22	6	26	34
3. a new people that will be formed here?"	6	0	7	10
Total %	100	100	100	100
N	245	83	63	99
Median	1.20	1.03	1.24	1.39

Table 2 State of Israel as a continuation of Jewish history
"In your opinion is the State of Israel a continuation of Jewish history?"

	All Respondents	Religious	Traditionalist	Non-Religious
1. Yes, of all periods.	54	63	55	46
2. Yes, only of the period when Jews lived here.	28	21	30	33
3. Yes, only of the period when Jews lived abroad.	2	1	3	1
4. No, it has opened a new page of history.	16	15	13	20
Total %	100	100	100	100
N	248	82	64	102
Median	1.42	1.29	1.41	1.62

Table 3 Negative aspects of Jewish behavior during the Holocaust

	All Respondents	Religious	Traditionalist	Non-Religious
1. Passivity: going as sheep to the slaughter	55	36	45	70
2. Collaboration with the Nazis	23	40	31	10
3. Blindness to reality (the danger of Nazism)	13	17	10	13
4. Lack of internal cooperation and cohesiveness	8	7	14	7
Total %	100	100	100	100
Total number of answers	142	42	29	71

Table 4 Positive aspects of Jewish behavior during the Holocaust

	All Respondents	Religious	Traditionalist	Non-Religious
1. Heroism and active opposition	59	43	67	73
2. Self-sacrifice for the sake of the group	3	2	11	1
3. Mutual help	5	6	3	5
4. Internal organization and cohesion	4	4	5	4
5. Passive resistance and maintenance of identity (*Kiddush Hashem*, facing death unflinchingly, faith in God, observance of *mitzvot* under stress, preservation of Jewishness)	29	45	14	17
Total %	100	100	100	100
Total number of answers	217	98	37	82

Table 5 Identification with suffering of Jews in Holocaust
"Do you identify with Jews who suffered in the Holocaust?"

	All Respondents	Ashkenazim	Orientals
1. Yes, to a large extent	46	47	38
2. Yes	39	37	44
3. Only to a slight extent	13	13	10
4. No	3	2	8
Total %	100	100	100
N	253	201	52
Median	1.61	1.57	1.76

Table 6 Identification with Jews who suffered from attacks in Islamic countries
"Do you identify with Jews who suffered from attacks in Islamic countries?"

	All Respondents	Ashkenazic	Oriental
1. To a large extent	30	26	43
2. Yes	38	38	37
3. Only to a slight extent	25	27	18
4. No	7	9	2
Total %	100	100	100
N	245	193	51
Median	2.04	2.14	1.68

Table 7 Possibility of repetition of Holocaust
"In your opinion can another Holocaust occur?"

	All Respondents
1. Yes, in all countries.	17
2. Yes, in most countries.	11
3. Yes, in some countries.	56
4. No, in no country.	16
Total %	100
N	250
Median	2.85

Table 8 Duty of Jews to see themselves as survivors of the Holocaust
"Do you agree with the statement 'Every Jew in the world should see himself as a survivor of the Holocaust?'"

	All Respondents	Religious	Traditionalist	Non-Religious	Ashkenazic	Oriental
1. I agree completely.	59	78	58	45	61	55
2. Only those from Europe.	11	9	9	14	12	6
3. Only those whose parents were there.	3	5	2	3	3	4
4. Only those who themselves suffered.	10	4	8	16	11	4
5. No, don't agree at all.	17	5	23	22	13	31
Total %	100	100	100	100	100	100
N	245	81	64	100	193	52
Median	1.34	1.14	1.36	1.86	1.37	1.41

Table 9 Definition of Zionism
"How do you define Zionism?"

	All Respondents
1. Actual *aliyah*	33
2. Desire to immigrate	18
3. Assistance in the up-building of Israel	8
4. Recognition of Israel as the homeland	22
5. Love of the Land of Israel	17
6. Other answers	2
Total %	100
Total number of answers	158

Table 10 Self-definition as a Zionist or Non-Zionist
"Do you see yourself as a Zionist?"

	All Respondents	Religious	Traditionalist	Non-religious
1. Yes	65	77	63	58
2. No	35	23	37	42
Total %	100	100	100	100
N	227	70	60	97
Median	1.27	1.15	1.29	1.37

Table 11 Closeness to American Jews (a) Willing (b) Unwilling to Immigrate

	Closeness to those willing to immigrate	Closeness to those unwilling to immigrate
1. Very close	38	1
2. Close	39	3
3. Moderately close	17	17
4. Slightly close	4	43
5. Not close at all	2	36
Total %	100	100
N	240	240
Median	1.82	4.18

Table 12 Possibility of Eradication of Anti-Semitism
"In your opinion, will it be possible to overcome anti-Semitism in the foreseeable future?"

	All Respondents
1. Yes, in all countries	16
2. Yes, in most countries	24
3. Yes, in some countries	13
4. No, in no country	47
Total %	100
N	239
Median	3.25

Table 13 Anti-Semitism and the Characteristics & Behavior of Jews
"Do the characteristics and behavior of the Jews contribute in any way to the spread of anti-Semitism?"

	All Respondents
1. Yes	80
2. No	20
Total %	100
N	235
Median	1.13

List of Tables

II. *In Supplement B*

Notes

Chapter 1

1. We are using the term "ethnic" in a broad sense similar to that in which it is employed by Klineberg in the following definition. "An ethnic group may be defined . . . as one which is set off from others by inherited physical type (or 'race'), by religion, language, or national origin, or any combination of these." O. Klineberg, "The multi-national society: some research problems," *Social Sciences Information* 6 (1967): 81–99. *Cf. also* J. Harding, H. Proshansky, and I. Chein, "Prejudice and Ethnic Relations," in *Handbook of Social Psychology,* ed. G. Lindzey (Cambridge, Mass.: Addison, Wesley, 1954), pp. 1021–1061.
2. Some studies of national character (when it is equated with modal personality structure, i.e., "the mode or modes of the distribution of personality variants within a given society") provide an initial basis for such analysis. For a review of such studies *see* A. Inkeles and D. J. Levinson, "National Character: The Study of Modal Personality and Sociocultural Systems" in *Handbook of Social Psychology,* ed. G. Lindzey, pp. 977–1020.
3. "Reinforcing national identity becomes even more important *after* independence. Independence revives the centrifugal tendencies which had been suppressed during the

struggle for independence. The claim of the new government to legitimacy is a rational-legal one, and this claim is as yet insecure. To reinforce the loyalty of the citizens, the governments feel the need to have recourse to tradition." I. Wallerstein, "The Search for National Identity in West Africa: The New History" in *Sociology and History,* ed. W. J. Cahnman and A. Boskoff (New York: Free Press, 1964), pp. 303–313.

4. *Cf.* K. W. Deutsch, "The Trend of European Nationalism— The Language Aspect" in *Readings in the Sociology of Language,* ed. J. A. Fishman (The Hague: Mouton, 1968), pp. 598–608.

5. Preface to N. Glazer and D. P. Moynihan, *Beyond the Melting Pot* (Cambridge, Mass.: M.I.T. Press, 1967).

6. Ibid., p. 314.

7. Thus, for example, the demand for Black studies has stimulated a demand for Jewish studies on the part of Jewish students.

8. For a discussion of the nature of the majority culture see M. Himmelfarb, "Secular Society? A Jewish Perspective," *Daedalus,* 96 (1967), 220–236. "The West has become secular—but not all that secular. From the perspective of Jewish experience and of contemporary Jewish reality, the Western secular society is Christian as well as secular— and that includes America," p. 230.

9. M. M. Gordon, *Assimilation in American Life* (New York: Oxford Univ. Press, 1964), S. Goldstein and C. Goldscheider, *Jewish Americans: Three Generations in a Jewish Community* (Englewood Cliffs, N.J.: Prentice Hall, 1968). *See also,* M. Sklare, "Assimilation and the Sociologists," *Commentary* 39 (May 1965), pp. 63–66.

10. M. L. Hansen, "The Third Generation in America." *Commentary* 14 (Nov. 1953), 492–500: W. Herberg, *Protestant-Catholic–Jew* (Anchor Books, 1960); B. Lazerwitz and L. Rowitz, "The Three-Generations Hypothesis," *Amer. J. of Sociol.* 49 (1964), 529–538; Goldstein and Goldscheider, *Jewish Americans.*

11. M. Sklare and J. Greenblum, *Jewish Identity on the Suburban Frontier* (N.Y.: Basic Books, 1967), p. 331.

12. I. Greenberg, "Jewish Survival and the College Campus," *Judaism* 17 (Summer 1968), 259–281.

13. Elie Wiesel, *The Jews of Silence* (N.Y.: Holt, Rinehart and Winston, 1967); L. Eliav, *Between Hammer and Sickle* (Philadelphia: Jewish Publication Society of America, 1967).

14. S. N. Herman, *American Students in Israel* (Ithaca, N.Y.: Cornell University Press) 1970.

15. For an example of a comparative approach to contemporary Jewish life, *see* M. Davis, "Centres of Jewry in the Western Hemisphere: A Comparative Approach," *The Jewish J. of Sociol.* 5 (1963), 4–26.

16. Sklare and Greenblum. New ground in the field of Jewish community studies is broken by *Jewish Identity on the Suburban Frontier,* which deals perceptively with problems of Jewish identity in a pluralistic society.

Chapter 2

1. D. R. Miller, "The Study of Social Relationships: Situation, Identity, and Social Interaction," *Psychology: A Study of a Science,* ed. S. Koch (N.Y.: McGraw-Hill, 1963), p. 674.

2. Ibid., p. 673.

3. R. C. Wylie, *The Self-Concept: A Critical Survey of Pertinent Research Literature* (Lincoln, Nebraska: Univ. of Nebraska Press, 1961), p. 3.

4. J. R. P. French, Jr., and J. Sherwood, "Self-actualization and Self-identity Theory," in J. R. P. French, Jr., *"Self-actualization and the Utilization of Talent"* (Cooperative Research Project No. E–066, Univ. of Michigan, 1963).

5. Miller, "The Study of Social Relationships . . . ,p. 673.

6. E. H. Erikson, *Childhood and Society* (N.Y.: Norton, 1950), p. 213.

7. E. H. Erikson, "The Problem of Ego Identity," in M. R. Stein et al., *Identity and Anxiety* (Glencoe, Ill.: Free Press, 1960), p. 38.

8. C. H. Stember et al., *Jews in the Mind of America* (New York: Basic Books, 1966), pp. 27–28.

9. For a study of Jewish-Gentile relationships in medieval and modern times *see* J. Katz, *Exclusiveness and Tolerance* (N.Y.: Schocken, 1962).

10. K. Lewin, *Field Theory in Social Science,* ed. D. Cartwright (N.Y.: Harper & Row, 1951), p. 148. *Cf. also,* D. T. Campbell, "Common Fate, Similarity and other indices of the status of aggregates of persons as social entities," *Behavioral Science,* 3 (1958), 14–25.

11. M. Deutsch, "A Theory of Cooperation and Competition," *Hum. Relat.* 2 (1949), 129–152.

12. *See* J. R. P. French Jr., and R. L. Kahn, eds., *J. Soc. Issues* 18 No. 3 (July, 1962);M. Rosenberg, *Society and the Adolescent Self-Image* (Princeton, N.J.: Princeton Univ. Press, 1965).

13. *See* "The Friendship Ties of the Lakeville Jew," in Sklare and Greenblum, *Jewish Identity on the Suburban Frontier* (N.Y.: Basic Books, 1967), p. 289. "Since it is an unresolved question whether the old pattern of prejudice and discrimination will occur in the future (it has already declined sharply), the Jewish clique may represent a residual form of Jewishness, a 'holding operation' preliminary to the assimilation of the individual—or of his offspring—into the majority community."

14. E. H. Erikson, "The Problem of Ego Identity," p. 38. *See also* idem, "The Concept of Identity in Race Relations. Notes and Queries" in *The Negro American,* ed. T. Parsons and K. B. Clark (Boston: Beacon Press, 1965), p. 243. ". . . identity also contains a complementarity of past and future both in the individual and in society; it links the actuality of a living past with that of a promising future."

15. For examples of such studies, *see* Erikson, "Growth and Crises of the Healthy Personality," in *Personality in Nature, Culture and Society,* ed. C. Kluckhohn and H. R. Murray (N.Y.: Knopf, 1953), p. 185–225; R. Kastenbaum, ed., *New Thoughts on Old Age* (N.Y.: Springer, 1964); Lewin, *Field Theory in Social Science,* pp. 140–142.

16. *Cf.* Kurt Lewin's comparison between the morale and time perspective of the Zionists and of other Jews in Hitlerist Germany. "For decades they (the Zionists) had tried to study their own sociological problems realistically, advo-

cating and promoting a program that looked far ahead. In other words, they had a time perspective which included a psychological past of surviving adverse conditions for thousands of years and a meaningful and inspiring goal for the future. As a result of such a time perspective this group showed high morale—despite a present which was judged by them to be no less foreboding than by others." K. Lewin, *Resolving Social Conflicts,* ed. Gertrud Lewin (N.Y.: Harper, 1948), p. 104.

17. Yonina Talmon, "Pursuit of the Millenium: The Relation between Religious and Social Change," *European J. of Sociol.* 3 (1962), 125–148.
18. Lewin, *Resolving Social Conflicts,* pp. 103–124.
19. R. Kastenbaum, "The Structure and Function of Time Perspective," *J. of Psychological Researches* 8 (1964), 1–11.
20. S. M. Lipset, "The Study of Jewish Communities in a Comparative Context," *The Jewish J. of Sociol.* 5 (1963), 157–166.
21. K. Lewin, *Field Theory in Social Science,* pp. 267–272.
22. R. G. Barker et al., "Adjustment to Physical Handicap and Illness: A Survey of the Social Psychology of Physique and Disability," *Soc. Sc. Research Council, N.Y., Bulletin 55* (1953), pp. 37–46.
23. By "life space" is meant the totality of facts determining the behavior of a person at a given moment. The reference is to the psychological environment,i.e., the environment as it exists for the person. The psychological environment is composed of "regions" surrounded by boundaries. For a systematic review of the concepts of Lewinian field theory, *see* D. Cartwright, "Lewinian Theory as a Contemporary Systematic Framework," in *Psychology: A Study of a Science,* ed. S. Koch, Vol. 2, 7–91. *See also* M. Deutsch, "Field Theory in Social Psychology," in *Handbook of Social Psychology,* ed. G. Lindzey, pp. 181–222.
24. Barker, pp. 39–40.
25. Lewin, *Resolving Social Conflicts,* p. 20.
26. Lewin, *Field Theory in Social Science,* p. 123.
27. For a fuller discussion of salience, *see* S. N. Herman and E. O. Schild, "Ethnic Role Conflict in a Cross-Cultural Situation," *Human Relations* 13 (1960), 215–228. It should be noted that Miller, "The Study of Social Relationships

..., p. 681, uses the term "salience" in a different sense from that which we adopt here.

28. H. H. Kelley, "Salience of Membership and Resistance to Change of Group-anchored Attitudes," *Hum. Relat.* 8 (1955), 275–289; W. W. Charters and T. M. Newcomb, "Some Attitudinal Effects of Experimentally Increased Salience of a Membership Group" in *Readings in Social Psychology,* 3rd ed., ed. E. E. Maccoby, T. M. Newcomb and E. L. Hartley (New York: Holt, Rinehart & Winston, 1958), pp. 276–281; W. E. Lambert et al., "The Effect of Increased Salience of a Membership Group on Pain Tolerance," *Journal of Personality* 18 (1969), 350–357.

29. For a given milieu a certain pattern of behavior is perceived as fitting. The milieu together with the pattern of behavior perceived as fitting has been termed a "behavior setting": R. G. Barker and H. F. Wright, *Midwest and its children: the Psychological Ecology of an American Town* (Evanston, Ill.: Row, Peterson, 1954), pp. 7–10.

30. T. M. Newcomb, R. H. Turner and P. E. Converse, *Social Psychology* (N.Y.: Holt, Rinehart and Winston, 1965), p. 59.

31. K. Lewin, *A Dynamic Theory of Personality* (N.Y.: McGraw-Hill, 1935), p. 51.

32. Lewin, *Field Theory in Social Science,* p. 270.

33. Barker et al., *Adjustment to Physical Handicap and Illness,* pp. 39–42.

34. Herman and Schild, "Ethnic Role Conflict . . . ."

35. Kelley, "Salience of Membership. . . . "

36. For details of the composition of the sample and the methods of the study, see Appendix 1.

Chapter 3

1. *Ariel* (A Quarterly Review of the Arts and Sciences in Israel) 17 (1966), 5–6.

2. An eloquent exponent of this theme is Israel's President Shazar. Israel's obligation to concern itself with the welfare of Jewish communities dispersed in distant lands was emphasized by him in his address to the Knesset on the occasion of his first inauguration as President of the State.

3. Georges Friedmann, *The End of the Jewish People?* (Garden City, L.I.: Doubleday, 1967), p. 238.
4. Melford Spiro, *Children of the Kibbutz* (Cambridge, Mass.: Harvard Univ. Press, 1958), p. 388.
5. *Molad* 2, no. 10 (1949), 226–229.
6. The program for the inculcation of "Jewish consciousness" *(toda'ah yehudit)* has been further extended in recent years. Among the additions is a course dealing with events in Jewish life in the last hundred years.
7. The prosecutor, Gideon Hausner, began his address with the words: "When I stand before you here, Judges of Israel, I am not standing alone. With me are six million accusers . . ."
8. Friedmann, *The End of the Jewish People?*, p. 120.
9. For such historical reviews, *see* B. Halpern, *The Idea of the Jewish State* (Cambridge, Mass.: Harvard Univ. Press, 1961); A. Hertzberg, ed., *The Zionist Idea: A Historical Analysis and Reader* (Philadelphia: Jewish Publishing Society of America, 1959), particularly the Introduction, pp. 15–100; I. Kolatt, "Theories on Israel Nationalism," in *In the Dispersion* (Jerusalem: World Zionist Organization, 1967), Vol. 7, pp. 13–50. For a review of the ideological background to discussions of Israeli-Jewish identity, *see also* R. Cahane, "Patterns of National Identity in Israel," in S. N. Eisenstadt et al., *Readings in Education and Society in Israel* (Jerusalem: Akedemon, 1968), in Hebrew.
10. For a discussion of the various *aliyot* (immigration waves), *see* S. N. Eisenstadt, *Israeli Society* (London: Weidenfeld and Nicolson, 1967), pp. 7–33.
11. For examples of the extension of the "collective pioneering image," *see* Eisenstadt, *Israeli Society,* p. 390.

Chapter 4

1. The position is different with Israeli Arabs in whose case there is a strict compartmentalization between "being Arab" and "being Israeli." S. N. Eisenstadt and Y. Peres, "Some Problems of Educating a National Minority," mimeographed research report, U.S. Office of Education Project No. E-6-21-013.

2. S. N. Herman, *American Students in Israel* (Ithaca, N.Y.: Cornell University Press, 1970).
3. Sklare and Greenblum, *Jewish Identity on the Suburban Frontier;* I. Chein, "The Problem of Jewish Identification," *J. of Soc. Studies* 17 (1955), 219–222; *cf.* I. L. Child, *Italian or American? The Second Generation in Conflict* (New Haven, Conn.: Yale Univ. Press, 1943).
4. I. Chein, "The Problem of Jewish Identification," p. 220.
5. E. H. Erikson, *Insight and Responsibility* (New York: Norton, 1962), p. 92.

Chapter 5

1. S. N. Herman, *American Students in Israel* (Ithaca, N.Y.: Cornell University Press, 1970).

Chapter 6

1. *The Government Legal Adviser v. Adolf Eichmann* (Jerusalem: Government Printer, 1962), pp. 38–46.
2. S. N. Herman, Y. Peres and E. Yuchtman, "Reactions to the Eichmann Trial in Israel: A Study in High Involvement," *Scripta Hierosolymitana* 14 (1965), 98–118. In a further substudy we also found an association ($\gamma = .33$) between consciousness of being in the position of a survivor and valence of Jewishness.
3. *See* M. Weinreich, "Yidishkayt and Yiddish: On the Impact of Religion on Language in Ashkenazic Jewry" in J. A. Fishman, *Readings in the Sociology of Language* (The Hague: Mouton, 1968), pp. 382–413.
4. S. N. Herman, "Explorations in the Social Psychology of Language Choice," *Hum. Relat.,* 14 (1961), 149–164.
5. An unpublished M.A. dissertation by Uri Farago in the Department of Sociology, Hebrew University of Jerusalem.
6. M. Sklare, "Intermarriage and the Jewish Future," *Commentary* 37 (1964), 46–52; M. Davis, "Mixed Marriage in Western Jewry: Historical Background to the Jewish Response," *Jewish Journal of Sociology* 10 (1968), 177–220.

Davis uses the term *out-marriage* to cover both inter-marriage and mixed marriage. He differentiates between these two terms. *Mixed marriage* is defined as "marriage between a Jew and a non-Jew in which neither partner renounces his religious faith" whereas in *intermarriage* "one of the partners adopts the faith of the other before marriage in attempt to achieve a religious unity in the family."

Chapter 7

1. B. Litvin and S. B. Hoenig, *Jewish Identity: Modern Response and Opinions on the Registration of Children of Mixed Marriages* (N.Y.: Feldheim, 1965).
2. Ibid.
3. "Judgment in the High Court Application of *Oswald Rufeisen v. The Minister of the Interior*" (Jerusalem: Ministry of Justice, 1963.)
4. Ibid., pp. 13–18. The wide interpretation given by Justice Silberg to the circumstances in which a convert to another religion would still be regarded as a Jew under religious law has been questioned by some authorities.
5. Ibid., p. 18.
6. Ibid., p. 20.
7. Ibid., p. 46. For a review of another issue in regard to which the question of "who is a Jew" became pertinent—the discussions around the status of *Benei Israel,* a Jewish group from India, *see* S. N. Eisenstadt, *Israeli Society* (London: Weidenfeld and Nicolson, 1967), pp. 312–314.
8. *Cf.* "The Image of the Good Jew in Lakeville" in M. Sklare and J. Greenblum, *Jewish Identity on the Suburban Frontier* (New York: Basic Books, 1967), Ch. 10.
9. R. K. Merton, *Social Theory and Social Structure* (New York: Free Press, 1957), p. 314.

Chapter 8

1. An unpublished study by the author of this volume.

Chapter 9

1. This is an illustration of the pervasive influence of a value-system. M. Rokeach has, in our view, rightly stressed the need for greater attention by social psychologists to the study of values. *See* his paper "A Theory of Organization and Change within Value and Attitude Systems," *Journal of Social Issues* 24 (1968), 13–33. For an empirically-based study of the religious factor, *see* G. Lenski, *The Religious Factor: A Sociologist's Inquiry* (N.Y.: Doubleday, 1963).
2. The reference is to the relative homogeneity in the value system of the religious students in this study who attend the state schools and belong to what is known as the "national-religious" sector of the population. This does not include students from religious groups, such as Agudath Israel, who maintain independent schools (see Appendix I). Marked differences are likely to be found between the religious students in our study and the other religious groupings, particularly on Israeli issues.
3. *See* "Jewish Ethnicism" in S. W. Baron, *Modern Nationalism and Religion* (Jewish Publication Society of America, 1960), Chapter VII; B. Halpern, *The Idea of the Jewish State* (Cambridge, Mass.: Harvard Univ. Press, 1961), pp. 16–18.

Chapter 10

1. For an analysis of the composition of the *aliyot, see* J. Matras, *Social Change in Israel* (Chicago: Aldine, 1965).
2. *See* the statement by the then Minister of Education (Z. Aranne) in S. N. Eisenstadt et al: *Readings on Education and Society in Israel* (Jerusalem: Akedemon, 1968), pp. 121–130. For a critical analysis, with constructive suggestions, *see* H. Adler, ibid., pp. 215–225.
3. Y. Peres, "Ethnic Identity and Relations among Ethnic Groups in Israel" in S. N. Herman, J. E. Hofeman and Y. Peres, *The Identity and Cultural Values of High School Pupils in Israel* (Washington, D.C.: U.S. Office of Education), Cooperative Research Project OE-4-21-013.

4. We have limited ourselves to a few general statements as a necessary background to the discussion which follows on communal differences in respect to Jewish identity. For the broader aspects *see* C. Frankenstein, ed., *Between Past and Present* (Jerusalem: Henrietta Szold Foundation, 1953); S. N. Eisenstadt, *Israeli Society* (London: Weidenfeld and Nicolson, 1967); A. Weingrod, *Israel: Group Relations in a New Society* (London: Pall Mall, 1965); Y. Peres, "Ethnic Identity and Relations among Ethnic Groups in Israel" in S. N. Herman, et al., *The Identity and Cultural Values of High School Pupils in Israel.*

5. *See* S. N. Eisenstadt, *The Absorption of Immigrants* (London: Routledge and Kegan Paul, 1957); J. Shuval, *Immigrants on the Threshold* (N.Y.: Atherton, 1963).

6. *Cf.* E. Katz and A. Zloczower, "Ethnic Continuity in an Israeli Town," *Hum. Relat.* 14 (1961), 293–327.

Chapter 11

1. P. Jacob, *Changing Values in College* (New York: Harper & Row, 1957); J. Coleman, *The Adolescent Society* (New York: Free Press, 1961).

2. K. Lewin, *Resolving Social Conflicts,* ed. Gertrud Lewin (New York: Harper & Row, 1948), p. 4.

3. S. N. Herman, "The Attitudes of Israeli Youth to their Jewishness and to Jews Abroad," mimeographed (Jerusalem: 1967), Ch. VI.

4. For the tables, ibid.

5. Ibid.

Chapter 13

1. S. W. Baron, *Modern Nationalism and Religion* (Philadelphia, Penna.: Jewish Pubn. Soc. of Amer., 1960); B. Halpern, *The Idea of the Jewish State* (Cambridge, Mass.: Harvard Univ. Press, 1961).

2. M. Sklare and J. Greenblum, *Jewish Identity on the Suburban Frontier* (New York: Basic Books, 1967); *cf. also,* N.

Glazer, *American Judaism* (Chicago, Ill.: Univ. of Chicago Press, 1957).

3. J. Zellermayer: "The psychosocial effect of the Eichmann trial on Israeli society," *Psychiatry Digest* (Nov. 1968), 13–23.

4. *See* Samuel Gringauz, "Jewish Destiny As the DP's See It: The Ideology of the Surviving Remnant" in Nahum G. Glatzer, ed., *The Dynamics of Emancipation: The Jew in the Modern Age* (Boston: Beacon Press, 1965), pp. 127–137. "Nothing must permit Hitler a final triumph by the destruction of the Jews through the circumstances of the post-war world or through inner disintegration. Judaism, as a nation and a collectivity, must be preserved despite all its enemies, and shall emerge from the great catastrophe healthier and morally purified, shall experience a new renaissance and shall lead a normal life on its own soil," p. 129.

5. S. N. Herman, *American Students in Israel* (Ithaca, N.Y.: Cornell Univ, Press, 1970).

6. For the viewpoint of a leading Israeli thinker, himself a traditionally observant Jew, *see* E. E. Urbach, *On Judaism and Education* (Jerusalem: Hebrew University School of Education and The Ministry of Education, 1967), pp. 26–28 (in Hebrew).

7. G. W. Allport, *The Nature of Prejudice* (Cambridge, Mass.: Addison-Wesley, 1954).

8. K. Lewin, *Resolving Social Conflicts,* ed. Gertrud Lewin (New York: Harper & Row, 1948), pp. 186–200.

9. *Cf.* C. Wagley and M. Harris, *Minorities in the New World* (New York: Columbia Univ. Press, 1958), pp. 229–230.

10. *See* Yeheskiel Kaufman, "Anti-Semitic Stereotypes in Zionism," *Commentary* 7 (1949), 239–245. Among the writers exemplifying the view are Berdichevski and Brenner.

Chapter 14

1. A. Shapiro, ed., *Si'ach Lochamim (The Warriors Talk),* (Tel Aviv, Federation of Kibbutz Movements, 1968) in Hebrew. Discussions with members of Kibbutzim who fought in the Six Day War. An insightful analysis of the

interviews in the book is provided by Zvi Zinger, "The Iron in the Rock," *Jerusalem Post* (April 12, 1968).
2. Ibid.
3. Ibid.
4. Ibid.
5. S. N. Herman, *American Students in Israel* (Ithaca, N.Y.: Cornell Univ. Press, 1970).
6. A. Shapiro, *Si'ach Lochamim.*
7. Ibid.
8. *In the Dispersion* Vol. 7 (1967): 10.
9. M. Tsur et al., *Among Young People: Talks in the Kibbutz* (Tel Aviv: Am Oved, 1969), [in Hebrew]; Zvi Zinger, "An Israeli Dilemma: Tradition and/or Faith," *Jerusalem Post* (Sept. 12, 1969). *See also* numerous articles in journals such as *Shdemot* and *Petahim.*
10. Prognostications by officials of the Jewish Agency suggest that there will be further increase in the volume of immigration in 1970.
11. S. N. Herman, "American Jewish Students in Israel," *Jewish Soc. Studies,* 24 (1962), 3–29, at p. 16.

Appendix I

1. S. N. Herman, *American Students in Israel* (Ithaca, N.Y.: Cornell Univ. Press, 1970).
2. L. A. Goodman and W. H. Kruksal, "Measures of Association for Cross Classification," *J. of Amer. Statistical Assoc.* 49 (1954): 732–764.

Appendix II

1. The study in the agricultural school was carried out by John Hofman and Itai Zak, reported in an unpublished manuscript. One aspect of this study is discussed in "Interpersonal Contact and Attitude Change in a Cross-cultural Situation," by Hofman and Zak, *Journal of Social Psychology* 78 (1969): 165–171.
2. Ibid., pp. 115–116.

Glossary of Hebrew Terms

aliyah—(literally, "ascent") immigration to Israel

avodah—labor

bar mitzvah—religious celebration of the thirteenth birthday by a boy at which time he is initiated into full religious duties

dati (pl. *dati'im*)—religiously observant

derech eretz—courtesy, respect

Eretz Israel—Land of Israel

Galuth, Golah—Exile

garin—nucleus of agricultural settlement group

Gemara—record of the discussions of Jewish law in the Rabbinical academies; a part of the tracts of Jewish law comprising the *Talmud*

goy (pl. *goyim*)—gentile

Haftorah—a chapter from the Prophets read in the synagogue after the portion from the Pentateuch

Haganah—(literally, "defense") Jewish defense organization before the establishment of the State of Israel

halacha—Jewish religious law

Hanukah—Festival of Lights commemorating the victory of the Maccabees

Hashomer—(literally, "The Watchman") a defense organization in the early days of Jewish settlement

heder—an elementary religious school

Kabbalat Shabbat—(literally, "the reception of the Sabbath") ceremony on Friday evening welcoming the incoming of the *Shabbat*

kashrut—dietary laws

kibbutz (pl. *kibbutzim*)—collective settlement

kibbutz galuyot—(literally, "in-gathering of the exiles") in-gathering of Jews from the Diaspora

Kiddush—(literally, "sanctification") blessing over wine or bread *(halah)* on Sabbath and festivals

Kiddush Ha-Shem—sanctification of God's name, martyrdom

kipah—skull-cap worn by observant Jews

lo-dati (pl. *lo-dati'im*)—non-observant

madrich—counselor

matzah (pl., *matzot*)—unleavened bread for Passover

melah—Jewish ghetto in North Africa

mizug hagaluyoth—(literally, "integration of the exiles") integration of Jews coming to Israel from various countries of the Diaspora

mitzvah (pl., *mitzvot*)—religious obligation, commandment

moshav ovdim—smallholders' settlement

m'sorati (pl., *m'sorati'im*)—traditionalist

Nachal—a group combining military service with work in an agricultural settlement

oleh (pl., *olim*)—immigrants

olim chadashim—new immigrants

Rosh Hashana—New Year

Rosh Yeshiva—head of religious academy

sabras—(from *tsabar*) local-born Israelis

Seder—the ceremonial meal on the first night of Passover (first two nights outside of Israel)

shtetl—(from the Yiddish) Jewish village in Eastern Europe

Simchat Torah—the Festival of the Rejoicing of the Law (on completion of the reading each year of the Pentateuch)

Succah—a booth erected for *Succot,* the Festival of Tabernacles commemorating the wanderings of the children of Israel in the desert

Tanach—Bible

tephillin—phylacteries

Tisha Be'av—ninth day of the month of Av, commemorating the destruction of the Temple

toda'ah yehudit—Jewish consciousness

Torah—Pentateuch, also used more broadly to refer to the teachings of Judaism

Tsofim—Scouts
yerida—(literally, "descent") emigration from Israel
yeshiva—religious academy
yeshiva gedola—advanced Rabbinical academy
yeshiva tichonit—a religious secondary school
Yidishkayt—(from the Yiddish) Jewishness
Yishuv—the Jewish community in Israel
Yom Ha'atzmaut—Independence Day
Yom Kippur—Day of Atonement
yored (pl. *yordim*)—an emigrant from Israel
zemirot—Sabbath and Festival songs (hymns)

Bibliography

Agnon, S. Y. "Address at Nobel Prize Award Ceremony," *Ariel (A Quarterly Review of the Arts and Sciences in Israel),* XVII (1966), 5–6.

Allport, G. W. *The Nature of Prejudice.* Cambridge, Mass.: Addison-Wesley, 1954.

Barker, R. G., *et al.* "Adjustment to Physical Handicap and Illness: A Survey of the Social Psychology of Physique and Disability," *Social Science Research Council Bulletin,* LV (1953), 37–46.

————, and Wright, H. F. *Midwest and Its Children: The Psychological Ecology of an American Town.* Evanston, Ill.: Row, Peterson, 1954.

Baron, S. W. *Modern Nationalism and Religion.* Philadelphia: Jewish Publication Society of America, 1960.

Cahane, R. "Patterns of National Identity in Israel," *Readings in Education and Society in Israel,* ed. S. N. Eisenstadt, *et al.* Jerusalem: Akedemon, 1968. [In Hebrew]

Campbell, D. T. "Common Fate, Similarity and Other Indices of the Status of Aggregates of Persons as Social Entities," *Behavioral Science,* III (1958), 14–25.

Cartwright, D. R. "Lewinian Theory as a Contemporary Systematic framework," *Psychology: A Study of a Science,* ed. S. Koch. II, 7–91.

Charters, W. W., and Newcomb, T. M. "Some Attitudinal Effects of Experimentally Increased Salience of a Membership

Group, *Readings in Social Psychology,* ed. E. E. Maccoby, T. M. Newcomb, and E. L. Hartley. pp. 276–81. 3rd edn. New York: Holt, Rinehart and Winston, 1958.

Chein, I. "The Problem of Jewish Identification," *Journal of Social Studies,* XVII (1955), 219–22.

Child, I. L. *Italian or American? The Second Generation in Conflict.* New Haven: Yale University Press, 1943.

Coleman, J. *The Adolescent Society.* New York: Free Press of Glencoe, 1961.

Davis, M. "Centres of Jewry in the Western Hemisphere: A Comparative Approach," *Jewish Journal of Sociology,* V (1963), 4–26.

———. "Mixed Marriage in Western Jewry: Historical Background to the Jewish Response," *Jewish Journal of Sociology,* X (1968), 177–220.

Deutch, K. W. "The Trend of European Nationalism: The Language Aspect," *Readings in the Sociology of Language,* ed. J. A. Fishman, pp. 598–608. The Hague: Mouton, 1968.

Deutsch, M. "A Theory of Cooperation and Competition," *Human Relations,* II (1949), 129–52.

———. "Field Theory in Social Psychology," *Handbook of Social Psychology,* ed. G. Lindzey, I, 181–222. Cambridge, Mass.: Addison-Wesley, 1954.

Eisenstadt, S. N. *Israeli Society.* London: Weidenfeld and Nicolson, 1967.

———. *The Absorption of Immigrants.* London: Routledge and Kegan Paul, 1957.

———., and Peres, Y. "Some Problems of Educating a National Minority." Washington, D.C.: U.S. Office of Education Project No. E-6-21-013, 1968.

Eliav, L. *Between Hammer and Sickle.* Philadelphia: Jewish Publication Society of America, 1967.

Erikson, E. H. *Childhood and Society.* New York: Norton, 1950.

———. "Growth and Crises of the Healthy Personality," *Personality in Nature, Culture and Society,* ed. C. Kluckhohn and H. R. Murray. New York: Knopf, 1953.

———. *Insight and Responsibility.* New York: Norton, 1962.

———. "The Concept of Identity in Race Relations. Notes and Queries," *The Negro American,* ed. T. Parsons and K. B. Clark, pp. 227–53. Boston: Beacon Press: The Daedalus Library, 1965.

_____. "The Problem of Ego Identity," *Identity and Anxiety,* ed. M. R. Stein, *et al.* Glencoe, Ill.: Free Press of Glencoe, 1960.

Frankenstein, C., ed. *Between Past and Present.* Jerusalem: Henrietta Szold Foundation, 1953.

French, J. R. P., and Kahn, R. L. "A Programmatic Approach to Studying the Industrial Environment and Mental Health," XVIII (1962), 1–47.

French, J. R. P., and Sherwood, J. "Self-Actualization and Self-Identity Theory," *Self-Actualization and the Utilization of Talent,* ed. J. R. P. French, Jr. Ann Arbor, Mich.: University of Michigan Cooperative Research Project No. E–068, 1963.

Friedmann, G. *The End of the Jewish People?* New York: Doubleday, 1967.

Glazer, N. *American Judaism.* Chicago, Ill.: University of Chicago Press, 1957.

_____, and Moynihan, D. P. *Beyond the Melting Pot.* Cambridge, Mass.: M.I.T. Press, 1967.

Goldstein, S., and Goldscheider, C. *Jewish Americans: Three Generations in a Jewish Community.* Englewood Cliffs, N.J.: Prentice-Hall, 1968.

Goodman, L. A., and Kruksal, W. H. "Measures of Association for Cross Classification," *Journal of American Statistical Association,* XLVII (1954), 732–64.

Gordon, M. M. *Assimilation in American Life.* London and New York: Oxford University Press, 1964.

Greenberg, I. "Jewish Survival and the College Campus," *Judaism,* XVII (1968), 259–81.

Gringauz, S. "Jewish Destiny as the DP's See It," *The Dynamics of Emancipation: The Jew in the Modern Age,* ed. N. G. Glatzer, pp. 127–37. Boston: Beacon Press, 1965.

Halpern, B. *The Idea of the Jewish State.* Cambridge, Mass.: Harvard University Press, 1961.

Hansen, M. L. "The Third Generation in America," *Commentary,* XIV (1953), 492–500.

Harding, J., Proshansky, H., and Chein, I. "Prejudice and Ethnic Relations," *Handbook of Social Psychology,* ed. G. Lindzey, pp. 1021–61. Cambridge, Mass.: Addison-Wesley, 1954.

Herberg, W. *Protestant-Catholic-Jew.* New York: Anchor Books, 1960.

Herman, S. N. "American Jewish Students in Israel," *Journal of Social Studies,* XXIV (1962), 3–29.

———. *American Students in Israel.* Ithaca, New York: Cornell University Press, 1970.

———. "Explorations in the Social Psychology of Language Choice," *Human Relations,* XIV (1961), 149–64.

———. "The Attitude of Israeli Youth to their Jewishness and to Jews Abroad." Research Report, Jerusalem, 1967. Mimeographed.

———. Peres, Y., and Yuchtman, E. "Reactions to the Eichmann Trial in Israel: A Study in High Involvement," *Scripta Hierosolymitana,* XIV (1965), 98–118.

Hertzberg, A., ed. *The Zionist Idea: A Historical Analysis and Reader.* Philadelphia: Jewish Publication Society of America, 1959.

Himmelfarb, M. "Secular Society? A Jewish Perspective," *Daedalus,* XCVI (1967), 220–36.

Hofman, J. E., and Zak, I. "Interpersonal Contact and Attitude Change in a Cross-Cultural Situation," *Journal of Social Psychology,* LXXVIII (1969), 165–71.

Inkeles, A., and Levinson, D. J. "National Character: The Study of Modal Personality and Socio-Cultural Systems," *Handbook of Social Psychology,* ed. G. Lindzey, pp. 977–1020. Cambridge, Mass.: Addison-Wesley, 1954.

Jacob, P. *Changing Values in College.* New York: Harper and Row, 1957.

Judgement in the Case of the Government Legal Adviser vs. Adolf Eichmann. Jerusalem: Government Printer, 1962.

Judgement in the High Court Application of Oswald Rufeisen vs. The Minister of the Interior. Jerusalem: Ministry of Justice, 1963.

Kastenbaum, R., ed. *New Thoughts on Old Age.* New York: Springer, 1964.

———. "The Structure and Function of Time Perspective," *Journal of Psychological Researches,* VIII (1964), 1–11.

Katz, E., and Zloczower, A. "Ethnic Continuity in an Israeli Town," *Human Relations,* XIV (1961), 293–327.

Katz, J. *Exclusiveness and Tolerance.* New York: Schocken, 1962.

Kaufman, Y. "Anti-Semitic Stereotypes in Zionism," *Commentary,* VII (1949), 239–45.

Kaznelson, B. "Youth and Jewish Fate," *Molad,* X (1949), 226–29. [In Hebrew]

Kelley, H. H. "Salience of Membership and Resistance to Change of Group-Anchored Attitudes," *Human Relations,* VIII (1955), 275–89.

Klineberg, O. "The Multi-National Society: Some Research Problems," *Social Sciences Information,* VI (1967), 81–99.

————, and Zavalloni, M. *Nationalism and Tribalism Among West African Students.* Paris: Mouton, 1969.

Kolatt, I. "Theories on Israeli Nationalism," *In the Dispersion,* VII (1967), 13–50.

Lambert, W. E. "The Effect of Increased Salience of a Membership Group on Pain Toleration," *Journal of Personality,* XVIII (1969), 350–57.

Lazerwitz, B., and Rowitz, L. "The Three-Generations Hypothesis," *American Journal of Sociology,* IL (1964), 529–38.

Lenski, G. *The Religious Factor: A Sociologist's Enquiry.* New York: Doubleday, 1963.

Lewin, K. *A Dynamic Theory of Personality.* New York: McGraw-Hill, 1935.

————. *Field Theory in Social Science,* ed. D. Cartwright. New York: Harper, 1951.

————. *Resolving Social Conflicts,* ed. Gertrud Lewin, New York: Harper, 1948.

Lipset, S. M. "The Study of Jewish Communities in a Comparative Context," *Jewish Journal of Sociology,* V (1963), 157–66.

Litvin, B. *Jewish Identity: Modern Responsa and Opinions on the Registration of Children of Mixed Marriages,* ed. S. B. Hoenig. New York: Feldheim, 1965.

Matras, J. *Social Change in Israel.* Chicago: Aldine, 1965.

Merton, R. K. *Social Theory and Social Structure.* New York: Free Press of Glencoe, 1957.

Miller, D. R. "The Study of Social Relationships: Situation, Identity and Social Interaction," *Psychology: A Study of a Science,* ed. S. Koch, V, 639–738. New York: McGraw-Hill, 1963.

Newcomb, T. M., Turner, R. H., and Converse, P. E. *Social Psychology.* New York: Holt, Rinehart and Winston, 1965.

Peres, Y. "Ethnic Identity and Relations Among Ethnic Groups in Israel," *The Identity and Cultural Values of High School Pupils in Israel,* ed. S. N. Herman, J. E. Hofman, and Y.

Peres. Washington, D.C.: U.S. Office of Education Cooperative Research Project OE–4–21–013.

Rabin, Y. "Address at a Hebrew University Graduation Ceremony," *In the Dispersion,* VII (1967), 9–12.

Rokeach, M. "A Theory of Organization and Change within Value and Attitude Systems." *Journal of Social Issues,* XXIV (1968), 13–33.

Rosenberg, M. *Society and the Adolescent Self-Image.* Princeton, New Jersey: Princeton University Press, 1965.

Shapiro A., ed. *Si'ach Lochamim* [The Warriors Talk]. Tel Aviv, Federation of Kibbutz Movements, 1968.

Shuval, J. *Immigrants on the Threshold.* New York: Atherton, 1963.

Sklare, M. "Assimilation and the Sociologists," *Commentary,* May 1965, pp. 63–66.

————. "Intermarriage and the Jewish Future," *Commentary,* 1964, pp. 46–52.

————, and Greenblum, J. *Jewish Identity on the Suburban Frontier.* New York: Basic Books, 1967.

Spiro, M. *Children of the Kibbutz.* Cambridge, Mass.: Harvard University Press, 1958.

Stember. C. H., *et al. Jews in the Mind of America.* New York: Basic Books, 1966.

Talmon, Y. "Pursuit of the Millennium: The Relation Between Religion and Social Change," *European Journal of Sociology,* III (1962), 125–48.

Tsur, M., *et al. Among Young People: Talks in the Kibbutz.* Tel Aviv: Am Oved, 1969. [In Hebrew]

Urbach, E. E. *On Judaism and Education.* Jerusalem: Hebrew University School of Education and the Ministry of Education, 1967. [In Hebrew]

Wagley, C., and Harris, M. *Minorities in the New World.* New York: Columbia University Press, 1958.

Wallerstein, I. "The Search for National Identity in West Africa: The New History," *Sociology and History,* ed. W. J. Cahnman and A. Boskoff, pp. 303–13. New York: Free Press of Glencoe, 1964.

Weingrod, A. *Israel: Group Relations in a New Society.* London: Pall Mall, 1965.

Weinreich, M. "Yidiskayt and Yiddish: On the Impact of Religion on Language in Ashkenazic Jewry," *Readings in the Sociology of Language,* ed. J. A. Fishman, pp. 382–413. The Hague: Mouton, 1968.

Wiesel, E. *The Jews of Silence.* New York: Holt, Rinehart and Winston, 1967.

Wylie, R. C. *The Self-Concept: A Critical Survey of Pertinent Research Literature.* Lincoln: University of Nebraska, 1961.

Zellermayer, J. "The Psychosocial Effect of the Eichmann Trial on Israeli Society," *Psychiatry Digest,* November 1968, pp. 13–23.

Zinger, Z. "The Iron in the Rock," *Jerusalem Post,* April 12, 1968.

———. "An Israeli Dilemma: Tradition and/or Faith," *Jerusalem Post,* September 12, 1969.

Indices

INDEX OF SUBJECTS

INDEX OF AUTHORS

About the Author

SIMON N. HERMAN is an associate professor at the Institute of Contemporary Jewry and in the Department of Psychology at the Hebrew University of Jerusalem. After completing his studies in social psychology in South Africa, Professor Herman came to the U.S.A., where he worked under the late Professor Kurt Lewin, founder of the Research Center for Group Dynamics (then at M.I.T.).

In Israel, the focus of his research has been on problems of ethnic identity, cross-cultural education and sociolinguistics. His papers on these subjects have appeared in a number of scholarly journals, and he is the author of a recent book, *American Students in Israel.*